Also available from Macmillan

Patrick Dunleavy, Andrew Gamble, Ian Holliday
and Gillian Peele (eds)
DEVELOPMENTS IN BRITISH POLITICS 4

Peter Hall, Jack Hayward and Howard Machin (eds)
DEVELOPMENTS IN FRENCH POLITICS

Gillian Peele, Christopher Bailey and Bruce Cain (eds)
DEVELOPMENTS IN AMERICAN POLITICS

Gordon Smith, William E. Paterson, Peter H. Merkl
and Stephen Padgett (eds)
DEVELOPMENTS IN GERMAN POLITICS

Stephen White, Alex Pravda and Zvi Gitelman (eds)
DEVELOPMENTS IN SOVIET AND POST-SOVIET POLITICS

Forthcoming

Patrick Dunleavy
ANALYSING BRITISH POLITICS

Developments in East European Politics

Edited by

Stephen White
Judy Batt
Paul G. Lewis

150th YEAR
M
MACMILLAN

First published 1993 by
THE MACMILLAN PRESS LTD
Houndmills, Basingstoke, Hampshire RG21 2XS
and London
Companies and representatives
throughout the world

ISBN 0–333–59189–5 hardcover
ISBN 0–333–59190–9 paperback

A catalogue record for this book is available
from the British Library.

Printed in Great Britain by Mackays of Chatham PLC, Chatham,
Kent

Contents

PART THREE: PATTERNS OF POLITICS IN POST-COMMUNIST
EASTERN EUROPE

Preface

It used to be easy to define 'Eastern Europe'. Broadly speaking, it was a group of states on the far side of what was for many years an Iron Curtain. Most of them bordered on the Soviet Union, and most of them were bound to the Soviet Union by economic and military alliances as well as by a close interconnection at the level of their communist party leaderships. Their fate, it appeared, had been largely determined at the end of the Second World War, when Europe had been divided – however provisionally – into rival spheres of influence. Yugoslavia had successfully separated itself from the Soviet alliance in the late 1940s, and from the 1960s Albania and Romania were increasingly independent. All of the states in the region none the less remained under communist leadership, state ownership was dominant, and public life was framed by the requirements of Marxism-Leninism.

The dramatic changes of the late 1980s and early 1990s have shattered these earlier patterns, and brought an end to the division of Europe and – in most parts of the region – to communist rule itself. The changes that began in 1989 took a variety of forms, and governments changed more quickly than political systems and forms of ownership, still less the habits and practices that had developed over forty years of communist rule – and in many cases over a much longer period. By the early 1990s, none the less, East European states were facing a largely similar set of challenges. Could they develop forms of rule, including party systems and structures of participation, that would replace the authoritarianism of the communist years? Could they find a balance between effective leadership, often through a presidency, and accountability, typically to an elected parliament? Could they reverse the economic decline of the late communist years, and could they best do so through 'shock therapy' or by a more gradual process? And could they carry out programmes of change with popular support, notwithstanding the sacrifices that were involved and the increasingly difficult position of students, the elderly, the handicapped, and a growing number of unemployed?

These are just some of the issues that are addressed in this collection, which brings together a number of leading specialists from the European countries and from North America. Our first two chapters set out the context of change, and explore some of the features that mark out a distinctively East European group of systems. We turn, in the second part, to a series of chapters that consider the process of transition in a number of individual states in the region: in Poland, the Czech and Slovak republics, Hungary, Bulgaria, and what has become known as the 'former Yugoslavia'. Our third part deals more comparatively with processes of change, including parties and parliaments, leaderships and the mass public, and the difficult transition from central planning to the market and a greater degree of social differentiation. Our fourth and final section examines the comparative politics of the region in a postcommunist era, and the place of Eastern Europe in a broader international environment; and we conclude with the voices of East Europeans themselves as they contemplate an uncertain future.

Developments in East European Politics is intended as a guide to the common patterns, as well as the individual variety, among a group of states that were formerly modelled on the Soviet Union but are now a distinctive and independent presence in a postcommunist international system. We hope that not only our students, but also our colleagues and readers in other walks of life, will find something of value in the result.

Stephen White
Judy Batt
Paul G. Lewis

Note: in the interests of reader-friendliness, accents and diacriticals have been omitted from Eastern European names.

Notes on the Contributors

Judy Batt is Lecturer at the Centre for Russian and East European Studies, University of Birmingham, and is currently on secondment to the Foreign and Commonwealth Office, London. Her publications include *Economic Reform and Political Change in Eastern Europe* (1988) and *East Central Europe from Reform to Transformation* (1991).

John D. Bell is Professor of History at the University of Maryland in Baltimore and President of the Bulgarian Studies Association of North America. As well as numerous articles on modern Bulgarian history, he is the author of *Peasants in Power* (1977) and *The Bulgarian Communist Party from Blagoev to Zhivkov* (1986).

Chris Corrin is Lecturer in Politics at the University of Glasgow in Scotland. A specialist on East-Central European and women's issues, she is the author of *Magyar Women: Hungarian Women's Lives 1960s–1990s* (1993) and co-author of *Superwomen and the Double Burden: Women's Experience of Change in Central and Eastern Europe and the Former Soviet Union* (1992).

Bob Deacon is Reader in Social Policy at Leeds Metropolitan University in Leeds, England. His publications, as author or co-author, include *Social Policy, Social Justice and Citizenship in Eastern Europe* (1992) and *The New Eastern Europe: Social Policy, Past, Present and Future* (1992).

Jan Ake Dellenbrant is Reader in Political Science at the University of Umea, Sweden. He has published books and articles on political and economic change in Russia/USSR, the Baltic States and Eastern Europe, including *Gorbachev and Perestroika: Towards a New Socialism?* (with Ronald J. Hill, 1990) and *The New Democracies in Eastern Europe: Party Systems and Political Cleavages* (with Sten Berglund, 1991).

Judy Dempsey works for the *Financial Times*. A graduate of Trinity College, Dublin, she is currently based in Germany and specialises in East-Central Europe.

Krzysztof Jasiewicz is director of electoral studies at the Institute of Political Studies of the Polish Academy of Sciences, Warsaw, and is currently visiting professor of sociology at the Washington and Lee University in Lexington, Virginia. He was the co-author of a series of political attitude surveys known as *The Poles of '80, '81, '84, '88* and *'90*, and has recently contributed to the *Journal of Democracy* and to the *European Journal of Political Research*, as well as to professional symposia.

Paul G. Lewis is Senior Lecturer in Government at the Open University, Milton Keynes, England. A specialist on Polish and comparative politics, his books include *Poland: Politics, Economics and Society* (with George Kolankiewicz, 1988), *Political Authority and Party Secretaries in Poland 1975–1986* (1989), *Democracy and Civil Society in Eastern Europe* (edited, 1992) and *Political and Economic Dimensions of Modernity* (co-edited, 1992).

David S. Mason is Professor of Political Science at Butler University, Indianapolis. A specialist in Polish politics and public opinion in East Central Europe, his books include *Public Opinion and Political Change in Poland* (1985) and *Revolution in East-Central Europe* (1992). He is currently coordinating a 12-nation survey project on popular perceptions of social, economic and political justice.

Daniel N. Nelson is Director of the Graduate Programs in International Studies at Old Dominion University in Norfolk, Virginia. During 1990–1 he was Senior Foreign and Defense Policy Advisor for the Majority Leader of the US House of Representatives, Richard Gephart, and he was previously a Senior Associate at the Carnegie Endowment and a Professor of Political Science at the University of Kentucky. His most recent books are *Romania after Tyranny* (1992) and *Security after Hegemony* (1993).

George Schöpflin is Lecturer in the Political Institutions of Eastern Europe at the London School of Economics and at the School of Slavonic and East European Studies. His recent publications include *Politics in Eastern Europe 1945–1992* (1993).

Jim Seroka is Professor of Political Science and Public Administration at the University of North Florida in Jacksonville, Florida. He is the author of numerous scholarly articles and monographs on Yugoslav domestic and international politics, co-author of *Political Organizations in Socialist Yugoslavia* (1986) and co-editor of *The Tragedy of Yugoslavia: The Failure of Democratic Transformation* (1993).

Nigel Swain is Deputy Director of the Centre for Central and Eastern European Studies at the University of Liverpool. His publications include *Hungary: A Decade of Economic Reform* (with Paul Hare and Hugo Radice, 1981), *Collective Farms which Work?* (1985), *Hungary: The Rise and Fall of Feasible Socialism* (1992) and *Eastern Europe since 1945* (with Geoffrey Swain, 1993). He is currently researching the impact on rural society of the transition to private agriculture in Central Europe.

Ray Taras teaches politics at Tulane University in New Orleans. He studied at the universities of Montreal, Sussex and Essex, and at the University of Warsaw in Poland, and has taught at US universities since 1982. The author of *Ideology in a Socialist State: Poland 1956–1983* (1983) and *Poland: Socialist State, Rebellious Nation* (1986), Ray Taras has also edited *Leadership Change in Communist States* (1990) and *Handbook of Political Science Research on the USSR and Eastern Europe* (1992).

Stephen White is Professor of Politics and a Member of the Institute of Russian and East European Studies at the University of Glasgow. A specialist on Soviet, Russian and comparative politics, his books include *The Origins of Detente* (1985), *The Bolshevik Poster* (1988), *Communist Political Systems: An Introduction* (3rd edn, 1990) and *After Gorbachev* (4th edn, 1993). He is presently working on a survey-based project on democratic values in Russia, Ukraine, Hungary and the former Czechoslovakia.

Gordon Wightman is Lecturer in the School of Politics and Communication Studies at the University of Liverpool. His articles on Czechoslovak politics have appeared in *Electoral Studies, Parliamentary Affairs* and the *Journal of Communist Studies*, and in professional symposia. He is presently engaged in an inter-university research project on 'Regime change in East-Central Europe', sponsored by the UK Economic and Social Research Council under its East–West Initiative.

Map of Eastern Europe

PART ONE

Perspectives on Eastern Europe

1

Eastern Europe after Communism

STEPHEN WHITE

At first sight, the nations of Eastern Europe are hardly a coherent group of political systems. Their languages are Slavonic, Romance and Finno-Ugrian. Their religions are Orthodox Christian, Roman Catholic, Lutheran and Muslim. Their historical experience falls partly within the mainstream of European civilisation, and partly outside it. And their relations with each other have hardly been harmonious: even today, national boundaries are under challenge, and there are substantial minorities beyond national boundaries – like the Hungarians in Romania, or the Poles in Lithuania – that are a constant source of tension. After the communist era, the very designation of the 'lands in between' has become controversial. The region can hardly be called 'Slavic', if the Hungarians and others are to be included. But should be known as Eastern Europe, with its connotations of Soviet control, or Central Europe, or East-Central Europe? Is there a distinct and separate 'Balkan' identity, embracing Greece as well as the post-communist states of the area? Indeed, can any single term adequately encompass such a variety of cultures and political experiences?

We have tried, in this volume, to take account of the distinct identities of the countries within what we have generally called Eastern Europe; but we have also focused on the common features that unite them. In particular, we shall be concerned to examine the complex legacy of what can best be called post-communism. Not all the countries with which we are concerned remained within the

Soviet sphere of influence; and in some of them communist influence is still strong. And yet for more than forty years these were systems modelled closely on the USSR, and a part of what was formerly the Eastern bloc. Their politics were dominated by single ruling parties; their economies were based upon public ownership and state planning; their social and cultural life was heavily politicised; and their international alliances were based upon the Warsaw Treaty Organisation and the Council for Mutual Economic Affairs (CMEA), which sought to integrate military and economic policy across the area. The USSR's closest allies, in this relationship, were known as the 'socialist community of nations'; the sixteen communist-ruled nations, in Asia and Latin America as well as Eastern Europe, were known as the 'world socialist system'; and all of them were part of a still broader association of communist parties and movements.

The nations of Eastern Europe, accordingly, have shared the common heritage of communist rule, and its implications for social and economic as well as political life. Equally, in the 1990s, they confront many similar problems. For most of them, the central task is to rebuild their economies on market principles, and not simply to resume the patterns of growth that had faltered in the late communist period but to resume them on a basis that is ecologically sustainable and technologically literate. The societies of post-communist Europe face a similar challenge, as the basic but comprehensive welfare provision of the former regimes is replaced by more limited and contributory systems, and at a time when government revenues have generally been falling and levels of poverty and unemployment have been mounting. And there have been similar challenges in political life, as the countries of the region have sought to develop forms of government that allow presidents and governments to act effectively, but which also allow a genuine role for parliament, political parties, and a wider range of forms of participation than were permitted under communist rule. It is this common heritage, and these common challenges, that are considered on a country by country and then on a broader comparative basis in *Developments in East European Politics*.

The Communist Inheritance

Communist rule in Eastern Europe dates from World War II, and from the division of the continent into rival spheres of influence that took place at the Teheran, Moscow, Yalta and Potsdam conferences between 1943 and 1945. In some cases there was little domestic support for communist policies and the new government was effectively installed by the Red Army, as in East Germany, Poland and Romania. In Bulgaria the communist party had enjoyed a considerable degree of popular support, but the country sided with the Axis powers during the war and it was occupied by the Red Army in 1944, with whose support a communist government came into being two years later. In Czechoslovakia and Hungary, on the other hand, the communist party did enjoy a substantial degree of popular support and the Red Army, despite occasional excesses, was seen by many as the agency by which these countries had been liberated from the Nazis. In Czechoslovakia the communist party in fact secured 38 per cent of the vote, the largest for any party, in the relatively free elections of 1946, while in Hungary the communists became the largest single party after the rather less freely held elections of 1947. In both cases coalition governments were established within which communists swiftly assumed a dominant position.

In Yugoslavia and Albania a rather different path was followed, and communist rule, as in Russia, was more 'indigenous' than 'imposed'. Communists, in both Yugoslavia and Albania, had headed a wartime partisan struggle against German and Italian occupation, and they had come to power with little or no support from the USSR. They tended, for these reasons, to have a greater degree of at least initial popular support than other communist governments, and it may have encouraged them to take a more independent attitude towards Moscow than the regimes that were simply imported 'in the baggage train of the Red Army'. The Yugoslav leadership initially maintained close ties with the USSR but a breach occurred in 1948, after which Tito and his associates took a more independent line in foreign affairs with the support of the Western powers, particularly Britain. Yugoslavia was not at any time a member of the Warsaw Treaty Organisation; Albania, under the leadership of Enver Hoxha, became a Chinese ally during the 1960s and 1970s.

Whatever their origins, the communist governments of Eastern Europe had a number of institutions that bound them together and – at the same time – subordinated them to Soviet purposes. The CMEA, or Comecon, was the first of these to be established; it was set up in 1949 by the USSR and the East European states largely as a response to the Marshall Plan and the formation of the Organisation for Economic Cooperation and Development by the major Western powers. Albania was one of the early members, but took no part in the work of the CMEA after 1961; its other members, in the 1980s, were Bulgaria, Hungary, the German Democratic Republic, Poland, Romania, Czechoslovakia and the USSR, as well as Cuba, Mongolia and Vietnam. The CMEA was regulated by a statute, which came into force in 1960, and by an agreement on the 'basic principles of the international socialist division of labour', which was approved in 1962. A more elaborate 'complex programme' was approved in 1971, and in 1988, after a period of inactivity, a 'collective concept of the international socialist division of labour' was approved for implementation from 1991 onwards. Most CMEA members traded most heavily with other members, ranging from Hungary (about 45 per cent in the late 1980s) to Bulgaria (nearly 80 per cent), but the real purposes of the organisation were political rather than economic. Military integration was assured by the Warsaw Treaty Organisation, established in 1955 and headquartered in Moscow.

Whether or not they were members of the Warsaw Treaty or the CMEA, the states of Eastern Europe shared the central features of the 'Soviet model'. The first of these was a formal commitment to Marxism-Leninism, which provided the vocabulary of politics in these states as well as the basis upon which their rulers claimed to exercise authority. Indeed a commitment of this kind was normally written into the constitution: in Albania, for instance, the constitution straightforwardly declared 'Marxism-Leninism is the dominant ideology in the People's Republic of Albania. The entire socialist social order evolves on the basis of its principles'. The commitment to Marxism-Leninism was less direct in the other states of the region, but their constitutions did define them as 'socialist' and in most cases (Bulgaria, Czechoslovakia, the German Democratic Republic and Romania) there was a further commitment to the eventual achievement of communism. It was in this sense that communist-ruled states were called 'ideocratic', or simply an 'ideology in power' (Wolfe, 1969); they were states in which a single official theory dominated the mass media, the educational system and public discourse, and in which other views of society were illegitimate and difficult to communicate because of controls over the flow of information within and across national boundaries.

A second defining feature of the East European states up to the 1980s was public ownership and management of economic life. There were some important exceptions: in Poland and Yugoslavia, for instance, most land was privately owned and managed, and in the

German Democratic Republic were were, until the 1970s, a small number of actual capitalists. There were other forms of ownership, such as cooperative ownership, that were important, and limited forms of private ownership and economic activity were permitted in virtually every case. The predominant pattern, however, was of state ownership that included at least the 'commanding heights' of the economy, such as heavy industry, finance and foreign trade, and this was combined with state direction through a series of five-year plans. There was certainly no doubt of the dominance of public ownership during the period of communist rule: the state accounted for well over 90 per cent of industrial output in all the East European states in the 1970s and 1980s, and for over 90 per cent of national income everywhere but Poland. The plan, under these arrangements, was a law, not simply a recommendation; managers were appointed by the state to fulfil it; and the centre allocated the necessary resources, set prices and determined wages.

A third central feature, and probably the crucial one, was that political life was dominated by a ruling party within which power was highly concentrated. The model for a party of this kind had been supplied by Lenin's book *What is to be Done?* as early as 1902; as Lenin made clear, a vanguard party of this kind should have a relatively restricted membership based upon a high level of political consciousness, and it should be based upon a high level of discipline with members and branches responsible for implementing the decisions of the leadership, not challenging them. This was most clearly formulated in the doctrine of 'democratic centralism', by which decisions were made by the majority but in practice unanimously and in a form that was mandatory for lower levels. And there were ways in which the party leadership were strengthened, including a 'ban on factions' and an insistence in the party rules that – in the words of the Socialist Unity Party of East Germany – the party manifest a high degree of 'ideological and organizational unity' and 'conscious discipline' (White and Simons, 1984, p. 192). Party leaders, protected from their members by such practices, often held office for long periods. Todor Zhivkov, the Bulgarian first secretary, became party leader in 1954 and held the same post until 1989. Romania's Nicolae Ceausescu was party leader from 1965 until the regime itself was overthrown in December 1989; and the Socialist Unity Party of East Germany had just two leaders from 1950 to 1989, Walter Ulbricht and (from 1971) Erich Honecker.

A fourth features of East European communism was the broad

scope of the party's 'leading role'. In liberal democracies, the courts, the press and bodies such as the trade unions are independent of government and one of the means – together with competitive elections – by which political leaderships are held periodically to account. In the East European countries, on the contrary, the separation of powers was repudiated and there was no division between government and the administration of justice. Bodies like the trade unions, women's organisations and sports clubs were defined as 'transmission belts' and directed in all their activities by the party authorities. And the mass media were closely controlled: their editors were party appointees, and their coverage was determined at weekly briefings in party offices. The media and all other forms of information were in addition subject to a detailed but still secret system of censorship. In Poland, for instance, this prescribed that certain subjects could not be mentioned at all – such as price increases, road accidents, epidemics or meat exports to the USSR – while others could be only be discussed in a limited and formulaic manner. The whole system became public knowledge when an official from the Krakow censorship defected to the West in the 1970s, taking his instructions with him (Curry, 1984).

The Transition from Communist Rule

Communist rule was still expanding in the 1970s, at least in Africa and Asia, and it appeared well established in the countries of Eastern Europe. Some of the communist governments still attracted the popular authority that came from heading a successful struggle against the Nazis, or in Tito's case against Stalin. Nor had they simply resisted change. There had been uprisings in East Berlin in 1953, a popular reform movement in Czechoslovakia in 1968, and unrest in northern Poland in the early 1970s. And yet reform of a more modest character had continued. There was a steady extension, for instance, in the range of alternatives available at elections. Poland, in 1956, was the first communist government to establish a choice of candidates, if not of policies; Hungary followed in the 1960s, and Romania in the 1970s. Local councils gained in power in most of the countries of the region, and the originally very limited powers of communist parliaments were strengthened. The ruling parties increased their memberships, again with some exceptions, and leaderships broadened into consultative oligarchies. The official ideology became less

8 Eastern Europe after Communism

TABLE 1.1 Average annual rates of growth, 1951–88 (percentages)

	1951–5	1955–60	1961–5	1966–70	1971–5	1976–80	1981–5	1986–88
Bulgaria	12.2	9.7	6.7	8.8	7.8	6.1	3.7	5.6
Hungary	5.7	5.9	4.1	6.8	6.3	2.8	1.3	1.7
GDR	13.1	7.1	3.5	5.2	5.4	4.1	4.5	3.5
Poland	8.6	6.6	6.2	6.0	9.8	1.2	–0.8	3.9
Romania	14.1	6.6	9.1	7.7	11.4	7.0	4.4	5.1
Czechoslovakia	8.2	7.0	1.9	7.0	5.5	3.7	1.7	2.4
CMEA as a whole	10.8	8.5	6.0	7.4	6.4	4.1	3.0	3.0

Source: Adapted from Statisticheskii ezhegodnik stran-chlenov SEV 1989 (Moscow: Finansy i statistika, 1989) pp. 18–28.

restrictive, state ownership became less monopolistic, and bodies like trade unions and churches secured more autonomy than ever before.

The collapse of communist rule throughout the region was accordingly a surprise, not only to Western observers, but also to many of the peoples that were directly concerned. With the benefit of hindsight, there were several critical failings. Arguably the most important was the steady fall in rates of economic growth throughout the region (see Table 1.1). In the 1950s, communist governments had been able to expand their economies at rates much higher than those that had been achieved in the capitalist West. The Soviet Union, speaking for the communist countries as a whole, could promise in 1961 that the United States would be overtaken by 1970, and that a fully fledged communist society would be developed from 1980 onwards. The East German party declared in 1963 that the transition from capitalism to socialism was the 'main content and the fundamental development law of our epoch'; the Czechoslovak party simply declared that its own programme was the same as that of the CPSU. With the rapid rate of growth that was secured during these years, competing interests could all be satisfied; and the population at large could be persuaded, through an implicit 'social contract', to accept a limited range of political liberties in exchange for a modest but steadily improving standard of living.

The collapse of communist economic performance, and even negative growth in some countries by the 1980s, prejudiced this tacit understanding between the regimes – which had at no stage been freely elected – and the societies over which they ruled. The collapse of economic growth sharpened social divisions, as prices rose and shortages worsened and the elderly, the infirm and the less skilled were left behind. The worsening of shortages, in turn, made the privileges of communist leaderships less acceptable. One of the factors that led to the emergence of Solidarity in Poland, for instance, was the formation of a group of privileged officeholders known as the 'owners of People's Poland'. The party leader of the time, Eduard Gierek, was reported to live in a villa set in 4000 acres of parkland, with a dining room that seated forty and a private cinema; one of his closest associates, the former head of Polish television, had a fleet of yachts and cars, a harem of prostitutes, and a foreign bank account of which he made use when taking safari holidays in Africa. Greater openness in the media made it possible to report matters of this kind more directly, and it was one of the demands of the Gdansk shipyard workers in 1980 that action be taken to 'abolish the privileges of the citizens' militia, the security service and the party apparatus by equalising family allowances, ending special sales and so forth' (*Glos Pracy*, 2 September 1980).

Economic circumstances, for all their importance, were not the only factor at play. Indeed domestic factors of this kind were themselves part of a larger international environment. One element in this wider picture was the position of the Soviet Union. Under Brezhnev any departure from socialist principles was regarded as a threat to the socialist community as a whole, and the doctrine of 'socialist internationalism' was written into the 1977 Constitution. Under Mikhail Gorbachev, after 1985, the suppression of the Prague spring was officially condemned and it was made clear that the communist governments of the region would not necessarily be sustained by the might of Soviet armed forces. There was also a 'demonstration effect', as the overthrow of communist government in one country after another led to its collapse in the remainder. Even before this, the government of the GDR had been fatally weakened by another exogenous factor: the mass exodus of young workers and professionals that took place through Hungary to what was then the Federal Republic. Later still, it was the knowledge of what had happened in Poland and in Hungary that helped to bring about the massive but peaceful revolutions in Czechoslovakia, Romania and the former GDR.

The transition itself began in Poland, where (as we show in Chapter 3) the partly competitive elections of June 1989 led to an overwhelming victory for Solidarity and the first non-communist prime minister in Eastern Europe for forty years. At the end of the year the Polish parliament removed the 'leading role' from the constitution, and changed the name of the state from 'People's Republic' to 'Republic of Poland'; the communist party, demoralised and declining in membership, had meanwhile collapsed and been partly reconstituted as a Social Democratic party. In Hungary, as we show in Chapter 5, the process of transition had also begun from above, as the ruling Hungarian Socialist Workers' Party abandoned its leading role in early 1989 and committed itself to multiparty politics. A process of discussion followed in which it was agreed that open, competitive elections should take place at the earliest opportunity. At those elections, in March–April 1990, the conservative Democratic Forum secured 42.5 per cent of the vote and formed the country's first non-communist government; the former communists, renamed the Hungarian Socialist Party, had to be content with 8.5 per cent, and even less in the local elections that took place later the same year.

The process of political change took still more dramatic forms in East Germany, Romania, Czechoslovakia and Bulgaria. In the former GDR the transition began with the outflow of population through Hungary to West Germany, and developed into a widespread popular resistance led by the Lutheran Church and an oppositional coalition known as New Forum. Party leader Erich Honecker was forced to resign in October 1989, and later placed under house arrest; but the demonstrations continued, with up to half a million appearing weekly on the streets of Leipzig, and further concessions followed including the breaching of the Berlin Wall in November 1989. The ruling Socialist Unity Party changed its name to Party of Democratic Socialism in December, and elected a new leader; another reform-minded communist became prime minister. The new leadership announced that competitive, multiparty elections would take place the following year; at those elections, in March 1990, the conservative Christian Democratic Union won 40.8 per cent of the vote and began to move rapidly towards union with the Federal Republic. The former communists did badly, with just 16.4 per cent of the vote, although they came second in Berlin. A treaty of unification was signed on 31 August, and at midnight on 2 October 1990 the former German Democratic Republic became part of a larger German state under a Christian Democratic government.

The process of change in Czechoslovakia was also largely peaceful (see Chapter 4), although it began with police attacks on huge public demonstrations in November 1989. The demonstrations, the largest for twenty years, were led initially by students and increasingly involved the population as a whole. Just a week after the demonstrations had started, on 24 November, the communist leader Milos Jakes and the whole of the Politburo resigned; the government followed on 7 December, and on 10 December a largely non-communist adminstration took office. At the end of the month Alexander Dubcek, leader of the 1968 reform movement, was elected chairman of the Czech parliament, and the following day the popular playwright and former political prisoner, Vaclav Havel, was elected president. In Bulgaria mass demonstrations in November 1989 led to the resignation of party leader Todor Zhivkov and attacks upon the 'totalitarian' regime he had established (see Chapter 6). The leading role of the party was swiftly abandoned, the communists changed their name to the Bulgarian Socialist Party, and although they emerged as the largest single grouping at the elections that took place in June 1990 they were eventually obliged to form a coalition government. At further elections, in October 1991, the former communists lost further ground and were forced into opposition.

Most spectacular of all, perhaps, was the overthrow of Nicolae Ceausescu, party leader and virtual dictator of Romania since 1965. There had been little obvious threat to Ceausescu at the Romanian Communist Party's 14th Congress, in late November 1989; the leader's own speech was interrupted by no fewer than 125 standing ovations, and the resolutions that were adopted showed little sign of compromise. The fall of the regime in fact began shortly afterwards, with demonstrations in the largely Hungarian city of Timisoara, which were crushed with exceptional ferocity. The protest nonetheless spread to other towns and cities and to the capital Bucharest, where Ceausescu, addressing a public rally on 21 December, was ignominiously shouted down. The following day he fled the capital by helicoptor but was captured and brought to trial after further street fighting had claimed thousands of lives. On 25 December Ceausescu and his wife were sentenced to death and summarily executed; reports began to circulate at the same time of the extraordinary opulence in which the former dictator had lived, including a house crammed with art treasures and a nuclear bunker lined with marble. The functions of government were carried on, after Ceausescu's overthrow, by the National Salvation Council, a close coalition within which there appeared to be substantial communist influence. At the multiparty elections which took place in May 1990 the Front and its presidential candidate, Ion Iliescu, won convincing victories; Iliescu won again in 1992.

The transition from communist rule, initiated in 1989, was largely complete by 1992. In Yugoslavia (see Chapter 7), the ruling League of Communists abandoned its guiding role in early 1990; power in most of the republics passed into the hands of noncommunists, and by the following year the federation had effectively ceased to exist. In Albania a wave of anti-government demonstrations in the summer of 1990 led to the legalisation of opposition parties in December; a communist government was again returned at elections in March 1991, but at further elections in March 1992 the oppositional Democratic Party secured 68 per cent of the vote and the former communists left office. A year later the collected works of Enver Hoxha, party leader until 1985, were being turned into cardboard boxes. Within the USSR, meanwhile, the Communist Party had abandoned its leading role in March 1990 and had then been suppressed entirely following an unsuccessful coup in August 1991. By December the state itself had ceased to exist. The Council for Mutual Economic Assistance had no role to perform in these circumstances, and formally dissolved itself in September 1991. The Warsaw Treaty Organisation had already decided to disband in July, bringing to an end the international framework within which communist rule had been sustained since the 1950s.

Eastern Europe after Communism

The transition from communist rule took a variety of forms; so too did the construction of a postcommunist order. Indeed in many cases the distinction was of limited value. Former communist parties remained influential at the polls, sometimes even winning elections; and former party members were well represented in government and at all levels of the society. A large part of the economy in the early 1990s was still in public hands, and 'administrative methods' were being used much more widely in a system in which market and legal institutions were still weakly developed. In the varied, complex and transitional system that had succeeded communist rule, at least three issues were central to the political agenda throughout the region.

First of all, what kind of *political order* would take the place of centralised, ruling communist parties? Would it be a system based around a powerful executive presidency of the American or French kind, or a parliamentary system of the kind that existed in the United Kingdom and Italy? At a time of great economic difficulty there were strong arguments in favour of decisive leadership, based around a presidency with the ability to issue decrees, to appoint the government, and perhaps even to suspend parliament. And yet how were the decisions of such a presidency to be put into effect when there was no 'presidential party' to sustain them, and no system of laws and courts to impose them if necessary? And what could protect society against the danger that a powerful executive presidency might infringe the civil and political rights of ordinary citizens in much the same way that the communist system had done? A parliamentary system, with a government accountable to elected representatives, offered a different way forward. And yet political parties were weakly developed throughout the region, without clear identities or mass memberships; they were often little more than the personal followings of their leaders, and they tended to split whenever their leaders disagreed with each other. All of this contributed to a disorderly and ineffective parliamentary process, and to a low level of public support for representative institutions in general (these issues are discussed further in Part Three of this book).

Postcommunist governments in Eastern Europe also confronted a number of difficult choices in the formation of *public policy* (see Chapters 12 and 13). It was widely agreed that 'there was no alternative to the market'. But it was less clear how to make a transition from a system of state ownership to a viable economy based upon market relations. There was often no tradition of entrepreneurship, and none of the institutions that were necessary for its existence such as a stock market, accountants or commercial banks. There were other problems inherited from the communist period; factories were typically very large, making it difficult for governments to allow them to go bankrupt, and they were often monopolistic, allowing them to charge whatever they wanted for their production. Very few countries had attempted to privatise their economies under such circumstances, and at the same time to deal with complicated problems of ownership, foreign control, and reinvestment. Very few governments, moreover, found it easy to cope with the social and political consequences of the transition to market relations. Levels of inflation and unemployment started to rise sharply, and whole sections of the society, particularly those on state or fixed incomes, found themselves in serious difficulty. Public services like health and education began to experience budgetary problems as their supplies

TABLE 1.2   '*In general, do you think things in our country are going in the right or in the wrong direction?*'

	Right direction	Wrong direction
Albania	77	17
Slovenia	62	22
Czech republic	58	34
Slovakia	46	47
Bulgaria	42	40
Romania	42	49
Poland	27	56
Hungary	20	67

Source: Adapted from *Central and East European Barometer*, 1993.

became more expensive and their staff became impossible to pay at a level that was adequate to the rise in prices. Meanwhile, trade unions and other organised interests began to rediscover their original purposes, and outside bodies like the IMF and the World Bank became more interventionist but without providing the kind of resources that were necessary to fulfil their instructions.

What, finally, did the *East European public* make of these rapid and far-reaching changes? One of the changes that had taken place was itself the ability to examine popular attitudes through large-scale surveys; their results suggested a wide measure of disillusion, but also a considerable variation from country to country. Most of the countries concerned wanted a closer relationship with the European Community (from 73 per cent, in Bulgaria, up to 92 per cent, in Slovenia, favoured full membership), and more of them saw a future relationship that was associated with the EC than with Russia, the CIS or the United States. Many, however, thought that things were 'going in the wrong direction' in their own country (see Table 1.2), and there were serious reservations about the market economy and the pace of reform, particularly in the Czech and Slovak republics. The great majority intended to vote in the next general election, but relatively fewer in Poland and Hungary; and there was much more dissatisfaction than satisfaction with 'development of democracy' in each of the countries in the region, with the Hungarians (22 per cent satisfied but 72 per cent dissatisfied) again the least content. More Hungarians and Poles thought things were better for them under the communist system than thought things were better under the system that had succeeded it, and there was widespread concern about economic hardship, crime and minority rights throughout the region

(*Central and East European Barometer*, no. 3, 1993; see also Rose, 1991, and and Rose and Haerper, 1992). These were scarcely the kind of conditions in which it would be easy to develop an open, stable but competitive political system and a society that was largely self-governing and tolerant of diversity.

2

Culture and Identity in Post-Communist Europe

GEORGE SCHÖPFLIN

The political culture of Central and Eastern Europe was probably never more fluid than in the early 1990s, in the immediate aftermath of the collapse of communism. Various value systems were on offer, some derived from the pre-communist past, some conditioned by the anticipatory socialisation of communism and some structured by expectations of 'entering Europe'. Elements taken from all three broad possibilities were combined in a variety of ways to produce an uneasy and complex situation, in which no one political culture could be described as dominant. Nor was there a universally or generally accepted official political culture; on the contrary, after four decades of communism, the idea that the state should play a significant role in the shaping of social, political and economic attitudes was strongly contested. Different social categories sought to emphasise their own values and to insist that theirs should be used by the new order as its basic building block. Political parties were as much involved in the establishment of basic values as in the representation of interests. Indeed, the definition of interest was a crucial feature of the new politics. The political conflicts of the early years of post-communism centred essentially on the determination of the kinds of institutional frameworks that would most successfully articulate one or other of these cultures.

The historical dimensions are helpful in unravelling this complexity, though they cannot provide a full explanation. In broad historical terms, a distinction must be made between lands of

16

Western and Eastern Christianity and particular attention must be paid to the interface between the two. An understanding of the characteristics of the two main currents of Christianity in the context of Central and Eastern Europe is significant in illuminating the deeper levels of attitudes and values towards morality, power and the roles of state and society. These do not, of course, offer operationalisable models of behaviour, but provide information concerning how those models came to be constructed (see Chirot, 1989).

Thus it can be argued in an ideal-typical way that post-Reformation Western Christianity tended to emphasise the role of the individual conscience over the collectivity, that it provided space for the working-out of individual rather than collective salvation and that it allowed for a degree of reciprocity and mutual obligation. When translated into politics, this gave saliency to a two-way relationship between rulers and ruled that avoided the most extreme forms of absolutism found outside Europe and gave rise to a principle that the ruler was not absolute in himself, but owed a duty of obligation to some other, external agency. It followed logically that expectations were created thereby that power would be exercised within certain broad restraints and that some means of arbitration, external to the exercise of power, would be admitted in the relationship between rulers and ruled (see Schöpflin, 1993). In secular terms, this gave rise to the expectation of the external legitimation of power, an autonomous system of judicature and, ultimately, to popular sovereignty. Above all, it is a key feature of this political model that the ruler does not have exclusive control of legitimation, but must seek legitimacy in a dynamic relationship with the ruled.

In Central Europe, this ideal-typical model was beset with serious shortcomings, but it was nevertheless a recognisable variant of it. Western Christianity was accepted relatively early, but in a somewhat modified form, essentially because in these lands Western Christianity was in competition with Eastern variant and was under threat from pagan incursions, so that the role of the secular ruler was strengthened over the church. The kind of reciprocity that evolved further west was weaker in Central Europe and when this came to be translated into political arrangements the state emerged as a far more powerful actor. Above all, through the doctrine of the discretionary power of the state, the ruler came to exercise a dominance over society that gravely weakened the patterns of reciprocity found in the West. In effect, society was never able to develop the institutional and cultural strengths to challenge the ruler.

Furthermore, the weakness of native political institutions meant that, one after the other, all these polities succumbed to foreign rule, making imperial overlordship a shared experience. It was to shake off imperial power that the local élites turned to nationalism in the nineteenth century as their favoured instrument of mobilisation. A word is essential here about the very particular role played by intellectuals in Central and Eastern Europe. Because society was weak, the rise of a secular intellectual stratum with the Enlightenment produced a social configuration palpably different from that of Western Europe. While in the West the intellectuals had to contend with a reasonably well-established bourgeoisie and a confident ruling stratum in their attempts to secure their authority, further east they were virtually unchallenged. Consequently, when the intellectuals encountered nationalism, they were able to construct a programme that fused their claim to be moral, political and social legislators with the claim for national independence (Bauman, 1987). This gave Central and East European politics a very striking quality, in that the ethnic and civic agendas of politics were consistently confused and collective and individual freedoms were combined and sometimes confounded.

The political constellation that came into being in the last century, which survived until the coming of communism with greater or lesser modifications, was one where a bureaucratic state was run by a relatively small élite using the discretionary power of the state to marginalise challengers. It was not necessarily hostile to modernisation, understood as the reaching of Western levels of industrialisation and economic performance, but would block initiatives that threatened its own hegemonial control of power. It successfully coopted the intelligentsia – the possessors of technical knowledge – into the ambit of the state through its position as preeminent employer and its influence in the private sector and equally through the prestige of political power. The bulk of intellectuals, the creators of values, were likewise closer to the system than against it and helped to legitimate the political élite's position, mainly by explaining it in nationalist terms. It was only a minority of intellectuals that protested. Protest, therefore, tended to be polarised and be sympathetic to either left or right-radical solutions. Nationalist discourse thus tended to be the dominant mode of political expression, which it was extremely difficult to challenge effectively. It should be noted, however, that the system was not totalitarian, but permitted islands of pluralism, with their own independent sources of power and legitimacy, to coexist within the system.

The majority of the population was subjected to political power without having much ability to influence it. It was socialised into hierarchical authoritarian modes, the acceptance of a degree of arbitrariness and the remoteness of power. Power itself was thus legitimated partly by reference to nationhood and partly tradition; on occasion, this might be strengthened by the emergence of a charismatic or semi-charismatic leader. The pre-communist system was thus relatively stable, heavily state-centred and tending towards stagnation. By and large civil society found it difficult to emerge, because attempts to construct autonomous space ran into the obstacles of state power.

The state of affairs in South-Eastern Europe – the Balkans – was analogous to what has just been sketched but was, if anything, even more marked by the dominance of the collectivity over the individual and the state over the subject. Society was very weak and dependent and this dependence was reinforced by the historical experience which these lands had undergone. Eastern Orthodoxy, unlike Western Christianity, placed little emphasis on the individual conscience and favoured control by the community over control by internal conviction. In other words, these cultures were structured by externalisation rather than internalisation. The intensity of this varied, but the pattern as a whole persisted.

A second relevant factor was that alien rule – in this instance, rule by the Ottoman Empire – was, in addition to being alien in historical and political terms, also alien in religion. The way in which this empire influenced the states that it conquered again differed from the Austrian, Prussian and Russian empires, in that the Ottomans suppressed local élites unless they converted to Islam and insisted on retaining a political monopoly for Muslims. Conversion took place in Bosnia and Albania; elsewhere, Orthodox Christian peasantries were ruled over by the Ottoman administration. Romania constituted a half-exception to this, in that the Danubian provinces were never fully incorporated into the empire, but paid tribute to it and its rulers held power only with the consent of the Porte. The response, however, was analogous. Retreat into Orthodoxy and into subsistence cultivation were accompanied by a deep suspicion of a politics and the emergence of various compensatory myths, especially among the Serbs.

The coming of independence to South-Eastern Europe in the nineteenth century and to Central Europe in the twentieth was, therefore, a major change, in as much as it propelled rather inexperienced élites into power and they had simultaneously to construct a new state administration, create infrastructure, mobilise the nation and transform the existing passive culture into an active, participatory one. Also relevant in this connection was that religion gained an added salience, because it became the primary institution of national self-identification in the Balkans; religion had been used by the Ottoman Empire as the main basis of taxation and that in turn enhanced the role of the collectivity in the life of the individual.

The modes of legitimation adopted by these new élites relied very heavily on nationalism, and given the relative poverty of the tradition of nationhood in the political realm – no real history as a political nation for many centuries – myths were used as a substitute. This reliance on myth, coupled with externalisation, frequently made it hard for these political cultures to come to terms with existing realities, like economic backwardness and political irrelevance, which then gave rise to new compensatory myths of alien hostile conspiracy. This distorted view of the world was essential in explaining away why, despite independence, society remained poor and its prospects dim. For all practical purposes, civil society did not come into being in any recognised sense in South-Eastern Europe and power was monopolised by the political and intellectual élites.

Societies during this period ranged in terms of economic development from backward to semi-developed. In general, as argued, there was a small, usually urbanised, sometimes formerly aristocratic élite that ruled over a vast and generally barely literate peasant mass – literate both in the strict sense of the word, but also more broadly in respect of its understanding of politics, procedures and complexity. Its attitude was hostile to complexity, which it regarded as inauthentic by the criteria of the traditional village community, and at the same time it sensed that its powerlessness in respect of both politics and the market left it exposed to the vagaries of external forces over which it had no control. The Czech lands (and former East Germany) constituted an exception to this pattern, although even here there were some similarities, as will be argued later.

The Coming of Communism

Communism brought sweeping changes to this rather passive, backward political culture, reinforcing some aspects and blocking others.

There was, however, one irreversible change, a transformation the achievement of which had eluded the pre-communist élites. This was the resolution of the peasant problem. Communism took the great peasant mass and used it as clay to mould a working class out of it, in its own image. The enormous mobilisation of the 1945–70 period, which reduced the rural population from around 50 per cent of the total to around 25 per cent, created a new working class with what can only be described as a nineteenth-century configuration. Its sociological characteristics were its inexperience of urban patterns, its vulnerability to political manipulation and its effective exclusion from access to the advantages of urbanisation, including not just access to political power but also an understanding of the purposes of politics. From the standpoint of the newly mobilised peasantry, however, the massive demographic shift, with all its attendant traumas, did offer one great benefit – a steady income.

By contrast with life on the land, where in bad years the poor peasantry starved, industrial working offered a steady income and a degree of existential security backed up by low level of collective consumption much preferred to marginal living on the land. Politically, on the other hand, this stratum remained marginal. Political power continued to be monopolised by the élite, albeit now claiming to rule in the name of the ex-peasant proletariat and calling itself communist. The new working class, for its part, remained suspicious of power and complexity, was slow in regarding its position in the political situation as influential and responded to political challenges only *in extremis*, usually when mobilised by a sense of threatened nationhood (see Connor, 1979).

The peasant tradition, with its reluctance to come to terms with the impersonal patterns of organisation and institutions in industry, in this sense added up to a windfall benefit to the communists, by making atomisation that much easier to sustain. The second generation, those born in the 1950s and after, inherited some, though not all of these attitudes. It tended to see politics in relatively homogeneous terms, to be hostile to power in any institutional form and to see a deep gulf between itself and the élite. The Solidarity experience in Poland was a classic illustration of this attitude (Ash, 1983; Staniszkis, 1984).

The impact of communism on élites was similarly far-reaching. In the first place, the power, authority and legitimacy of the old ruling élites was definitively broken; indeed, it is worth remarking here that this great historic step was ironically accomplished by the radical right, rather than the radical left, although the latter claimed the credit for it. It was the wartime activities of Nazi Germany and its local allies that destroyed the political preeminence of the old élites for good. The communists were the beneficiaries of this historic turning point and, where necessary, they completed the process (as in Bulgaria and Czechoslovakia).

The creation of a new élite followed ineluctably. It was recruited from talented low-status individuals and was fairly rapidly socialised into the new system of values. It came to accept high levels of state intervention and control as desirable, hierarchy and denial of choice to the individual as justified in the name of the secular utopia that the party was notionally constructing, and took the view that its rule could and should be imposed, coercively if necessary, on those who believed in alternatives. Thus, this new élite was relatively authoritarian in its attitudes, supported étatism and understood redistribution by the state in a bureaucratic manner, without reference to society, as fully justified. In a word, it was technocratic and believed in the correctness of its strategies because it thought that it possessed a monopoly of knowledge and efficiency. The élite was suspicious of initiatives from below, disliked change and widening choice and was comfortable with its own rather static, undemanding view of the world, from which alternatives were excluded.

This ethos was transmitted to the next generation of bureaucrats and permeated the system. It affected both the style and content of the exercise of power, and tended to promote inexperience and depoliticisation on the part of the wider population. In addition, as the original ideological impulse weakened, which it began to do by the 1960s, the purposiveness of the bureaucracy was subtly altered from the construction of socialism to the administration of the system, from which it was quite legitimate for the bureaucracy to take a disproportionate share. The values of accountability and responsibility were not rated highly in this culture. Indeed the doctrine of collective responsibility was effectively used to avoid assuming it. The demands articulated by Solidarity in 1980 concentrated expressly on these two issues.

The evidence of popular values from the communist period is contradictory and somewhat misleading as a guide to what has emerged under post-communism. The nature of popular values, as these surfaced in Hungary in 1956, in Czechoslovakia in 1968 and in Poland in 1980–81, could be read as well disposed towards reciprocity and democracy. Yet with the benefit of hindsight this was too simplistic. The popular values that emerged during these upheavals pointed in another direction, that of homogeneity and oversimplification. One of the clearest expressions of this was during the Solidarity period, understandably given that it lasted longest. The Solidarity programme, adopted at the congress of September–October 1981, was a clear indicator of this tendency. Attitudes were essentially structured by a very strong sense of good and evil, with society cast in the role of the former, and 'them', the party-state, in the role of the latter.

The value system that gave this emphasis to moralising was counterpointed by a far-reaching weakness in the ability of society, whether as a whole or as individuals, to identify interests in material terms. Material interests were submerged or subsumed in the relationship with the party–state and could not be identified as long as the system subsisted. The key point here is the totalising nature of the Soviet-type system and the superimposition of the political sphere on all others. As long as the legitimating ideology of the system made the claim to transcend all else, that there was no area of life which the system could not regulate and rearrange in theory – even if the practice had become rather less intrusive – society felt constrained to devise counter-strategies. The obvious and most effective one was to claim a moral superiority to the official ideology. The superiority might be grounded in human rights (the line taken by the democratic opposition) or in nationalism or in religion.

Again with the benefit of hindsight, it seems clearer after the collapse of communism that the transmission of traditional values was stronger throughout the communist period than was understood at the time. This transmission is frequently perceived as the survival of values antagonistic to communism, like nationalism and religion. To some extent they did serve to delegitimate the communist system, but that did not in itself make them open to democratic ideals. If anything, the constant reference to totalising communism made its antagonists more like communists. And in any case, both nationalism and religion contain clear homogenising imperatives, which are hostile to the bargaining and compromise demanded by democracy.

Some of this anti-communist value system consisted of salvaging idealised elements of the pre-communist past, particularly through nationalism, which created the illusion that national freedom would lead ineluctably to individual freedom and economic well-being, both conceived of as a mythicised version of the West. The practical articulation of this was through the construction of competing thought-worlds. The establishment of competing or alternative institutions was, of course, impractical or even dangerous, as the party-state was able to liquidate these in very short order through its monopoly of coercion. Individuals were, therefore, prevented from gaining the experience of dealing with each other in any terms other than those created by the system (seen as illegitimate) or by society (wildly idealised).

The outcome was that individuals saw their lateral relationships very much in these high-level, abstracted terms and were unused to seeing each other as partners in more everyday arrangements, where interactions were structured by voluntarily assumed obligations, consent and the expectations of mutual benefit. The difficulty of structuring such interactions by moral categories is that these are generally useless in governing a whole range of problems, where other codes apply. Indeed, moral categories tend to homogenise expectations, to raise them very high and to weaken the self-regulating mechanisms by which society becomes capable of running its own affairs without excessive external intervention. In this way, the Soviet-type system and its totalising ideology produced a counter-ideology that successfully infantilised society, made it incapable (or almost) of dealing with other members without immediately escalating demands to the highest levels. That, of course, made compromise almost impossible to achieve and tolerance likewise, given that moral categories can hardly be bargained away, precisely because they belong to the sphere of morality (see Staniszkis, 1985–6; Feher *et al.*, 1983).

Post-Communism: Competing Political Cultures

It is only with the disappearance of communism that the shape of the society it created has started to become visible. It has several striking features, as already noted. Looked at by its horizontal divisions, there is a sizeable bureaucracy or series of bureaucracies, which largely encompass the intelligensia; this is changing only slowly as the private sector expands to absorb the bearers of specialised knowledge (engineers, architects, economists and so on). Intellectuals have for the time being been drawn into the political élite, so much so that the autonomy of intellectual thought is questioned and their objectivity or neutrality is impugned.

This may be a passing phenomenon, but it does have consequences in respect of the intellectualisation of politics and the language of political discourse, of the peculiarly abstract, often impractical, quality of political debates and their distance from everyday concerns. This phenomenon in turn influences perceptions of politics on the part of society at the very moment when the new system is actually being established. The old communist elite, the *nomenklatura*, has lost much of its political power – the power derived from officeholding – but it has successfully salvaged a not inconsiderable part of its power by moving into the private sector of the economy. This is not popular, but it can be seen as an automatic outcome of the way in which power was transferred by the communists in what can be termed a negotiated revolution. The transfer of power as such has barely affected the bulk of the population in terms of re-empowerment, although sections of society have concluded that this state of affairs should change.

The political–cultural scene, as it began to emerge under post-communism, was marked by the shared experience of communism, but the responses to that experience and to the demands of constructing a new political system or systems were extraordinarily various and inconsistent. Having undergone homogenisation, elites and societies were motivated by wildly different aspirations, ideals and expectations. There were three unifying concepts, but they were understood so differently that for the time being, diversity or indeed disunity was the most marked feature of the scene. In the first place, there was a widespread desire for economic improvement, for a much higher standard of living than existed and, with it, for all the most obvious material features of Western culture. Second, there was the legacy of having lived under a system that was persistently regarded as lacking legitimacy by large sections of the population. And third was the hope invested in the supposed magical properties of nationalism and nationhood.

The aspiration for economic improvement was directly and causally linked to the collapse of communism. The communist system fell apart not least because it was no longer able to keep its economic promises and the West represented a far more attractive, though heavily mythicised, alternative. In the eyes of many, democracy was understood as meaning 'a high standard of living', thereby divorcing the political system and its values from the perceived high consumption of the West. The inability of the newly elected and therefore 'democratic' governments to transform the post-communist economies with the wave of a wand has fuelled impatience and an unfocused radicalism.

It is noteworthy in this connection to recognise the widespread difficulty of many people in understanding the nature of the economic interactions in a market situation (see Sytompka, 1991). The idea of the market was perceived as a synonym for prosperity, and not as a complex system of prices and wages, supply and demand, which would result in differentiation and differential access to goods and services. The ethos of state dependence, the idea that the state would and, indeed, should bail out the individual was very strongly assimilated. In effect, the level of economic literacy was low.

To this should be added the problem of the weakness or absence of internalised values. Because the communism system was imposed from the outside, society rejected its values and conformed to them only externally, while transmitting a competing set of norms. Whilst this may have been a useful strategy under communism, it is obviously counterproductive under a political system that supposedly rests on choice. It tends to mean that duties are not understood as duties – i.e. individuals act out of either a moral sense or a long-term collective advantage – but rather that they do what they have to solely or overwhelmingly from a sense of fear. The transformation removed this ever present fear, but it has been replaced by a void. The fear was already disappearing before the end of communism, as evidenced by rising criminality, the growth of subcultures, the emergence of punk groups, bikers, drugs, and so on. But in the immediate aftermath of communism, there was no one, or even more than one idea, around which a community could cohere – indeed, this, the definition of such a constitutive idea, was what much of the post-communist contest was about.

Communist institutions were regarded as inauthentic, because they were the emanation of a system that was regarded as inauthentic and alien. This tended to promote an attitude of mind that considered all institutions as fraudulent, as a device foisted on the population by the deceitful and manipulative elite. There was very little understanding of the role of institutions as stabilising agents, helping to reduce arbitrariness and prevent power from being accumulated by a small minority. The consequence is that personal relations are regarded as far more authentic than institutional ones, and the codes appropriate to persons, rather than the impersonal world of institutions, are what tend to dominate politics. Personal loyalty and disloyalty are employed to make sense of power flows and political interactions, but because these are often unhelpful and do little to explain the existing realities, there is a tendency to take refuge in conspiracy theories. In this context too the communist legacy was negative, in as much as it destroyed or weakened the trust by which a community regulates itself and replaced it with atomisation.

A part of the chaos of the post-communist scene was that occasioned by the disappearance of familiar landmarks, institutions, organisations, procedures, emblems and vocabulary, even when this was considered desirable. This was profoundly disquieting for anyone over a certain age and produced various responses. In some there was be a holding on to the old, of seeking to make as much of the old system work as possible, including rewriting history, and claiming that at least under the communists there was plenty of say, security; this was obviously happening in Romania. Communism promoted a very simplistic concept of change, which then came largely to be interpreted as the arrival of plenty and complete licence.

In a very real sense, conspiracy-mindedness is a product of ideological thinking. In the realm of ideology, the relationship between cause and effect, between input and output is transparent and perfect. When this is applied to the muddy interactions of the real world, where chance, accident and coincidence have their roles, where results are highly imperfect, it is a very easy step to assume that the failure of a particular aspiration was the result of malign intervention by hidden forces that have yet to be 'unmasked'. In effect, the cognitive categories of those emerging from communism into post-communism make a very bad fit with the requirements of democracy.

The rise of nationhood as the source of potential salvation is explained by these factors. Where the institutional framework is weak, the identities represented in the public sphere by institutions are likely to be similarly weak. But something has to fill the resulting vacuum and, given that the national identity is the only public identity available, it follows that nationhood will acquire a role far more salient than in the West, where institutions have had several generations to gain popular acceptance.

Here the role of nationhood in the communist period is also relevant. While the communists were able successfully to eliminate the institutions of the pre-communist period, and thereby to destroy the incipient civic identities that they articulated, they could not do this with the ethnic identities of the people over whom they ruled. Ethnicity is very deeply rooted and has an authentic function in the maintenance of communities and the representation of communal identities, for all that ethnic identities can say very little in respect of the distribution of power. Hence during the communist period, reference to nationhood was evidently significant in delegitimating communism, but could put nothing in its place, other than illusions. These illusions centred on the vague, inchoate idea that once the nation was free to decide over its future, the failures experienced under communism would disappear.

In reality, the ethnic dimension of nationhood has next to nothing to offer in the definition of government, institutions and markets; these processes are determined by the civic dimension of nationhood. Hence with the disappearance of communism, the population turned almost automatically to nationhood, expecting near instant salvation, but lacked the cognitive categories, yet again, to make sense of the illusory nature of the promises of nationalism and nationalist leaders.

Post-Communist Societies

The most persuasive attempt to define the kinds of societies that have emerged under communism and are thus politically influential under post-communism is the one sketched at the very outset of this chapter. Post-communist societies are deeply divided into three broad, vertical categories – a traditional society, a society brought into being by communism and still influenced by it, and what might be termed a 'liberal' society, which accepts and understands the values of political and economic competition. The concepts and aspirations of the three are very different; there is limited communication between them and considerable mutual misunderstanding, even antagonism.

Traditional society can be described as defined by the area's rural past. Traditional peasant and, where appropriate, neo-feudal values have survived the communist modernisation, often in despite of the communist attempt at forcible transformation. Its ideas are strongly collectivist, negatively egalitarian or hierarchical, anti-intellectual, distrustful of politics and, thanks to its lack of political sophistication, vulnerable to manipulation by populist demagogues. Elements of the past were conserved in the peasant attitudes and mingled with those of the present, retarding it, refracting it and crucially leading to a situation where popular control of power was not the norm, but where a wide variety of illusions were entertained about what could be done *with* power. Where these illusions failed to materialise, explanations and comfort were sought in compensatory myths. These myths were of a total transformation, and could include aspirations of a very high level of material consumption, but – being myth-derived

29

- without any sense of the intermediate steps needed to bring them into the real world.

A further irony in all this was that the low level of political literacy had the automatic corollary of promoting the role of the state and dependence on it. As these traditional sections of the population found it difficult to come to terms with the complexity of industrial life, they were inevitably forced into a one-way relationship with the incomprehensible state and, unwillingly, they were constrained into an acquiescence in étatism.

Although the emphasis in this section has been on the ex-peasantry, this term is used emblematically and the actual situation varied from country to country. Thus in Poland the peasantry was still very much a reality, largely because of the inability of the communist authorities to complete collectivisation in the 1950s and 1960s. The impact of this still fairly traditional peasantry on Polish political life has been to introduce an element of unpredictability, impatient radicalism and unreliability into an already volatile political scene. In the Czech lands, the absorption of the peasantry into industry took place much earlier, having begun before the First World War, but given the particular nature of Czech industrialisation, a social formation was created that remained isolated from many of the technological and economic processes that might have favoured a more relaxed attitude towards mobility and change. The Czech working class was, therefore, deeply imbued with conservative values of hierarchy and immobility (Rupnik, 1982). In the former East Germany, the transformation was experienced in a more or less colonialist fashion, with West German values and institutions, as well as personnel, being superimposed on East German society. The attitude of the working class was resentful and dissatisfied, being determined to gain access to the symbols and reality of Western levels of consumption, but hostile to the methods imported from the West. Above all, the cognitive categories of the former East German population found it hard to cope with the new models of expected behaviour and the people tended to retreat into myths, resentment or apathy.

Possibly the most enduring feature salvaged from the rural past has been the deep distrust of the city. Communism imposed a terrible experience on traditional society, which it bore sullenly, unforgivingly and reluctantly, preserving what it could from the past, but changing in unperceived ways as well. This was an altogether different form of urbanisation from that undergone by the West, which was much more organic and effected a fairly successful integration. The disappearance of communism thus meant an end to the sense of humiliation and, equally, an opportunity for revenge. The particular irony of this is that whereas in the West communism was perceived as having created a world of especially soulless industrialisation, remote from the Western experience, for the peasantry that underwent communist modernisation the distinction between the integrated Western process and the failure of the communist process was non-existent. In this sense, communist modernisation was conflated with Westernisation, with the triumph of the hated and sinful city over the pure and authentic values of the countryside.

The collapse of the communism should logically have meant an easy return to those pure values, except of course that the clock cannot be put back and the semi-urbanised masses were thus ready to give an attentive ear to the ex-peasant intellectuals, who were making false promises of a simpler life. This ex-peasant intellectual stratum deserves special attention. Its members were recruited under communism and enjoyed the rapid upward social mobility that the system provided, but instead of embracing its values unquestioningly, they were repelled by it and had the articulateness to give voice to the lost world, not least because their vision of power was one of a simpler, more straightforward, more transparent set of relationships, where cause and effect were directly related.

The ideology voiced by this intellectual stratum is hostile to modernity, to industry, to the density and complexity symbolised by the city and its most extreme manifestation can be observed in the war of Yugoslav succession. The senseless destruction of Vukovar, Sarajevo or Dubrovnik is best interpreted in this context as the ritual killing of the city. This Serbian example also illustrated something else that was evident to the outside observer – the futility of the war against modernity. But this futility was not at all obvious to the ex-peasantry, which was ready to believe its leaders that a better world was round the corner once its alien, sinful enemies had been extirpated. All this says a great deal about the superficiality of the communist modernisation process, which failed to offer those affected enough of a material, moral or political vision to foster a complete integration.

For the post-communist experiment in democracy, the existence of this sizeable, still collectivist-minded and homogenised traditional society does not augur well. Its broad attitudes towards a social and political system orientated towards complexity, change and choice has already been described. Its outstanding characteristic is its malleability, even manipulability and credulousness, as well as its hostility to opposing points of view. The sections of society that voted for Meciar's HZDS in Slovakia, the Greater Romania party, the Smallholders in Hungary, the Bulgarian Socialist Party and, of course, the Peasant Parties in Poland can be regarded as having opted in favour of illusory solutions. They are bound to be disappointed with the nostrums purveyed by populist leaders and will continue to be a volatile element in the political spectrum.

The second vertical segment is the one brought into being by communism. Obviously, there will be some overlap here with the traditional segment, but that fact does not invalidate the separation of this category. Probably the single most salient feature of this group is its positive attitude towards dependence on the state. If it can be described as having been created by the hyper-étatism of communism, it has retained the characteristics of its origins. It continues to regard the state as the best guarantor of both individual and collective well-being, it is not hostile to hierarchy and it believes that the communist system, while imperfect, was the source of its status, achievements and identity.

Unlike the traditional segment, this étatist stratum does accept modernisation in the form of industrialisation, but considers the state to be the most effective instrument of this process. It further accepts that bureaucracy and transformation from above, rather than by personal endeavour, is the most rational and most just method of change. The lower echelons of this segment see their security and livelihood as intimately bound up with the state and are fearful of the implications of the market, not least because many of them fear that their qualifications will not be adequate in a competitive atmosphere to provide them with the standard of living and the status that they have acquired.

Again unlike the traditionalists, this segment has a sizeable intelligentsial – the one brought into being by the communist modernising revolution – and some intellectuals are sympathetic as well. Indeed, there is an argument to be made that a significant proportion of those who consider themselves Western and European in the post-communist world owe their elevation to the communist system. Also important is that many in this segment have considerable political and administrative experience and the self-confidence that goes with that experience.

The upper echelons of the étatists, the former *nomenklatura*, have been among those who have converted their political power under the communist system into economic power under post-communism through *nomenklatura* privatisation, much to the dismay of the traditionalists. This phenomenon has provided the fuel for the populist anger and for the proposition that these countries have been 'robbed' of their revolution. But the étatist segment as a whole is not itself inclined to listen to attentively to the radical message. Rather, it prefers to delay the introduction of market disciplines and tends to vote for parties which promise something along these lines, most obviously for the ex-communist, now socialist parties.

At first sight, the étatists ought to be an ally of the third, liberal segment, but for one important reason. Once the initial pro-Western democratic euphoria of the immediate aftermath of the collapse of communism wore off, many highly placed functionaries discovered that they could salvage some of their political power by a rapid ideological conversion to nationalism. This is the origin of the phenomenon called 'chauvino-communism'. This is very marked in Slovakia, Bulgaria, Romania and, of course, in the country where it was effectively invented and practised with the greatest success, Serbia. The post-communist party in Czech lands, the Left Bloc, has been in the forefront of the campaign against making any concessions of those Sudeten Germans who are demanding that they be included in property restitution plans. The rise of chauvino-communism makes nonsense of the conventional left–right divide and requires a new ideological and party political classification.

Finally, there is the liberal or, perhaps, civic segment. It is characterised by its openness to new ideas, to the market, to initiative, to risk-taking, to technological change in economics and to the recognition that a flexible political system based on compromise and making provision for the entry of new political actors is the one that serves their interests most effectively. This segment was never very strong in Central and Eastern Europe. The values of the market were often promoted by ethnically alien entrepreneurs, especially Jews, and much of the capitalist development of the pre-communist era was, in reality, dependent on the state.

The communist revolution destroyed this tradition and put central planning in its place. However, the idea of independent exchange, of buying and selling as a way of meeting low level disequilibria in supply and demand, could not be stamped out. This kind of activity was, at best, a poor relation of the market, but it did help to keep alive the ethos of trade in a system that regarded it with the utmost disfavour. The rise of the secondary economy in the 1970s and 1980s greatly expanded the potential for an entrepreneurial ethos, even though the secondary economy was in a symbiotic relationship with the first and to an extent was parasitical on it.

Through the secondary economy and partly independently of it, a section of the working class acquired some experience of a labour market. Wherever labour was allowed the freedom of changing its place of work, a kind of surrogate low-level wage bargaining could take place, whereby workers would move from one enterprise to another in order to raise their wages. Where workers had access to a particularly marketable skill – electricians, plumbers – they could move directly into the secondary economy. The upshot of this development was that some sections of the working class became able to recognise their material interests as articulated through wages and prices. This applied even more to various middle strata, including some of the intelligentsia though not so much intellectuals, who were likewise able to market their skills. Clearly, the extent of this varied from country to country. It was far-reaching in Yugoslavia and Hungary, it had some strength in Poland, but was virtually impossible in Romania.

With the end of communism, with marked variations, sections of the population concluded that opportunities to make money through economic activity were possible. These groups were frequently undercapitalised, low in their knowledge of economic methods and technology and had little idea of finance or the nature of credit. On the other hand, they were ready to learn and to assume risk. They would have had some knowledge of the West and, while still harbouring expectations of state support, they had the minimal understanding needed for a proto-entrepreneurial stratum.

In political terms, they were anti-communist and were reasonably well disposed to an anti-étatist message. The greatest political capital of this segment lay in the legitimating ideology of democracy, indissolubly associated with the market economy, which claimed the kudos of having overthrown communism, the support of a sizeable – though weakening – section of the political elite and beyond that, the prestige of the West.

The relative strengths of these three societies was hard to assess and it undoubtedly varied from country to country. It was evident that the chances of establishing a reasonably functioning democracy rested on the size of the third and second segments and, correspondingly, the weakness of the first. Some kind of an alliance between étatism and liberalism was feasible and could constitute the basis for the evolution of a civil society, even if there were major differences in approach between them. This appeared to be the state of affairs in Poland, Hungary and Slovenia. In the Czech lands, the political constellation was somewhat different, in that the Civic Democratic Party was elected on a very clear pro-market platform and the nature of traditional society was more industrial than agrarian; on the other hand, many of the processes, like the introduction of marketisation, had yet to reach high levels in the Czech lands, so it was unclear how the various segments would respond.

This implies that the character and responses of the segments are not fixed, but might well shift according to circumstances. While the essentials of the three broad segments were clear enough, the way in which they might influence politics and be influenced by political processes were still open. Furthermore, as suggested at the outset, these categories are rather fluid and individuals, even groups, could slide from one to another and then back again. The level of volatility was unusually high in the post-communist constellation, hardly surprisingly given the epoch-making transformation that these polities had undergone.

PART TWO

Models of Transition in Eastern Europe

3

Poland

DAVID S. MASON

Official name: Republic of Poland
Area: 120,725 square miles
Population: 38,377,000 (mid-1992)
Head of state: President Lech Walesa
Head of government: Prime Minister Hanna Suchocka

The formation of a non-communist government in Poland in
September 1989 opened the floodgates of reform and revolution in
East-Central Europe. Moscow's acquiescence in this change sent a
signal to the rest of the region, and led in short order to the popular
overthrow or collapse of every one of the European communist
regimes, and ultimately to the disintegration of the Soviet Union
itself. It was not entirely coincidental that Poland had led the charge,
since that country had always been an anomaly in the communist
bloc, and had had a long history of revolt and rebellion.

This anomalous situation was most apparent in the strong role of
the Roman Catholic Church. In a state that was officially atheistic,
there were over 20,000 priests and 15,000 churches and over 90 per
cent of the population professed belief in God. Even 80 per cent of
members of the communist party (the Polish United Workers' Party
PUWP) claimed to be believers.

The other main feature of Poland's unorthodoxy was the large
private sector of the economy – in agriculture. Everywhere else in the
communist world (except Yugoslavia), both land and industry had

36

been socialised, virtually eliminating private ownership. In Poland, however, after one of the country's periodic rebellions in 1956, farmers had been permitted to leave the state-owned and collectivised farms and to resume private farming. In the 1980s, three-quarters of all farmland was in private hands, and a quarter of the country's workforce were private farmers. Thus in both religion and agriculture, there were large sectors of the population, and important aspects of social life, that were largely outside of control by the communist authorities. It is doubtful that the term 'totalitarian' adequately described any East European state after the early 1950s, but it certainly did not apply to Poland. Even Joseph Stalin had admitted that 'communism fits Poland like a saddle fits a cow'.

The Erosion of Communist Rule

In the political sphere, Poland had a tradition of revolt, often against the Russians, that dated back to the eighteenth-century era of 'the Partitions' when the Polish state was gobbled up by its three powerful neighbours Russia, Prussia and Austria. This tradition continued even after the consolidation of communist power. The first major popular challenge to communist policies and power in East Europe occurred in Poland in 1956. In the western Polish city of Poznan, protests and demonstrations against food shortages and poor economic conditions became a riot that was brutally put down by internal security forces. The demonstrations spread to other cities, however, and led to demands for political reforms as well. The Polish party leader expressed sympathy for some of the demonstrations and political demands and finally agreed to step aside in favour of Wladyslaw Gomulka, the more independent-minded party chief in the early post-war years who had been purged for his nationalist tendencies. Gomulka assumed the party leadership, this time promising Poles a more 'Polish' form of communism; he eased pressure on the Roman Catholic Church, abandoned the collectivization of agriculture, and dismissed the Soviet general who was Poland's Defence Minister. Moscow tolerated these changes as long as the regime preserved communist party rule and maintained its commitments to the Warsaw Pact, the Soviet-led military alliance that had been formed the previous year.

Gomulka's liberalism in 1956 gradually eroded, as did the regime's legitimacy, especially in the eyes of young people and intellectuals. In

1968 students and professors in Warsaw staged huge demonstrations following the regime's closing of a performance of a nincteenth-century play (by the national poet Adam Mickiewicz) that contained the line: 'the only things Moscow sends us are jackasses, idiots and spies'. The Polish demonstrations took place as the liberalising reforms of the 'Prague Spring' were unfolding in neighbouring Czechoslovakia under the leadership of Alexander Dubcek. One of the slogans during the Warsaw student demonstrations was the rhyming 'Polska czeka na swego Dubceka' – Poland is waiting for its own Dubcek. The 1968 demonstrations were met with harsh reprisals and purges of students and professors, especially those of Jewish origin.

In 1970, the initiative returned to the workers, this time in the port cities of Gdansk and Szczecin, where they mounted huge demonstrations against a Christmastime increase in food prices. Gomulka fell from power the same way he had risen, on the basis of popular unrest, and was replaced as party leader by Edward Gierek. Gierek rescinded the price increases, but when the regime tried to raise them again in 1976, they were met by another round of strikes and demonstrations.

The 1976 strikes, and the subsequent crackdown by the authorities, brought workers and intellectuals into an alliance for the first time, with the formation by the latter of KOR, the Workers' Defence Committee. KOR was the first of a burgeoning movement of underground societies and organisations in Poland. Some of these, like KOR, were partly a response to the 1975 Helsinki Agreements, in which all governments of Europe, including the communist ones, had guaranteed to protect a wide range of civil rights and freedoms. The late 1970s saw the formation of the Movement for the Defence of Human and Civil Rights (ROPCiO in the Polish acronym), a Polish chapter of Amnesty International, and the nationalist Confederation of Independent Poland (KPN). All of these organisations produced their own *samizdat* publications which frequently reported cases of political arrests and the regime's violations of the country's Constitution or international covenants on human rights such as the Helsinki accords. In the mid-1980s, there were over 2,000 regular *samizdat* publications in Poland, some printed in tens of thousands of copies. All of this contributed to the development of what observers in both east and west called a 'civil society', independent of the formal structures of power, and the gradual weakening of the legitimacy and power of the communist party.

In 1978, there were two other developments that were to have major long-term consequences for Poland. That year, a small group of workers in the shipyards along the coast illegally formed a Committee of Free Trade Unions for the Baltic Coast. One of the founding members was a shipyard electrician named Lech Walesa. In October of the same year, Karol Wojtyla of Krakow was elected Pope of the Roman Catholic Church, taking the name John Paul II. On his triumphal visit to Poland the next year, he was welcomed by millions of Poles, and gave them a sense of both hope and power.

The stage was set for an even more powerful challenge to the regime. The spark came in July 1980 with yet another effort by the regime to raise retail food prices (which by this time were considerably below the cost of producing the product, requiring huge government subsidies). Strikes spread throughout the country, eventually centering on the coast again. By mid-August, 16,000 workers were on strike at the huge Lenin Shipyards in Gdansk. Lech Walesa assumed the leadership of that strike committee and then of the Interfactory Strike Committee (MKS), which represented and coordinated the strike activity at over two hundred enterprises.

When a Politburo delegation from Warsaw arrived to negotiate, the MKS presented them with a list of twenty-one demands, the first of which was 'acceptance of Free Trade Unions independent of both the Party and the employers'. After two weeks of negotiations inside the Lenin Shipyards, the government finally agreed to virtually all of the demands. Thus the government sanctioned the creation of the first independent trade union in the communist world, which the workers named 'Solidarity'.

Over the next sixteen months, some twelve million people (out of a total workforce of sixteen million) joined Solidarity or its rural affiliate. With this practically universal support, the organization became more and more powerful, and increasingly challenged the political prerogatives of the PUWP. At the same time, the party grew weaker and more indecisive, as hundreds of thousands of members resigned, and another million joined Solidarity. The weakening of the Polish party raised hackles in the Kremlin. Several times in 1980 and 1981, Warsaw Pact forces staged threatening military manoeuvres along the Polish borders. After the September 1981 Congress of Solidarity, the Kremlin condemned the session as an 'anti-socialist and anti-Soviet orgy'. In an ominous hint of things to come, in October 1981 the Polish party leader, Stanislaw Kania, was replaced by General Wojciech Jaruzelski, who was already Prime Minister and Defence Minister. Finally, under pressure from the Kremlin, on 13 December,

Jaruzelski declared martial law, arrested the Solidarity leadership, and banned the union.

In 1968, after Soviet forces had intervened in Czechoslovakia to crush the Prague Spring, the Soviet leadership had argued that such intervention was justified to protect the gains of socialism. This policy was dubbed the 'Brezhnev Doctrine' in the West. Though the Brezhnev Doctrine was not explicitly invoked in Poland in 1980–1, the crushing of Solidarity was a reaffirmation of the unwillingness of the Soviet leadership to tolerate the erosion of communist authority in Eastern Europe. But in Poland the results were different from Hungary in 1956 or Czechoslovakia in 1968. In the first place, the Soviet army had *not* intervened directly, apparently fearing massive national resistance to the use of Soviet troops. Secondly, the martial law abolition of Solidarity was not entirely effective. The union was reconstituted as an underground organisation, and continued its activities in organising strikes and demonstrations, publishing newsletters, and promoting independent initiatives in all spheres of society. What was most important, however, was the simple legacy of Solidarity. As Adam Michnik, a founding member of KOR and a Solidarity advisor, wrote:

> In 1980 the totalitarian state gave in and signed an agreement which allowed for the existence of the first legal and independent institutions of postwar Polish political life. They lasted but a short time; long enough, however, to convince everyone that after December 1981 it was not possible to speak again about 'socialism with a human face'. What remains is communism with its teeth knocked out. (Michnik, 1989, p. 184)

The Transition

After the martial law crackdown, Poland muddled along in political stalemate and economic stagnation. After 1981, most Poles turned apolitical and apathetic, reluctant either to support the martial law regime of General Jaruzelski or the underground opposition of Solidarity. Even after the lifting of martial law in 1983, neither the government nor the opposition could muster enough popular support to break the stalemate. People were disillusioned with the government and its policies – and with socialism.

The Jaruzelski government had initiated a decentralising economic

reform in 1982, but had little success in implementing it, due to
bureaucratic inertia, conservative opposition, and popular antipathy.
The economy experienced almost no growth from 1981 to 1985, and
only very small growth in the years after that. The country's huge
hard-currency debt continued to grow, reaching $40 billion in 1988.
The government's efforts to rationalise the pricing structure simply
led to skyrocketing inflation (60 per cent in 1988), workers' demands
for compensating wage increases, and a wage–price spiral that further
lowered the standard of living.

In 1988, a combination of circumstances led to yet another round
of Poland's periodic protests. Eight years after the founding of
Solidarity, there was a new generation of young people in the workforce, and some of them felt neither committed to the old organisation nor intimidated by the legacy of 1981. By now, there was a
reforming leadership in the Soviet Union, under Mikhail Gorbachev,
that would not necessarily support the conservatives in Warsaw. The
1988 protests were sparked by a new round of price rises that, as in
1956, 1970, 1976 and 1980, angered the workers and led them out into
two rounds of protests and strikes, first in the spring and then in
August.

In the spring of 1988 the strikers' demands were largely economic,
but in August they included calls for political changes, including the
legalisation of Solidarity. On 31 August (the anniversary of the
signing of the Gdansk agreements in 1980), Interior Minister Czeslaw
Kiszczak met with Solidarity leader Lech Walesa and offered to
discuss the legalisation of Solidarity if Walesa could persuade the
striking workers to return to work. After some difficulty with strike
leaders who feared a sellout, Walesa was able to prevail, and the
strikes came to an end. This cleared the way for a series of 'Roundtable Negotiations' among representatives of the government, the
Catholic Church and Solidarity.

The negotiations were concluded on 5 April 1989 with a path-
breaking set of agreements that had resonance all over Eastern
Europe. Solidarity would be reinstated and would receive air time on
radio and television as well as its own national and regional newspapers. New parliamentary elections would be called, and the
Solidarity-led opposition would be allowed to compete for 35 per cent
of the seats in the restructured lower house of the Polish parliament,
the Sejm. Even more far-reaching was the reconstitution of a second
legislative chamber, the Senate, for which elections would be completely free and open. At the signing ceremony of this historic pact,

Lech Walesa proclaimed 'this is the beginning of democracy and a free Poland'.

The elections were scheduled for early June 1989, just two months after the roundtable agreement. Under the agreements, the opposition was allowed to contest 161 of the 460 seats in the Sejm and all 100 seats in the new Senate. In the Sejm, the Polish United Workers' Party (or communist party) reserved 38 per cent of the seats for itself, the balance (27 per cent) going to its allied parties in the government. The Solidarity-led opposition was at an incredible disadvantage, trying in that short time to transform itself from illegal underground to legal electoral contestant. Despite the lack of time, resources, and organisation, the opposition staged a stunning victory, winning *all* of the contested seats in the Sejm and 99 of the 100 seats in the Senate. Lech Walesa had not run for the parliament, preferring to stay 'above' the fray of politics. But many veterans of Solidarity, KOR, and other opposition groups, including many who had spent years in internment or jail, were elected.

Solidarity's startling electoral success transformed the political climate in Poland. As agreed in advance, Jaruzelski was elected President by the new parliament, but with the absolute minimum number of votes necessary. In the election for Prime Minister, the PUWP's allied parties refused to support the communists' candidate, and instead swung their support behind Solidarity. With this unexpected turn of events, the party no longer commanded a majority in the parliament, and therefore the ability to form a government. Finally in September 1989 a coalition cabinet was formed under Tadeusz Mazowiecki, an attorney, editor, and Solidarity supporter. Communists remained in control of the military and internal security, with ministerial appointments to those two portfolios, but the rest of the government was non-communist. For the first time in the history of the communist bloc, a non-communist government was in power.

The roundtable negotiations, the election results, and the formation of the Solidarity-led government were increasingly blunt challenges to the principles of the Brezhnev Doctrine. In the past, maintaining the leading role of the communist party was the *sine qua non* for the people's democracies of East Europe. With the formation of the Mazowiecki government in September, the Polish communist party had lost this leading position, and was now in the unaccustomed role of an opposition party. But all through this process, the Kremlin looked on with equanimity, and even approval. Though the April roundtable agreements insisted neither on the preservation of party dominance nor on the preservation of socialism, the Soviet government newspaper *Izvestiya* (7 April 1989) treated the potential loss of communist dominance in an almost offhand way: the opposition 'will take their place in the parliament', it reported, 'where, incidentally, the PUWP will no longer have a majority'. That summer, a Gorbachev spokesman jokingly referred to Moscow's new 'Sinatra Doctrine'. This was a reference to Frank Sinatra's song 'My Way', and implied that the Soviet satellites would be allowed to go their own way. Soon after Mazowiecki's election as prime minister, he travelled to Moscow, where he was warmly received. The message for both Poland and the rest of the bloc was clear: the Brezhnev Doctrine was dead. Moscow was no longer an obstacle to systematic change. The floodgates of change were open.

The Mazowiecki government moved quickly to implement an economic plan to halt inflation and lay the groundwork for a market economy. The plan (see below) did succeed in reducing inflation and boosting the availability of consumer goods. But, as in every other country making the transition from plan to market, there were high costs in terms of declining consumer purchasing power, a drop in production, and a rapid rise in unemployment. Consequently, by the middle of 1990, the overwhelming early support enjoyed by the Mazowiecki government began to diminish rapidly. Walesa himself began to criticise the government as head of a new opposition coalition called the Centre Alliance. This was meant not to topple Mazowiecki, but to prod the government toward a more representative position. In response, Mazowiecki's supporters formed another coalition called Democratic Action (later renamed Democratic Union).

By the summer of 1990, Poland was in an anomalous and somewhat embarrassing situation: it was the first country in Eastern Europe to establish a non-communist government, but had still not experienced completely free parliamentary elections, which by that time had occurred in five other countries. There was increasing irritation in Poland, as well, about the continued presence in the presidency of Wojciech Jaruzelski, another remnant of the roundtable agreements. Bowing to these pressures, in September Jaruzelski announced that he would step down, clearing the way for new elections for the Presidency.

The presidential campaign was a strange one, to say the least. The two major candidates were Lech Walesa, the leader of Solidarity, and Tadeusz Mazowiecki, the leader of the Solidarity government.

Neither clearly defined the issues dividing them, and Walesa mostly banked on popular resentment with the economic reforms and his own charisma. The campaign became even more bizarre with the entry into the race of Stanislaw Tyminski, a Polish-born Canadian businessmen who had left Poland twenty years earlier. Making vague promises for rapid economic recovery and even vaguer warnings about anti-Polish conspiracies, Tyminski finished an astonishing second to Walesa in the November 1990 elections and forced a runoff two weeks later. Walesa won the runoff but Mazowiecki, who had won only 18 per cent of the vote in the first round, treated the results as a public vote of no confidence, so he and his government resigned.

After Walesa's inauguration as President, he nominated Jan Krzysztof Bielecki, an economist and private businessman, as Prime Minister to head up an apolitical 'government of experts' to manage the economic transition. During the first half of 1991, Walesa worked to strengthen the presidency and tried to deflect 'politics' from the Cabinet to his own office. But as the economic reform programme continued to inflict hardship on many Poles, the popularity of both Walesa and the Bielecki government declined, just as Mazowiecki's had.

The first totally free parliamentary elections were held in October 1991, under a complicated system of proportional representation. In some electoral districts, voters were faced with as many as 37 different party lists for the Sejm and 27 candidates for the Senate. Voter turnout was just 43 per cent and the vote was divided among 29 parties, with none winning more than 12 per cent. (Even the semi-serious Polish Beer Lovers' Party won 3.3 per cent of the vote and 16 seats in parliament.) The communists (by now renamed the Social Democrats) lost their guaranteed majority in the Sejm, but the multiplicity of parties created a new political stalemate that prevented the formation of a government for six weeks. Finally, Walesa reluctantly nominated Jan Olszewski, a critic of the free market economic reforms, as Prime Minister of a coalition government. Olszewski's government was also short-lived, and was replaced five months later first by one weak government and then by a another coalition of parties under yet another prime minister, Hanna Suchocka. The creation of a democratic political order solved some of Poland's problems, but it could not insure prosperity, harmony, or stability.

Issues in the Post-Communist Era

Economic 'Shock Therapy'

When Tadeusz Mazowiecki became Prime Minister in September 1989, Poland's financial situation was among the worst in the world, with inflation running at 40 per cent per month, widespread shortages of consumer goods, and a foreign debt of over $40 billion. Consumers and politicians alike were fed up with the many prior attempts to remedy economic ills with evolutionary reform programmes. Under the leadership of Deputy Prime Minister Leszek Balcerowicz, the new government developed a two-stage programme aimed first at curbing inflation and ending shortages, and then attempting to 'leap to a market economy' as quickly as possible through privatisation and deregulation. This strategy was dubbed 'shock therapy'. Balcerowicz and his economic team was assisted in this planning by a young economics professor from Harvard University, Jeffrey Sachs. Sachs had earlier made a reputation in advising the Bolivian government, where his prescriptions helped reduce inflation from 40,000 per cent to 15 per cent in a matter of months. As the Bolivian planning minister at the time explained, 'if you are going to chop off a cat's tail, do it in one strike, not bit by bit' (Sachs and Lipton, 1990, p. 56).

Consequently, the first stage of the 'Balcerowicz plan' was implemented all at once, and very quickly, beginning on 1 January 1990 – just months after the new Mazowiecki government took office. Effective in January, the Polish zloty was made 'convertible' with other currencies, with a new official exchange rate set at 9,500 to the dollar – about what the black market exchange rate had been. This allowed domestic enterprises to purchase foreign currency, and thereby import more goods from abroad. It also allowed exporters to easily convert foreign earnings into zlotys. Most trade barriers were eliminated, encouraging more imports, and the government began negotiations for reductions of other countries' restrictions on Polish imports.

Virtually all government price controls were lifted, allowing prices to respond to supply and demand, and thereby reach equilibrium at a realistic level. At the same time, most government subsidies of state enterprises were eliminated, forcing those companies to become profitable or go out of business. The elimination of subsidies helped to reduce the huge government budget deficits and reverse the growth of foreign debt. Anti-inflationary measures included restrictions on wage increases, reductions in the money supply and sharp increases in interest rates to restrain credit demand and stimulate savings.

The key element of the 'leap to the market' was the development of private property, and especially privatisation of state-owned enterprises. But here the government had to move more cautiously for two main reasons: (i) the question of *how* to sell off state industries (i.e. to whom and at what price); and (ii) the risk of massive unemployment in those industries that could not be sold. The Balcerowicz plan called for rapid small-scale privatisation, and a more deliberate pace for privatisation of major enterprises.

The former task was accomplished relatively quickly. Restrictions were lifted on private ownership, and immediately many *new* private shops and services popped up. Most small state enterprises, especially restaurants and stores, were sold to private owners. Some large enterprises were divided into several smaller units, which were then sold off. During 1990, over 500,000 new small private businesses emerged, while some 150,000 were liquidated. As a result private industrial production increased by 8.5 per cent in 1990, compared with a loss of 25 per cent in the much larger state sector.

The privatisation of large firms was more difficult. The Balcerowicz team, assisted by foreign consultants, the World Bank, and the European Bank for Reconstruction and Development, worked on the large-scale privatisation plan for almost two years before announcing the plan in June 1991. The plan called for the transfer of 400 state enterprises to private hands within six months, and giving a stake to every adult citizen by giving them vouchers for control of group stock funds. But the plan unravelled in late 1991 due to both political and economic objections. The Olszewski government that came to power after the October 1991 elections was not nearly as committed to privatisation, and the process slowed to a crawl. By the end of 1991, only a few state-owned enterprises had been sold off.

While the Balcerowicz reforms had brought some successes, they were also accompanied by terrible economic problems. While inflation *had* been reduced, from almost 2000 per cent in 1989, it still ran at an annual rate of 70 per cent in 1991, much more than expected or planned. Unemployment jumped from 7,000 at the end of 1989 to over 2 million two years later – 12 per cent of the workforce. Real wages declined by 20 per cent in 1990 and did not recover much in 1991. The country's GNP fell by almost 12 per cent in 1990 and another 7 per cent in 1991. Rising unemployment, declining production and the consequent decline in tax revenue led to a burgeoning budget deficit. The deficits violated Poland's agreements with the International Monetary Fund and the World Bank, which then suspended its $2.5 billion loan programme to Poland at the end of 1991.

Unemployment and production declines were exacerbated by the collapse of Poland's trade with the Soviet Union and other postcommunist states. The transition to hard-currency trade within the Council of Mutual Economic Assistance in January 1991 meant that Soviet and other East European firms were unable to purchase Poland's goods because of the lack of foreign exchange. In 1991, Poland's exports to the Soviet Union declined by 90 per cent, due in part to the USSR's own economic and political difficulties. In earlier years, the Soviet Union had absorbed about a third of Poland's exports.

Political Instability and the Growth of Populism

For all the post-communist states, the transition from command to market economy was expected to be a difficult one, and it was an open question whether the fragile new democratic governments could withstand the forces of economic discontent. Poland, being the first in East-Central Europe to launch both democratisation and economic liberalisation, was also the first to experience this political test. As we have seen, popular dissatisfaction with the results of the economic reform contributed to Mazowiecki's dismal showing in the presidential elections at the end of 1990 and to the defeat of the Bielecki government in the parliamentary elections of October 1991. But those elections produced a fragmented legislature that both reflected and exacerbated the many political tensions in the country.

In the Sejm (the lower house of the legislature), 18 parties were represented, with none of them having more than 12 per cent of the total seats, plus another eleven groups holding one seat each. Many of these 'parties' were actually more like electoral coalitions which continually changed as parties split, factions combined and organisations reformed themselves. The large number of small parties and their instability, combined with the large ideological spread, rendered it impossible to put together a stable majority coalition. It took six weeks even to hammer together a minority coalition under Jan Olszewski, and that government lasted only six months. This created another difficult and chaotic situation that resulted in the short-lived rise and fall of one prime ministerial candidate (Waldemar Pawlak) and then, in July 1992, the formation of a seven-party coalition under Prime Minister Hanna Suchocka. Six of the seven parties in the cabinet had a common heritage in the democratic opposition movement, but nonetheless it was a potentially explosive mix of liberals, social democrats, agrarians, Christian democrats and Catholic nationalists (see Table 3.1).

Even a united and strong government, however, would have had difficulties dealing with the many grave and pressing issues facing the country. The task of moving forward was often delayed by issues of the past. Olszewski's government was brought down, for example, after a bitter debate over the goverment's release of the names of alleged secret police collaborators occupying high public office. This issue was part of a larger debate, facing all of the post-communist states, of how to deal with the communist past. Olszewski and his supporters had argued for 'decommunisation' of Poland and a settling of accounts with the past. His opponents, including former Prime Minister Mazowiecki, argued for putting the past behind and moving ahead.

There were other difficult political issues as well. Hanna Suchocka, for example, was able to put together her broad-based coalition in part because her support for a bill banning abortion made her acceptable to the right-of-centre parties like the Christian National Union. But the abortion bill, also supported by the Roman Catholic Church, was a controversial and divisive one, and threatened to cause later problems for the governing coalition.

The fundamental political issue, however, continued to be economics. In the second half of 1992, there were some signs of economic recovery, with increases in industrial production and some declines in the rate of inflation. But for most Poles, the economy still seemed mired in a slump, three years after their exhilarating election of a non-communist government. As more and more factories were shut down or privatised, unemployment continued to grow, reaching 13 per cent in mid-1992. During the first half of 1992, real incomes fell by 5 per cent, and inflation continued at an annual rate of about 30 per cent. All of this contributed to an increasingly volatile political climate.

This became most evident in a dramatic increase in strike activity during 1992 (almost 6000 strikes nationwide by mid-year) culminating in a huge wave of new strikes in the summer. There were echoes of August 1980 when striking workers in the city of Tychy, near

TABLE 3.1   *The Polish parliamentary balance of power, July 1992*

Party	Number of seats
Seven-party governing coalition	
Democratic Union	62
Liberal Democratic Congress	37
Polish Economic Programme	12
Christian National Union	48
Peasant Alliance	19
Peasant Christian Alliance	10
Party of Christian Democrats	6
Supporting parties	
Solidarity	27
German Minority	7
Christian Democracy	5
Total support for coalition	233
'Soft' opposition	
Polish Peasant Party	50
Centre Alliance	30
Union of Labour	5
'Hard' opposition	
Democratic Left Alliance	59
Confederation for an Independent Poland (KPN)	49
Movement for the Republic	10
Real Politics Union	3
Total opposition to coalition	206
Unaffiliated deputies and minor parties	21
TOTAL	460

Source: Adapted from Louisa Vinton, 'Poland's Goverment Crisis: An End in Sight?', *RFE/RL Research Report*, vol. 1, no. 30 (24 July 1992) p. 22.

Katowice, issued a list of 21 Demands, just as the Gdansk strikers had done three years earlier. This list, however, called for 'liquidating unemployment' and abandoning the existing law on privatisation.

The continuing economic difficulties also increased support for 'stronger' government and emboldened nationalist and reactionary forces in the country. Public opinion polls showed that an increasing majority of the population favoured rule 'with a strong hand' and granting the government special powers to rule. In a disturbing sign of growing anti-Semitism, the same polls (reported in *Gazeta Wyborcza*, 11 August 1992) showed 40 per cent of the respondents believing that Jews 'played too big a role in the country's public life'.

Disillusion with the government, with Solidarity, and even with the Church, led many people to opt out of politics altogether (for example, abstaining even from voting) and others to turn to nationalist and populist parties and groups that promised quick and easy solutions. The nationalist Confederation for an Independent Poland (KPN) gained sharply in popularity during 1992, causing its leader, Leszek Moczulski, to predict the collapse of the Suchocka government, new elections, and a victory for the KPN which would, he pledged, settle the economic crisis within several months and totally eliminate unemployment within 3–4 years. This was demagoguery, but it had appeal.

It was difficult to see a positive solution to Poland's political and economic difficulties, given the weakness of government and the nature of its electoral system. Elections to the Sejm are based on proportional representation, with any party obtaining 100,000 signatures of support gaining a place on the ballot and state subsidies. In the October 1991 elections, as we have seen, over 100 parties competed for votes, and eighteen won seats in Parliament. No party has enough seats to govern alone, and coalitions of parties are inherently weak and unstable. A proposed new electoral law (including a 5 per cent threshold for entry to parliament in terms of votes cast nationally) would keep some of the smaller fringe parties from winning seats in the legislature, but the system of proportional representation will probably be retained. Thus, a new round of elections would probably not change this predicament very much.

Poland, therefore, was in a difficult and dangerous situation in the early 1990s. Unless the economy turned around, public apathy and antipathy was likely to increase. But in the absence of a strong and confident government, determined economic reform seemed doubtful. The alternative, unpleasant but increasingly likely, was the assumption of power by a strong and charismatic leader (Walesa? Moczulski?), the 'temporary' subordination of the democratic process, and the firm implementation of an economic plan – either toward the market or back toward state planning and control.

4

The Czech and Slovak Republics

GORDON WIGHTMAN

Czech Republic
Area: 78,864 square kilometres (30,442 square miles)
Population: 10,302,215
Head of state: Vaclav Havel
Head of government: Vaclav Klaus

Slovak Republic
Area: 49,035 square kilometres (18,934 square miles)
Population: 5,274,335
Head of state: Michal Kovac
Head of government: Vladimir Meciar

Despite the speed with which agreement was reached after the Czechoslovak parliamentary elections of 5–6 June 1992 to break up the 74-year-old 'common state' of Czechs and Slovaks and replace it with two independent republics, there was little evidence that the electorate in either part of the country had wished for such an outcome. With the exception of the separatist Slovak National Party, which attracted under 10 per cent of voters in Slovakia, all parties which won seats in the Federal Assembly and the parliaments in the two constituent republics claimed to favour maintaining a common state in some form. Yet the decision by the leaders of the most successful parties, Vaclav Klaus of the Czech-based Civic Democratic Party and Vaclav Meciar of the Movement for a Democratic

Slovakia, to go for what was quickly labelled 'a velvet divorce', less than three years after the 'velvet revolution' which brought an end to communist rule, was practically unavoidable given that the elections had produced majorities in the two republican parliaments for parties with divergent and irreconcilable programmes and a Federal Assembly where the only attainable consensus was an agreement to part company.

The decision to break up Czechoslovakia was all the more surprising insofar as it had appeared in 1989 to be the country in the Soviet bloc with the best prospects of achieving a relatively smooth transition to democracy. Alone in East-Central Europe it had maintained a stable parliamentary system intact during the period between the two world wars, and the revival of the democratic orientations which had underpinned that experience during the 1968 Prague Spring seemed to augur well for the post-communist future (Brown and Wightman, 1997). The country's economic prosperity, relative to its communist neighbours, also seemed likely to cushion the effects of the economic transformation envisaged after the end of communist rule and help to avoid a level of social unrest which might otherwise undermine the country's stability.

At the same time, Czechoslovakia suffered a number of disadvantages at the time of the communist collapse. The leadership which had remained relatively unchanged since it assumed power after the crushing of the Prague Spring was among the most repressive in the region. Its identification throughout the 1970s and 1980s as a loyal defender of 'real socialism' prevented anything other than superficial adaptation to the wind of change blowing from Moscow after the election of Mikhail Gorbachev in March 1985. Even the replacement of the party's General Secretary, Gustav Husak, in December 1987 made scant difference, since his successor, Milos Jakes, had been responsible for the mass expulsion from the Communist Party of the proponents of the very kind of reform Gorbachev was then trying to introduce in the Soviet Union.

Until the end of the 1980s, the population remained largely passive. Even ten years after its first appearance, the Charter 77 manifesto had been signed by no more than two thousand people and it was only in 1988 that dissent began to spread to larger numbers of independent civic initiatives. Even though in 1988 and 1989 there was evidence of increasing public willingness to take part in demonstrations (notably to mark the twentieth anniversary of the Soviet invasion in August 1968, the seventieth anniversary of the foundation of the republic on 28 October 1918 and the twentieth anniversary of the self-immolation of the student Jan Palach in January 1969), the Communist leadership appeared to remain unshaken.

On the other hand, the Communist regime itself was so hostile to reform that its fall from power, when it came, was as complete as it was unexpected. A week after the brutal police attack on a student demonstration, on 17 November 1989, which sparked off the 'velvet revolution', the entire Communist Party leadership, including its General Secretary, resigned. Two weeks after that, on 10 December, Husak gave up his remaining post as the country's President after swearing in a new Government of National Understanding led by Marian Calfa, a junior minister in the outgoing administration, and in which the Communists retained only ten of the twenty-one seats.

If this appeared to leave the Communists in a fairly strong position, the clearest signal that power had in fact shifted to their opponents came on 28 and 29 December when first Alexander Dubcek, the Communists' leader during the Prague Spring who had been expelled from the party in 1970, became chairman of the Federal Assembly, and then Vaclav Havel, the leading figure in Civic Forum, the new political movement created on 19 November, two days after the police attack, to coordinate the campaign to end communist rule, became Czechoslovak President.

The Transition

Czechoslovakia thus entered 1990 with a new government and a new President committed to preparing for free and competitive parliamentary elections. In mid-January it was agreed that these would be held for both the Federal Assembly and the Czech and Slovak National Councils on 8–9 June, using the party list system of proportional representation which had applied both in pre-war Czechoslovakia and in the last free elections in 1946, with two important modifications. To qualify for seats, contenders in the elections would be required to cross a threshold (set at 5 per cent for the Federal Assembly and the Czech National Council and 3 per cent for the Slovak parliament). Secondly, voters would be permitted to express a preference for up to four candidates on any particular list (see Wightman, 1990a, 1990b and 1991). If the first provision was designed to inhibit a proliferation of parties in the new parliaments, the second was intended to accommodate the perceived importance of individual personalities in an electoral system which tended to be weighted towards party officials who determined the composition of lists of candidates.

Those first six months of 1990 remained largely a period of consensus. Communist influence was reduced notably by the resignation from the party in January of Calfa and two of his senior ministers (the economists Valtr Komarek and Vladimir Dlouhy, both of whom had in any case been nominated to the government by Civic Forum), and the replacement of the Communist Frantisek Pitra who combined a post as deputy premier in the federal administration with that of Prime Minister in the Czech Republic by Civic Forum's Petr Pithart. (His counterpart in Slovakia, Milan Cic, who had combined a deputy premiership at federal level with the post of Slovak Prime Minister since December 1989, also resigned from the Communist Party in March.)

There was at this time little overt sign of the fundamental divergences between Czechs and Slovaks which were to emerge later. Slovaks had appeared as enthusiastic to end the Communists' power monopoly in November 1989 as their Czech counterparts and the emergence of a broadly-based political movement, Public Against Violence, to coordinate the campaign for democracy in Slovakia, seemed to augur well for the future.

The only major sign of dissensus came in March 1990 with what became known as the 'hyphen war', when demonstrations were organised in Bratislava to demand that Slovakia be made more 'visible' in the country's official name from which Havel had suggested the word 'socialist' be dropped. If the traditional Czechoslovak Republic was unacceptable to Slovaks, the hyphenated version they advocated was equally objectionable to the Czechs (for whom it was reminiscent of the short-lived period between the Munich Agreement in October 1938 and Hitler's occupation of Bohemia and Moravia in March 1939). The eventual compromise of Czech and Slovak Federative Republic appeared to satisfy both sides, but the dispute proved to be a forerunner of much more fundamental differences that were to surface soon after the elections.

The June 1990 Parliamentary Elections

The elections on 8–9 June 1990 provided resounding confirmation of support for the return to parliamentary democracy. As much as 96 per cent of the electorate took part, and if the Communist Party did better than some Czech commentators thought healthy with around 13.6 per cent of the vote in both republics, it was nevertheless a resounding defeat for a party which had won over 40 per cent of the Czech vote, and a third of that in Slovakia, in the last free elections in 1946.

Others, including President Havel, interpreted the vote as more a referendum on democracy (Havel, 1991, pp. 11–12) than an occasion on which the voters expressed their preferences for particular parties. This was certainly true of the Czech Republic, where around half the electorate cast their votes for Civic Forum as an affirmation of their commitment to democracy and where no other contender save the Communists attracted more than 10 per cent of the vote. Indeed, only two other parties succeeded in crossing the 5 per cent threshold in the Czech Republic: the Christian and Democratic Union (a coalition involving the former satellite Czechoslovak People's Party and the Christian Democratic Party led by former dissident Václav Benda), and the Movement for Self-governing Democracy – the Society for Moravia and Silesia, whose campaign for regional auton-omy had a particularly strong appeal in the two Moravian constituen-cies in the eastern half of the Czech Republic.

The elections were less of a plebiscite in Slovakia, where Public Against Violence attracted a lower share of the vote than Civic Forum had done among the Czechs. In the elections to the two chambers of the Federal Assembly, it won 32.5 per cent for the House of the People and 37.3 per cent for the House of the Nations and in those for the Slovak National Council it attracted an even lower 29.3 per cent. Leaving aside the half-million Hungarian min-ority whose votes went almost entirely to a coalition involving Coexistence (which had called for the support of all ethnic minorities in Czechoslovakia) and the Hungarian Christian Democratic Movement, Public Against Violence faced two important rivals for the Slovak vote: the Christian Democratic Movement and the Slovak National Party. The former's appeal to a Catholic constituency that was much stronger in Slovakia than in the Czech Lands attracted 19 per cent of the vote for the House of the People and the Slovak National Council and 16 per cent for the House of the Nations. The Slovak National Party's policy of separatism attracted 11 per cent for both chambers of the Federal Assembly and 13.9 per cent for the Slovak republican parliament.

While the distribution of seats in the Slovak National Council gave

Public Against Violence, with only 48 of the 150 deputies in that parliament, no alternative but to form a coalition with the Christian Democratic Movement, which had 31 (and with the Democratic Party which had failed to win any seats in the Federal Assembly but had crossed the lower 3 per cent threshold for the Slovak parliament and been awarded seven seats), the formation of relatively broad coalitions in the Czech Republic and at federal level reflected other considerations. The inclusion in the new Czech government of representatives of the Christian and Democratic Union and the Movement for Moravia and Silesia may be seen as an attempt to maintain a broad consensus in that parliament since, with 127 of the 200 seats, Civic Forum had a substantial majority in the Czech National Council.

The formation of a federal coalition which embraced deputies for the Christian Democratic Movement as well as Civic Forum and Public Against Violence, on the other hand, took into account the procedural difficulties facing any federal government which hoped to introduce substantial constitutional reform. A particular difficulty at federal level was the requirement that constitutional and other major legislative initiatives receive not only the approval of three-fifths of deputies in the House of the People but also the agreement of three-fifths of the 75 Czechs and three-fifths of the 75 Slovaks in the House of the Nations, voting separately. With 87 of the 150 members in the former chamber, Civic Forum and Public Against Violence were three short of that requirement. Civic Forum's 50 deputies in the House of the Nations were sufficient for the passage of such legislation in the Czech section, but a qualified majority of this kind could only be achieved among Slovak deputies in that chamber with the combined votes of the 33 Public Against Violence representatives and the 14 Christian Democrats. Intended to protect the interests of the Slovaks against being outvoted by the more numerous Czechs, these provisions were to prove a major obstacle to agreement on a range of controversial issues in the two years ahead.

Post-Electoral Discord

There was little reason to expect that the apparent harmony established between Czech and Slovak politicians and maintained within the victorious political movements up to the June 1990 elections would dissolve so quickly. Nevertheless, although much was to be achieved, particularly in the area of economic reform (legislation to privatise much of the retail and service sectors, to return property confiscated by the Communists to its rightful owners or their descendants, and to establish popular capitalism through 'voucher' privatisation of much of industry), the two-year term of the new parliaments was marked fairly early on by growing divisions between Czechs and Slovaks and a process of political differentiation first within Civic Forum and then within Public Against Violence.

At the heart of the crisis in Czech–Slovak relations, which was to dominate the second half of 1990 and erupt once more in late 1991, were different perceptions of the optimal constitutional relationship between the two nations. Czech politicians generally accepted that the highly centralised federal system inherited from the Communists had to be modified to transfer greater power to the republics and thus satisfy Slovak aspirations for greater control over their own affairs. Many feared, however, that too much devolution could be dysfunctional, inhibit a coordinated economic policy and even prove to be the first steps towards the break-up of the state.

From the outset, Slovak views were more diverse and indeed susceptible to change over time. There was some support for a federation, but the number of its proponents tended to decline as the arguments continued over constitutional reform. Vladimir Meciar, who replaced Cic as Slovak Prime Minister after the elections, for example, appeared in 1990 to be committed to a federal system, albeit one in which substantial powers would be devolved to the republics. A year later, after he had been dismissed from that post, he favoured a confederation and by the time of the 1992 elections was advocating what he termed a 'looser association' between the two republics. Jan Carnogursky, the leader of the Christian Democratic Movement, who succeeded Meciar as Slovak Prime Minister in April 1991, propounded the idea that Slovakia should remain within Czechoslovakia until it could obtain 'its own little star and its own seat' within the European Community at the turn of the century (*Rudé právo*, 5 November 1990; *Lidové noviny*, 20 December 1990).

If Czech unwillingness to contemplate anything weaker than a federal system was one obstacle to agreement, another was the apparent belief among many Slovak politicians that they could combine sovereignty and Slovakia's recognition in international law with membership of a 'common state' with the Czechs, and that the Czechs were so psychologically attached to that state that they would concede almost any Slovak demands to ensure its survival.

That this was far from the case was made clear after the 1992 elections, but well before then, divisions within both Civic Forum and Public Against Violence had come into the open and by mid-1991 both movements had split. Of the parties which emerged out of Civic Forum, it was the right-of-centre Civic Democratic Party, led by Vaclav Klaus, the then federal Finance Minister and father of the economic reform, which drew the largest following among Czechs, attracted to his vision of a prosperous, privatised free-market economy. In Slovakia, opinion swung in the opposite direction behind the Movement for a Democratic Slovakia, founded by Vladimir Meciar, after he broke with Public Against Violence in April 1991 following disagreements within the leadership of that movement over the nationalist and interventionist policies, as well as the confrontational style, that Meciar had favoured during his ten months as Slovak Prime Minister. Meciar's image as a defender of Slovak interests and his new movement's commitment, first to a confederation and then to a 'looser association' between the two republics, as well as to more protectionist economic policies, appealed to a public which wanted to see a greater devolution of power to Bratislava and which feared the consequences of marketisation and privatisation on an economy where unemployment was already several times higher than in the Czech Republic.

The June 1992 Parliamentary Elections

That divergence in public opinion within the two republics was confirmed in the parliamentary elections held on 5–6 June 1992. Standing in coalition with the small Christian Democratic Party, led by former dissident, Vaclav Benda, Klaus's Civic Democratic Party won a third of the Czech vote for both chambers of the Federal Assembly and 29.7 per cent for the Czech National Council. The two other main parties to emerge from Civic Forum drew little support by comparison. The centrist Civic Movement, which was led by the outgoing Foreign Minister Jiri Dienstbier and which embraced within its ranks many former reform Communists who had been prominent both in the dissident movement and in Civic Forum, failed to win any seats in either parliament. The Civic Democratic Alliance, a party which was close to Klaus in its policy goals but lacked his grass-roots organisation, was unsuccessful for the Federal Assembly but won fourteen seats, with 6 per cent of the vote, in the Czech National

Council (the Movement for Self-Governing Democracy – the Society for Moravia and Silesia suffered a similar fate, scraping through with the same share of the vote only for the Czech parliament).

Nor did any other contender in the Czech Republic come close to the level of support given the coalition between the Civic Democratic and Christian Democratic Parties. The successor to the Communists, the Left Block (a coalition embracing the Communist Party of Bohemia and Moravia and a small grouping called the Democratic Left), managed to obtain 14 per cent, and four other contenders succeeded in crossing the five per cent threshold. The centre-right Christian Democratic Union-Czechoslovak People's Party, with 6 per cent, was one of only two parties (the Communists were the other) to achieve re-election to both the Federal Assembly and the Czech National Council. Two left-of-centre newcomers, the Liberal Social Union (formed by the Czechoslovak Socialist Party, the Agricultural Party and the Greens) and the Czechoslovak Social Democratic Party, attracted around 6 and 7 per cent of the vote respectively, while the extremist, right-wing Association for the Republic-Republican Party of Czechoslovakia, which had also failed to cross the threshold in 1990, won 6 per cent for both parliaments this time round.

In Slovakia, the Movement for a Democratic Slovakia won a third of the Slovak vote for both houses of the Federal Assembly and an even higher 37.3 per cent for the Slovak National Council. Proponents of federalism and radical reform within Public Against Violence, who had transformed what remained of that movement after Meciar's departure into a political party called the Civic Democratic Union, failed to win any seats in either parliament.

Indeed, with the exception of the coalition involving the Hungarian Christian Democratic Movement and Coexistence, which retained the allegiance of the Hungarian minority in southern Slovakia, openly pro-federal parties did badly. The Democratic Party failed to win any seats. The Christian Democratic Movement saw its support halved to only 9 per cent, while the Social Democratic Movement in Slovakia succeeded in crossing the 5 per cent threshold only for the House of the Nations, thanks to the presence of Alexander Dubcek on its list of candidates for that chamber. Of the Slovak parties elected in 1990, only the Party of the Democratic Left (the successor to the Communist Party of Slovakia), with around 14.5 per cent, saw a slight increase in its share of the vote. Even the Slovak National Party saw its support fall, from around 11 per cent for the federal parliament in 1990 to 9.4 per cent in 1992, and from almost 14 per cent to 7.9 per cent for the Slovak National Council.

That decline in the Nationalists' vote confirmed that there was little support even among Slovaks for separatism and, given that neither Czechs nor Slovaks explicitly voted for the break-up of Czechoslovakia, the explanation for the rapidity with which Klaus and Meciar, as leaders of the most successful contenders, reached agreement on a 'divorce' between the two republics is to be found in the political stalemate created by the elections.

On the one hand, the elections had produced parliaments in the republics, in which strong governments of opposite political complexion could be formed relatively easily. In the Czech National Council, the electoral coalition between the Civic Democratic and Christian Democratic Parties had only 76 of the 200 seats, but with the two other right-of-centre parties, the Christian Democratic Union–Czechoslovak People's Party (which had 15) and the Civic Democratic Alliance (with 14), had a clear majority. In practice that was the coalition on which the new Czech government, sworn in on 2 July, was based, with Klaus as Prime Minister.

In the Slovak parliament, the Movement for a Democratic Slovakia, with 74 of the 150 seats, was only two short of an outright majority and could have formed an administration with either the Party of the Democratic Left (which had 29 seats) or the Slovak National Party (with 15). In practice, the latter proved the preferred partner and the new Slovak government, formed on 24 June 1992, comprised eleven members of the Movement for a Democratic Slovakia, one member of the Slovak National Party and, as Interior Minister, a non-party General.

In the Federal Assembly, by contrast, there was little prospect of forming a stable and effective government. Neither right-wing parties nor any other plausible coalition had even a simple majority in both chambers, let alone the qualified majority required for constitutional bills. Indeed, either of the two largest groups in the House of the Nations – the Civic Democratic Party–Christian Democratic Party coalition (with 37 of the Czech deputies) and the Movement for a Democratic Slovakia (with 33 of the Slovak representatives) – had more than the two-fifths needed to veto constitutional proposals they found unacceptable.

Given Meciar's insistence, during negotiations in the days following the elections, on Czechoslovakia's transformation into what Klaus interpreted as 'a defence and economic community and two states recognised in international law' (*Lidové noviny*, 10 June 1992), and Klaus's conviction that anything other than a federation would be unworkable and a threat to completion of economic reform, there was no room for compromise. The formation on 2 July of a 'grand coalition' embracing the Civic Democratic Party, the Movement for a Democratic Slovakia and the Christian Democratic Union–Czechoslovak People's Party, which could assume a caretaker role until the completion of 'divorce proceedings', seemed the only viable outcome.

The dissolution of Czechoslovakia was thus not the consequence of demands for independence from Slovakia. It was rather the result of a confrontation between divergent and incompatible beliefs about what was politically attainable, between an illusion on the part of many Slovaks that they could gain the trappings of independence (a declaration of Slovak sovereignty, and recognition of Slovakia in international law) while remaining in a common Czech and Slovak state, and a conviction on the part of many Czechs that anything other than a federal system was unworkable and to their disadvantage.

A Changing Political Agenda

By the end of 1992, the Federal Assembly had approved legislation terminating the Czech and Slovak Federative Republic at midnight on 31 December 1992 and dividing its property between the two successor republics. Agreement had been reached on a customs union, on maintaining the Czechoslovak crown until such time as separate currencies could be established, and a range of other matters. Nevertheless, hopes that the divorce settlement would permit relations between the two republics to start off on an amicable basis were not strengthened by Slovaks' questioning matters that appeared to have been settled. Cases in point were demands for compensation for their share of the costs of building the federal parliament in Prague, despite agreement that immovables would go to the republic in which they were situated, and the question of the federal gold reserve, from which Slovakia argued gold amassed by the wartime Slovak state should be deducted before the reserve was shared out on the agreed two to one ratio.

No attempt was made to obtain popular approval for the split. A referendum in Slovakia to ratify the agreements, originally planned for mid-December, was postponed for lack of time while, in the Czech Republic, a referendum (advocated by some opposition parties) was deemed neither useful nor expedient. While the new Slovak state was to some degree legitimised by its National Council's approval of a Declaration of State Sovereignty in July 1992 and the passage of a new Slovak Constitution in October, a suggestion by some Czech politicians that the new Czech Republic needed to be sanctified at least by the direct election of its first President was equally rejected. The Civic Democratic Party could argue that its commitment, since its congress in November 1991, to either a federation or a split, though played down in the election campaign, was sufficient mandate for the policy it was pursuing and that, in any case, a referendum could do little to overcome the impasse in the federal parliament.

While Slovakia had its new Constitution in place well ahead of independence, in the Czech Republic arguments continued well into December on a number of key issues. In the end, it was decided that the election of the President, as noted above, would remain within parliament's jurisdiction and views that parliament should remain unicameral were eventually turned down in favour of a bicameral assembly comprising a Chamber of Deputies and an 81-member Senate. The transformation of the existing 200-member Czech National Council into the Chamber of Deputies was a straightforward matter but the creation of the Senate was more problematical. No elections to the Senate seemed likely before 1994 and, as late as February 1993, proposals for the transfer of all or some of those deputies who had been elected in the Czech Republic to the new defunct Federal Assembly remained a subject of dispute between the parties.

If the transition from totalitarian rule proved fatal to Czechoslovakia, the prospects for democracy in the new Czech Republic remained reasonably good. The collapse of Civic Forum in 1991 and the failure of the Civic Movement in the 1992 elections ended illusions that the future lay in a new type of loosely structured political movement. The success of Klaus's Civic Democratic Party, which had been formed because of Klaus's determination to have a normal party capable of pushing a coherent programme, illustrated the attractions of a traditional political force with a strong membership base. Even if it fails to maintain the level of popularity it achieved in 1992, the Civic Democratic Party appears likely to remain a lasting feature of the Czech political landscape and to form one element in a new party system which had only begun to take shape by that time.

The 1992 elections had brought some progress in that direction. The Communists, it is true, remained an almost unregenerated force on the left and the support for the extremist Association for the Republic–Republican Party of Czechoslovakia on the right was an equally unwelcome indication of racist inclinations among some sections of the population. Yet the election of deputies for the Social Democratic Party, however few in number, brought the establishment of a conventional left–right spectrum closer, since its presence in parliament went some way to balance the stronger swing to the non-extremist right demonstrated in support for the Civic Democratic Party, the Civic Democratic Alliance and the Christian Democratic Union–Czechoslovak People's Party.

The Social Democrats and the People's Party were the only two parties with pre-communist roots to enter parliament on their own, the latter thanks to continuing support in its traditional rural and Catholic areas and despite its long years as a satellite party under Communist rule. The other Czech ex-satellite party, the Socialist Party, which also traced its origins to one of the major forces in pre-communist Czechoslovakia, only managed to win seats in 1992 as part of the Liberal Social Union which also embraced an organisation created to defend the interests of the cooperative farms, the Agricultural Party, and the Greens. A predictably unstable association of rather disparate interests, that Union was already under strain by the end of 1992 and seemed unlikely to take a permanent place in Czech politics.

The defeat of the Civic Movement was seen as a failure of the liberal centre in Czech politics but it also represented a defeat for the mainstream dissident movement and the 1968 reform communists, who had constituted much of the new elite after the collapse of communism. The government which led the Czech Republic into independence on 1 January 1993 was almost entirely comprised of people unknown in November 1989 and only one of its members, Jan Ruml the Interior Minister, stands out as having been a leading figure in dissent.

In Slovakia, by contrast, the transition to democracy seemed much less assured. Soon after the elections there were already intimations of a more authoritarian trend. Fears that the Movement for a Democratic Slovakia was aiming to gain control of the public media in order to silence its critics were increased by Meciar's demand immediately after the elections that federal television and radio should be closed down, by his government's re-nationalisation of Danubiaprint, which prints most of Slovakia's newspapers, and by a court case challenging the ownership of the most independent-minded Slovak daily, *Smena*. The attempt to remove the Vice-Chancellor of the new University of Trnava, Anton Hajduk, a political opponent, on the technical grounds that he was unqualified for the post (Havel, on making the appointment, had not been informed that Hajduk lacked the required status for the post – a matter he could have easily remedied at the time) and then government attempts to close down the University altogether, were ominous signs for academic freedom.

Slovakia attained independence with a party system that bore little resemblance to those of more conventional democracies, with a predominance of parties to the left of centre. The defeat of the right-wing parties, the Civic Democratic Union and the Democratic Party, was far from surprising. Their attachment to the federation and support for Klaus's free-market reforms were recipes for failure, reinforced by a lack of personalities with popular appeal. Nevertheless, the absence of a clearly pro-market party was a gap which the Slovak Nationalists, deprived of their main purpose, the attainment of independence, began to consider filling.

Party allegiance in Slovakia after the 'velvet revolution' was, however, relatively inconstant. (On the fluctuations in party support in 1989 and 1990, see Butora *et al.*, 1991.) The success of Public Against Violence in 1990 had suggested that the civil libertarian values it represented were more widely shared than might have been expected in a country where clericalism and nationalism had predominated in the past. In practice, civil libertarianism and clericalism proved weaker in the longer term as the national issue asserted its predominance.

The stringencies Slovakia seems likely to face without the advantages of redistribution of resources from the Czech Republic may well tempt its leaders to play the nationalist card. The prospect of a tough policy towards its Hungarian minority could well worsen relations with Hungary that are already uneasy because of Hungary's opposition to the Gabcikovo dam and hydroelectric project on the Danube, a matter of prestige in Slovakia.

On the other hand, Slovakia's application to join the Council of Europe suggests it accepts the rules of the democratic game, in principle. At the same time, it is by no means clear it is as enthusiastic as are the Czechs for integration in the European Community. Its geographical position has led some of its nationalist leaders to see advantages in closer trading links to the east, particularly with the Ukraine, and in that respect its future development may be very different from that of the westward-looking inhabitants of Bohemia and Moravia.

There was never any likelihood that discord between Czechs and Slovaks would lead to another Yugoslavia in central Europe. Czechoslovakia's disappearance nevertheless removes what had appeared to be an island of stability in the region and, insofar as it represents a failure to resolve national differences, is a move in the opposite direction from trends in what Czechs see as 'the civilised world' of Western Europe.

5

Hungary

NIGEL SWAIN

Official name: Republic of Hungary
Area: 93,000 square kilometres
Population: 10,335,000
Head of state: President Arpad Goncz
Head of government: Prime Minister Jozsef Antall

Hungary's transition from communism to post-communism was low-key. There was no bloodshed. There were few crowds. There were no big events to attract the world's media. Yet without Hungary the demise of communism in Europe – if it had happened at all – would have happened very differently. For it was Hungary's decision in September 1989 to permit the emigration through Austria of East German citizens (a logical extension of the decision taken the preceding May to dismantle the 'iron curtain' with Austria, a decision which was domestically unremarkable following the granting of full international passports to Hungarian citizens in January) that precipitated the fall of the Berlin Wall. Hungary's transition represented the quiet exhaustion of the communist economic system and its political masters. When pushed, the regime gave in and negotiated away all its powers. Furthermore, because dissident movements had enjoyed an almost accepted status for at least four years before 1989, and because the Communist Party (officially the Hungarian Socialist Workers' Party, hereafter Party) did not oppose change, the opposition, rather than unite against a common enemy, splintered early on into the precursors of the post-communist political parties. The

66

Hungarian transition, then, was gradual and peaceful; and an alternative pluralist politics in embryo was present even before the 'change of system' took place.

The End of the Communist Order

By the 1980s Hungary had gained a deserved reputation as the liberal exception in Eastern Europe, the result of the astute political skills of Janos Kadar who, having come to power with the aid of Soviet troops in 1956, had, during the course of the 1960s, negotiated two critical political compromises: a 'social compact' with the Hungarian people, and a power political bargain with the Soviet Union. In the latter, Kadar undertook to remain fiercely loyal to the Soviet Union in foreign policy matters (to the extent of joining in the invasion of Czechoslovakia in 1968) in return for the right to experiment domestically with economic and social reform. In his 'social compact' with the Hungarian people, he traded acceptance of the principle of single party rule by the Party for the promise of ever-increasing living standards and a depoliticisation of social life in line with the slogan 'he who is not against us, is with us'. This dual compromise had been exceptionally successful throughout the late 1960s and the 1970s; but by the 1980s it was beginning to fall apart on both fronts. Domestically, it proved increasingly difficult to provide increasing living standards (which from 1979 onwards stagnated or declined), while, internationally, the advent of Gorbachev and disappearance of the 'Brezhnev doctrine' removed the need for compromise at all.

Hungary's economic history is one of cycles of reform and recentralisation. The 'new economic mechanism' of 1968 was the most radical economic reform in the bloc, removing, as it did, all quantitative planning targets and central allocation of resources. The early 1970s had seen the pendulum swing away from reform, but, at the end of the decade, in a climate of increasing foreign indebtedness, reform came back onto the agenda. An austerity programme was introduced in 1978, and a series of measures between 1980 and 1988 radically overhauled the economic mechanism pushing it, after 1985, towards Yugoslav self-managed market socialism. In 1980–1 the number of ministries was reduced and the formation of small-scale semi-private (nominally cooperative) businesses stimulated. In 1982, Hungary joined the IMF and the World Bank and a fledgling capital market began as enterprises were permitted to offer interest-bearing

bonds. The right to issue equity shares followed in 1986 for a restricted number of joint stock companies (such as foreign joint ventures),
and stock exchange operations were introduced in January 1989 as
the right to establish joint stock companies became universal. (The
Stock Exchange proper was opened in June 1990.) In addition,
, stricter regulations concerning bankruptcy were introduced in 1986,
and financial institutions were created to handle enterprise insolvency
and restructuring. Banking reform followed in 1987, creating a bank
of issue and multiple competing commercial banks, rather than the
socialist system of non-competitive task-specific banks. And in 1988
Hungary adopted personal income and value-added taxes.

Much of the apparatus of a modern market economy was indeed in
place by the end of the 1980s although this did not alter its profoundly
non-market orientation, as borne out by enterprise behaviour following the XIIIth Party Congress in 1985 which signalled renewed economic growth for the first time since 1978. Hungary's by then
Enterprise Council-managed enterprises, like their 'self-managed'
Yugoslav counterparts, threw financial caution to the winds. The
result was mushrooming debt. Hungary's net convertible currency
debt, which had been held stable over the first half of the 1980s, after
nearly doubling between 1977 and 1979, more than doubled again
between 1985 and 1987, becoming the highest per capita debt in the
region. A short-term stabilisation plan was introduced in 1987, but
opposition reformists and government economists alike were finally
persuaded that introducing a veneer of market institutions was not
enough: the knotty problem of 'ownership reform' would have to be
addressed. The Companies Act which came into force on 1 January
1989 not only permitted the formation of private joint stock companies, it also allowed for the private ownership of shares in these
companies by private citizens – capitalism.

This undermining of the economic foundations of socialism was
part of a more general process. Hungary continued to be the liberal
and consumerist haven of Eastern Europe throughout the 1980s, but
it was in spite, rather than because of, socialist institutions. The only
dynamic part of the economy was the small-scale semi-private sector;
and citizens could only make ends meet by participating in this
economy *in addition to* their state sector jobs. The consequences of
this schizophrenic economy were a decline in public morale and the
emergence of extensive, if not mass, opposition. Social scientists
noted a decline in solidarist values and an increase in individualism,
while at the same time public opinion poll findings revealed a dra-

matic decline especially after 1986 in the population's faith in the government's ability either to solve the economy's problems or achieve socialist targets (Swain, 1992, pp. 7–32).

As the legitimacy of the regime was questioned, opposition activity increased. In 1985, although prominent dissidents failed in their bid to exploit electoral reform and enter parliament, a number of unofficial candidates succeeded, most notably Zoltan Kiraly; and a public two-and-a-half-day political gathering was held successfully at Monor. In 1986 and extending into 1987, opposition economists produced *Turnabout and Reform*, a radical critique of Hungarian economic performance which, finally, with the help of the increasingly prominent reform communist Imre Pozsgay, was brought into the public domain. In 1987, the 'democratic opposition' published a special issue of the samizdat *Beszelo* entitled 'The Social Contract' which called for political pluralism, an autonomous parliament and freedom for the press in June; in September, the 'populist' opposition and selected reform communists met in the village of Lakitelek and created Hungarian Democratic Forum (HDF); and in December, the Party opted to hold a special Conference in May 1988.

In the run-up to this Conference, a series of opposition public meetings was held in the Jurta Theatre in Budapest, while Kadar sealed his fate by expelling four prominent reformists from the Party. The bulk of the Party could not countenance a return to a politics of intolerance and expulsions, and Kadar was effectively removed from office at the Conference, where 'the most radical and most peaceful change of guard in a communist party leadership that has ever happened under normal conditions' took place (Lendvai, 1989).

As the nature or the Party subtly changed, the formation of *de facto* opposition parties (although technically associations or movements) carried on apace. In March 1988 FIDESZ (the Alliance of Young Democrats) was formed, as was the Network of Free Initiatives, out of elements of the former 'democratic opposition' and other opposition, peace and environmentalist groups. The following November the former 'democratic opposition' created the Alliance of Free Democrats (AFD) out of many of the organisations grouped under the Network umbrella, and the Independent Smallholders Party (ISP) reconstituted itself. Hungary's Social Democratic Party (HSDP) followed suit in January 1989, as did the Christian Democratic People's Party (CDPP) in March 1989.

By the end of 1988 Hungary's socialism was beginning to fall apart of its own accord. The old guard disappeared, a new guard had passed legislation which effectively permitted capitalist restoration; and inroads had been made into the Party's monopolistic control over public life by new forms of social organisation which, capitalising on reformist legislation passed in the mid-1980s, had established themselves independently of the Party-controlled Patriotic People's Front and now dared to produce openly political programmes. But even before the years of political transition, the opposition revealed itself to be divided ideologically. FIDESZ, whose members had reached maturity in the economic stagnation and ideological apathy of the 1980s, distanced itself from the former 'democratic opposition' whose members, twenty and more years earlier, had thought a reformed and humane socialism possible. When the former 'democratic opposition' created the AFD out of the Network of Free Initiatives, FIDESZ retained its independence. More important, following the HDF's failure to invite members of the 'democratic opposition' to the first Lakitelek meeting, the HDF and the AFD strove to maintain their separate nationalist and liberal identities.

The Transition

As has already been suggested, profound political transformations were underway in Hungary before the beginning of 1989. As a consequence, there was no single 'big bang' of revolutionary change; indeed, change was so gradual that Ash has suggested the neologism 'refolution' to describe events (Ash, 1990, p. 14). The more or less accepted characterisation of the Hungarian transition, however, has become 'negotiated revolution' (Bruszt, 1992). The legal framework for the 'change of system' emerged from protracted negotiations between government and opposition, negotiations which were ultimately successful because the opposition, despite the internal divisions noted above, defeated most Party attempts to divide and rule. The issue on which the Party did succeed in dividing the issue became a fault-line that would dominate Hungarian post-communist politics.

The history of the first nine months of 1989 is that of the process by which the two sides (communists who were willing to countenance negotiating away power and the Opposition Round Table) emerged, followed by the negotiations themselves. The first shot in the battle of reformists to take over the Party came with Pozsgay's announcement in January that the events of 1956 should be seen as a 'popular uprising' rather than a 'counter-revolution'. In the political in-fighting that followed, Pozsgay emerged victorious. On 11 February the Party's Central Committee formally accepted that Hungary would henceforth be a multi-party democracy, and in March it announced its readiness to participate in coalition government. Such formulations can cover a multitude of sins, and the opposition's immediate task was to ensure that Hungary's multi-party future should be more substantial than the nominally multi-party systems in its Warsaw Pact neighbours. For this a more unified front was required and, on 22 March 1989, at the suggestion of the Forum of Independent Lawyers, eight of the key opposition groupings (including FIDESZ, the AFD and the HDF) formed the Opposition Round Table. Its aims always remained restricted: to provide a framework in which negotiations with the Party could take place. After initial obduracy over issues such as the nature of the agenda, whom to invite to the talks (FIDESZ was initially excluded), whether discussions should be two-sided or three-sided (an issue the Party won), and after defeat by newly formed Reform Circles in its own ranks on the matter of holding an emergency congress rather than a conference in October and suspending work on the controversial Gabcikovo-Nagymaros dam on the Danube, the Party leadership agreed to the commencement of negotiations on 13 June 1989.

The pace and pattern of the talks were dictated by reformers within the Party, and they all but stalled when Pozsgay was not present. It was imperative for reformers that the negotiations should be successfully concluded before the emergency congress in October. The purpose of the negotiations was to agree certain 'cardinal laws' (the establishment of a new presidency, the creation of a Constitutional Court, an electoral law clarifying the status of political parties, and amendments to the criminal code) which the existing illegitimate parliament could pass, before holding elections for a new, legitimate parliament which might carry democratic transformation further. When the successful conclusion of the negotiations was announced on 18 September 1989, however, the AFD and FIDESZ caused a furore by refusing to sign. Both parties rejected four aspects of the agreement: the proposal that the election of a president by popular ballot should precede parliamentary elections; and the Party's refusal on three scores to relinquish its position of privilege – its failures to disband the workers' militia, to withdraw from workplaces, and to render a full account of its property. The divide within the opposition was such that the non-signatories forced a referendum on the four disputed issues.

Attention then turned to the Party and its emergency congress of 6–9 October 1989. After much in-fighting, the reformist proposal of creating a new party committed to social democratic values, rather than reforming the old one, carried the day. A new Hungarian Socialist Party (HSP) emerged carrying the bulk of the old Party with it, but leaving a rump Hungarian Socialist Worker's Party committed to reform communism in the Kadar tradition. By the conclusion of the Conference, the future political landscape seemed clear. Pozsgay, who enjoyed enormous personal popularity, would be elected president, and a Democratic Forum-led coalition (probably with Socialist Party support) would emerge from the parliamentary elections which would follow.

But this scenario did not reckon either with the fall of the Berlin Wall, or with the successful attempts of the AFD and FIDESZ to force a referendum on what had become the crucial issue of when (the question of how was left open) to elect the president. (Parliament had in the interim forced the HSP to comply with the other three contested issues.) In the referendum campaign the HSP argued for the prior election of the president by popular ballot, the HDF, sensing a changing political climate, urged abstention, and the AFD, FIDESZ, the Hungarian Social Democratic Party (HSDP) and ISP called for parliamentary elections to be held first. The referendum took place on 26 November 1989 and, with a turnout of 58 per cent, the AFD, FIDESZ and their allies won 50.07 per cent to 49.93 per cent. Despite this, in its dying days parliament accepted an amendment, initiated by the independent member of parliament Zoltan Kiraly, that the president should nevertheless be elected by popular ballot.

The November referendum marked a watershed in Hungarian multi-party politics. At this early date in the transition process, Hungarian citizens were asked to break the simple Party versus Opposition dichotomy and decide between competing opposition parties. It also marked the birth of the AFD as a mass party. The HDF suffered a momentary loss of prestige, but the biggest loser was the HSP. The referendum proved that the Party could be defeated, and, when socialist regimes were collapsing in Hungary's neighbours, the HSP's justifiable claim to be truly reformist cut little ice.

In the parliamentary election campaign that followed, between January and March 1990, the HDF learned the lesson of its referendum defeat. All idea of cooperation with the former socialists was abandoned as the HDF strove to outdo the AFD in rejecting the

TABLE 5.1 *Parliamentary elections 25 March and 8 April 1990*: *share of vote on regional list (per cent) and number of seats won*

Party	Regional list	Seats
Hungarian Democratic Forum (HDF)	24.73	165
Alliance of Free Democrats (AFD)	21.39	91
Independent Smallholders (ISP)	11.73	44
Hungarian Socialist Party (HSP)	10.89	32
Alliance of Young Democrats (AYD)	8.95	22
Christian Democratic People's Party (CDPP)	6.46	21
Hungarian Socialist Workers Party (HSWP)	3.68	
Hungary's Social Democratic Party (HSDP)	3.55	
Agrarian Alliance	3.13	1*
Other (incl. jointly sponsored)	5.49	10*

* Candidates won seats in individual constituencies outright in the first round even though their parties did not cross the 4% of the total vote threshold to enter parliament.

Source: Adapted from *Magyar Kozlony*, 1990, No. 25.

former system. The parties competed almost entirely on their stance towards the old system rather than on their vision for the new, and the accusation that the HDF had been ready to do a deal with the former communists was countered by the accusations that many prominent AFD members had been socialists in their youth and were the children of bolshevik cadres. The change of strategy paid off. As Table 5.1 indicates, under Hungary's mixture of proportional representation and first-past-the-post, although on the proportional representation lists and in the first round of the individual constituencies the results were quite close, in the second, individual constituency only round, the HDF picked up more votes and, crucially, even more seats, and emerged as the biggest party in parliament, the obvious leader of a new coalition government.

Some 84 parties had been formed by the time of the parliamentary elections, of which 64 were officially registered and 48 intended to run. Only ten parties registered sufficient candidate nominations to be included on the National List and stand a realistic chance of power, however, and only six parties crossed all the hurdles and entered parliament. These parties divided into three broad ideological groups: the conservative, nationalist-christian world view represented by the HDF, with its origins in the 'populist' dissidents, the ISP and the CDPP, both reconstituted versions of parties that had been active in the 1940s; the liberalism and social-liberalism, tinged with social democracy of the AFD and FIDESZ; and the social democracy of the HSP. All six supported variants of the 'social market economy', and favoured increasing the profile of the Hungarian cultural heritage. They disagreed on how much emphasis to place on that heritage, on priorities in social policy, on the pace of privatisation, on the desirable degree of state intervention in the economy, and most fundamentally, on the relative importance given to individual liberties versus collective obligations to family, Church and nation.

The former communist party's poor showing in the parliamentary elections is not surprising, but the total failure of social democracy is more noteworthy. It is attributable partly to the disarray in the HSDP (which spent half of 1989 squabbling and then elected the only woman party leader in Hungarian politics who conducted a campaign based on her personality rather than social democratic policies), but mostly to the population's rejection of anything to do with 'socialism'. Ivan Szelenyi and his colleagues have shown that many of the relatively high number of abstainers in the elections shared what are usually thought of as social democratic values (Szelenyi and Szelenyi, 1991; Szelenyi *et al.*, 1992). These votes are up for grabs in postcommunist politics; but it is by no means certain that they will go to social democratic parties, even with credible candidates. By September 1992 two new parties (Imre Pozsgay and Zoltan Biro's National Democratic Alliance, and Zoltan Kiraly and Andras Revesz's Social Democratic People's Party) were competing unsuccessfully for this terrain.

Political Issues in the Post-Communist System

As Hungary entered post-communist politics, not only was the process of party formation more or less complete, with a manageable number of parliamentary parties; a clear ideological divide had also emerged between a non-communist government and an equally non-communist opposition. The key political issues that the new government faced in constructing a post-communist politics can be grouped under three headings: creating a functioning pluralism, creating a post-communist conservatism, and creating a market economy.

Creating a Functioning Pluralist Political System

Although the HDF was the biggest party in parliament, it could not
command a majority alone, and its first task was to build a coalition.
The notion of a 'grand coalition' between all parties was not a serious
option after the robust electoral campaign. The Hungarian party
system could only be adversarial and Jozsef Antall, president of the
HDF, had to form a coalition with a comfortable working majority.
He was lucky on two counts. First, with only six parties in parliament,
a working coalition could be built out of compromises with only two
or three parties. Second, the ideologically similar ISP and CDPP had
sufficient votes for alliance with them to give him a working majority.
The new coalition government formally began work in May 1990.

But if the coalition was easy to form, it proved harder to hold
together. The main problem was the ISP. On the one hand, the
coalition failed the ISP on the one issue that it cared passionately
about – and reform. On the other, the ISP itself shifted further to the
right as the Jozsef Torgyan, exploiting discontent with the government's failure to produce an acceptable land reform, sought to take
over the party for his own ends. Antall retained good relations with
the ISP's parliamentary group, however, so that when Torgyan, who
became party president in June 1991, first split his party and then, on
21 February 1992, led his faction out of the coalition, the majority of
ISP MPs continued to vote with the government. The CDPP posed
less of a problem. Without CDPP prompting, the HDF supported
religious education in schools, the return of church property and the
reintroduction of army chaplains. Nevertheless, by the summer of
1992, it too was talking of itself as an opposition within the coalition.

Antall's immediate problem in the spring of 1990 was more complex than creating a workable coalition, however. Much of the legislation that all sides agreed to be fundamental for the new political
system necessitated constitutional amendments which required a two-
thirds majority in parliament. In order to implement these reforms,
the achievement of some sort of *modus vivendi* with parliamentary
parties outside the governing coalition was a major priority. This was
done by means of a pact agreed at the end of April on an individual
basis between Antall and Janos Kis, the first president of the AFD.
Under the terms of the pact, the AFD promised not to block legislation which required a two-thirds majority in return for a commitment
to the election of the president by parliament and to the retention of a
two-thirds majority requirement for constitutional amendments, local

government reform, electoral law, and legislation governing the press and media. The pact served its purpose in that the key constitutional amendments were passed; but it had its shortcomings. Because the membership of neither party had been consulted concerning the terms of the agreement, rank and file politicians felt themselves at liberty to criticise it openly and interpret it as they saw fit.

With an effective coalition in place, Antall could complete the construction of the new democratic political system. The critical outstanding issues were the status of the President of the Republic and the reform of local government. Although the HDF had favoured a popularly elected, strong president in late 1989, now that it was in control of parliament it became more sympathetic to the AFD's preference for a figurehead president elected by parliament. However, Kiraly blocked repeal of his amendment instigating the popular election of the president by calling for a further referendum on the issue. Held in July 1990 and supported mainly by organisations of the former socialist order, the referendum proved an embarrassing failure. With a 13 per cent turnout, it was invalid, and on 3 August 1990 parliament elected the AFD member Arpad Goncz president of the republic.

But that was only the beginning. Conflict between the president and government emerged as an unresolved tension in Hungary's post-communist political system, the unlikely consequence of the pact which obliged a coalition-dominated parliament to elect an opposition party president. Although the AFD was doctrinally in favour of a weak president, for its years in opposition at least, the presidency was a link with real power. AFD opinion swung in favour of the president exercising his powers to the full. Goncz happily obliged, and was twice accused of acting unconstitutionally, although on both occasions he was vindicated by the Constitutional Court. He further took the political initiative in May 1991 by refusing to sign the Restitution Bill before it had been assessed and passed by the Constitutional Court.

The government's behaviour in the construction of a functioning system of local government also reflected the tension between doctrinal purity and electoral success. In the precipitous dash for total democracy, outline local authority reform legislation and regulations for local authority elections were passed well in advance of legislation which clarified fully local authority powers. Prior to the elections, which the HDF was confident of winning (if only because it postponed making economic policy decisions that might adversely hit living standards until after them), talk was of the maximum decentra-lisation of power. Even the HDF suggestion to create powerful lord-lieutenants in each county was successfully removed from the legisla-tion (to be replaced by rather weaker republican representatives). In the event, however, the governing coalition was roundly defeated in the local authority elections, by the AFD and FIDESZ in the large towns, and by 'independents', many former Party members, in smaller settlements. Unsurprisingly, when the legislation concerning the extent of local government powers reached the statute book in May 1991, the authority of the centre was greatly increased at the expense of the locality. In the case of Budapest, since the Greater Budapest Council would have been opposition dominated, legislation passed in June 1991 increased the powers of each district at the expense of the centre.

In October 1990, the strength of the new political institutions was put to the test by the direct action of lorry and taxi drivers who blockaded towns, bridges, and border crossings during the course of the night of 25–26 October in protest against petrol price rises of 65 per cent. The country came to a standstill until the following Sunday evening. At first, the government took a firm line, but the situation then turned to stalemate as the Budapest police chief, prompted by the President, made it clear he would not use force against the crowds. Finally, negotiations on the Sunday, which were broadcast in their entirety live on television, were successful. The government withdrew the price rise, but only until such time as petrol prices were fully liberalised and hence outside the political domain.

If the new political institutions proved robust during the blockade, enthusiasm for the democratic process and the government coalition waned. At 65 per cent, the turnout for the first democratic elections in forty years was disappointing, but that for the local authority elections was 40 per cent in the first round and under 30 per cent in the second, and by January 1992 in one by-election turnout had fallen to below 10 per cent. Government popularity declined quickly after the May elections. Immediately after the taxi blockade in November 1990, after only six months in office, it inspired rather less confidence than the previous undemocratic government. The situ-ation did not improve. Indeed, despite its small membership and weakness at the grassroots level, FIDESZ more or less consistently headed the popularity ratings from January 1991 onwards, with the HDF usually third after the AFD. FIDESZ's reaction to popularity and possible success in 1994, when the next elections are due, was to suggest the removal of its age limit on membership (its current leaders would be nearing the limit by 1994). The AFD's popularity declined after the local elections, and the party entered a severe and enduring identity crisis. Former dissident Kis resigned in November 1991 and was replaced first by the more populist Peter Tolgyessy and then, in November 1992, by Ivan Peto, less populist and with better dissident credentials. The HSP meanwhile achieved a number of by-election successes following Pal Fillo's victory in Budapest's seventh district in April 1991. Internal divisions within the HDF were institutionalised in September 1992 as populists and liberals established their Hungarian Way Foundation and Liberal Forum Foundation respectively, lending credence to the view that further restructuring of the party system was a realistic possibility.

Creating Post-Communist Conservatism

As head of an avowedly conservative, nationalist-christian government, Antall did not simply face the task guiding the country in the formation of a functioning democratic politics, he also had to translate ideological conservatism into a concrete reality. This process took place slowly, not least because the HDF and its coalition partners had very few experts who could take over as civil servants and other administrators. Nevertheless, by 1992, a distinct brand of conservatism was becoming both a political and institutional reality.

Hungarian conservatism is interventionist, and in the economic sphere it has favoured state control rather than direction. Initially it could only ensure that the State Property Agency came under direct government, rather than parliamentary, control. Economic policy was left to Mihaly Kupa, not a party member, who believed in non-intervention and a firm monetary policy. From the last quarter of 1991, and certainly after the spring of 1992, the power of interventionists (Bela Kadar in the Ministry of International Economic Affairs and Istvan Szabo, the new Minister of Industry) increased, and by September 1992, even Kupa was talking of a change of emphasis in government policy in 1993. In like vein, in March 1992, Tamas Szabo, the new Minister without Portfolio with special responsibility for privatisation, intervened to postpone the second 'decentralised privatisation', and by the end of the summer of 1992 the government had published a list of enterprises it proposed permanently to keep in the state sector. It was also increasingly making political appointments to head state companies and other administrative and judicial offices. Yet the policy priority was control rather than direction. The proposals of the Economic Strategy Work Group published in June 1992 were bland and weak on specifics. Businessmen (many of them by this time HDF appointees) facing declining markets had been successful gaining the ear of government, but the government either did not have the skills or the will to convert control into a coherent national industrial policy which might conflict with the short-term objectives of individual companies.

Perhaps the most visible, acrimonious and long-lasting example of Hungarian conservatism's predilection for intervention concerned the media. The most contentious element of the government-opposition pact of April 1990 had been the inclusion amongst legislation requiring a two-thirds majority of laws on the media. The issue of press hostility to the government simmered throughout 1990 and 1991, and, when the creation of a new pro-government newspaper did little to correct its overall media image, the government attacked television and radio. The latest bout began in March 1992 when the head of television refused to resign; it continued through the summer when President Goncz refused to act on Antall's recommendation to sack him; it bordered on the absurd in early September when an HDF deputy announced that he was going on hunger strike until the issue was resolved; and it went into the streets at the end of that month with a large demonstration outside the television headquarters headed by Istvan Csurka, HDF deputy president and leader of its HDF populist wing. The issue remains unresolved.

The government's attempts to give a national-christian gloss to institutions under its control faced two problems. First, because of inexperience, it acted clumsily and unconstitutionally in the early years. Second, it had to be wary of the extremism of its own right wing since international acceptance required keeping nationalism within 'European' norms. A good example of the early inexperience was the fate of legislation in favour of churches. The government's first move in the summer of 1990, to make compulsory religious instruction in schools, had to be in large measure withdrawn. But, in the religious euphoria manufactured in the summer of 1991 by the reburial of Cardinal Mindszenty (victim of the Stalinist era) and the Pope's visit, parliament accepted a law returning church property. This represented an explicit exception to the general rule within the restitution legislation which required financial compensation rather than the actual return of property. Two attempts to exact retribution on the former regime (the Justicia Plan and the Zetenyi-Takacs Bill) also failed, the latter ruled unconstitutional in March 1992 after referral to the Constitutional Court by President Goncz.

Antall has twice been publicly embarrassed by the right wing of the party, in the autumns of 1991 and 1992. In 1991, in an internal document subsequently made public, Imre Konya, HDF leader in parliament, suggested that respect for democratic procedures had been simply a tactic to gain international respectability. That September, the opposition launched a Democratic Charter to defend the 'fledgling democracy under threat'. Just under a year later, Csurka, whose authority in the party had strengthened since the HDF Congress of December 1991, produced a study with strong nationalist and in places explicitly anti-semitic content. Antall was finally, but very belatedly, shamed into distancing himself publicly from Csurka's views in a parliamentary statement on 31 August. Torn between losing right-wing support at home and alienating the international community, he demonstrated the magnitude of his concern for the former. The Democratic Charter responded this time with a demonstration, which took place five days after the Csurka-led demonstration against the heads of the television and radio. Meanwhile, simmering ethnic tension between Hungarians and Gypsies reached crisis point with the murder of two gypsies, and the formation of the '1956 Anti-Fascist, Anti-Bolshevik Alliance' claiming to unite isolated skinhead groups in the cause of nationalism. There was a further example of the growing political significance of skinheads as the foot-soldiers of the ultra-right on 23 October 1991 – the new national holiday in memory of 1956 – when President Goncz was shouted down and prevented from making a speech by gangs of skinheads who had been invited up to Budapest by political groupings on the fringes of the ISP.

By the end of 1992 Antall had successfully moulded the state in an Hungarian, conservative image – but opposition to it was moving from parliament to the streets, and its robust nationalism was spawning ethnic unrest.

Transforming the Economy

Discussion of post-communist politics cannot avoid economic policy, since radical economic restructuring was recognised as a priority goal in the political transition (see Chapter 12). The economic problem was three-fold: creating a market-driven economy; stabilising that market-driven economy once in place; and creating private market agents to give substance to the market-driven form.

Hungary had entered 1989 with considerable economic reform in place, and when prices were liberalised by the Antall government the impact was not traumatic (the peak of inflation was around 40 per cent per annum). Once necessary pricing adjustments had rendered the Hungarian economy a potentially market-driven one, it proved easier to stabilise external relations than domestic ones. Control of inflation and restrictions on full currency convertibility (in conjunction with mechanisms guaranteeing profit repatriation) began a virtuous circle of domestic confidence in the forint and foreign enthusiasm for Hungary as an investment location. External trading relations also improved markedly. Despite, and partly because of, the collapse of the Soviet market, exports to the West increased in every year following the 'change of system'. In this context, the high level of external debt inherited from the communists appeared manageable, and Hungary maintained its policy of meeting all its external financial obligations.

The outlook for the domestic economy was less encouraging. The IMF was critical of the government's increasing budget deficit and further cuts in the social services were necessary if it was to conform with IMF prescriptions, on which future borrowings depended. Yet, after a slow start, as bankruptcies were enforced, unemployment reached Western European levels (around 11 per cent by the end of 1992) so increasing demands on the social services.

No market economy can operate on a long-term basis without private market agents, and in the immediate post-communist era in Hungary these simply did not exist. They had to be created, quickly, and in an economy with minimal domestic savings to devote to the purchase of enterprises, and little likelihood of foreign interest in purchasing companies with histories of world market failure. Here, too, Hungary had a head start, since the combined effect of legislation in 1984 and 1987 allowed state enterprises to establish limited liability subsidiary companies (Mora, 1990). State enterprises could become shell holding companies with numerous private subsidiaries into which their most profitable activities could be consolidated and foreign investment attracted. Enterprise restructurings of this type simply accelerated in 1989 when the Companies Act came into force. Reacting to popular anger at the asset undervaluation that was assumed to accompany such 'spontaneous privatisation', in March

1990 the socialist government created the State Property Agency to oversee the privatisation process.

The Antall government took over this structure and gradually staffed it with its own appointees; but it did not radically alter its mode of operation. Hungary determined from the outset that restitution for property confiscated or nationalised should be partial and indirect in the form of compensation vouchers (although the Restitution Act itself was only passed, after two rejections by the Constitutional Court, in June 1991). This allowed policy-makers to focus on privatising to new owners rather than reprivatising to the former ones. A grand privatisation strategy for twenty choice enterprises was announced in September 1990, but a year later only one enterprise had been fully privatised. Subsequent programmes were announced, and piecemeal privatisation of large-scale enterprises under ministerial control continued; but by the summer of 1991 it was accepted that policy should change. Rules for the 'self-privatisation' of smaller enterprises were published in September 1991, and a second round of 'self-privatisation', newly christened 'decentralised' privatisation, begun in the spring of 1992. Although the direct distribution to citizens of vouchers for the purchase of shares was consistently rejected in the early years, the use of 'employee share ownership plans' (ESOPs) and management buy-outs received government approval in 1992, and a new scheme to speed up privatisation was mooted which would be similar to the Czechoslovak voucher scheme, but, rather than give away assets, would give citizens the right to credit vouchers, repayable over fifteen years, for the purchase of state property. Privatisation was not on target for placing 50 per cent of economy into the private sector by 1994 as required by the government's programme, and this despite the tenfold increase in the number of private companies between December 1989 and December 1991.

Hungary entered post-communist politics with a head start in terms of economic reform and political party formation. As the Antall government sought, with increasing success, to mould institutions in conformity with its conservative, nationalist-christian ideology, the distinctiveness produced by this head start began to wane. Despite its deserved reputation for economic and political stability, by the early 1990s there was in Hungary a potentially dangerous cocktail of increasing unemployment, decreasing social welfare and growing political acceptance of the vocabulary of extreme nationalism.

6

Bulgaria

JOHN D. BELL

Official name: Republic of Bulgaria
Area: 42,858 square miles
Population: 8,950,000
Head of state: Zheliu Zhelev
Head of government: Lyuben Berov

The End of the Zhivkov Regime

During the communist era Bulgaria earned a reputation for passivity. The population appeared docile and, alone among the states of Eastern Europe, Bulgaria experienced no crisis in its relations with the Soviet Union. The long tenure of Todor Zhivkov, who became party leader in 1954, suggested an almost completely frozen political life. But if Bulgaria was politically stable, it experienced fundamental economic and social changes that laid the foundation for the dramatic political events of the late 1980s. At the end of the Second World War three-quarters of Bulgaria's population lived in villages, and the overwhelming majority of these villagers were engaged in small-scale, primitive farming. The communist regime was committed to transforming Bulgaria by developing industry and educating the population to include it in the 'scientific-technological revolution of the twentieth century'. By the 1980s, about two-thirds of the population was urban, and only about a fifth still directly involved in farming. Bulgaria came to rank among the most advanced nations in the

83

proportion of its eligible population receiving secondary and higher education. For the first time Bulgaria possessed the equivalent of the Western middle class; and though not a bourgeoisie in the classical Marxist sense of owning the means of production, in terms of its psychology and outlook, scepticism toward inherited dogmas, desire for material success and personal autonomy, it far more resembled its Western contemporaries than the generation of its parents and grand-parents. Signs of the growing influence of this social group were mainly cultural: the development of Sofia's Vitosha Boulevard as a Bulgarian Via Veneto of shops devoted to luxury goods; the opening of an aerobic dance studio; the growing popularity of tennis; the building of the country's first golf course; and the large number of pet dogs being walked in the country's parks. But there was also a political dimension, for this group proved extremely receptive to the new currents set in motion in the communist world by Mikhail Gorbachev. On the eve of Zhivkov's fall, State Security estimated that 95 per cent of the intelligentsia was hostile to the regime. And in the offices down the hall from Zhivkov's own, party officials mocked their leader and joked about party dogmas.

Because Zhivkov always stressed Bulgaria's fidelity to the USSR, stating that the two countries had 'a single circulatory system', it was inevitable that he would have to introduce his own version of Gorbachev's 'new thinking', even though he had little appetite for it, and in 1987 he inaugurated the 'July Concept', seeming to embrace the cause of reform wholeheartedly. Along with a wave of adminis-trative and economic reorganisation, the July concept called for several steps toward political democratisation, including an expan-sion of press freedom and experiments with multi-candidate elec-tions. Both of the latter proved short-lived. Following the exposure of several cases of official corruption, the press was again made subject to more stringent controls and uncompliant editors and reporters were fired. In the elections for mayors and regional and municipal councillors (held on 28 February 1988), local electoral commissions disqualified all but the officially approved candidates in 80 per cent of the electoral districts. In those districts where 'outsider' candidates managed to find a place on the ballot, the authorities ensured their defeat by trucking in large numbers of absentee voters from districts where there was no challenge to the official list and by changing the results on forms submitted by the election precincts.

Despite government persecution, dissidence in Bulgaria continued to build in several quarters and to emerge into the open to challenge the regime. The sociologist Zheliu Zhelev, who had been expelled from the Bulgarian Communist Party and was known for his classic *Fascism* (1968), inspired the formation of 'Clubs for the Support of Glasnost and Perestroika', which developed an organisation independent of the government and kept a critical spirit alive. The physician Dr Konstantin Trenchev and a few other intellectuals, inspired by Poland's Solidarity, announced the formation of *Podkrepa* (Support) as an independent trade union, and began to recruit members. In the city of Russe, being slowly poisoned by chlorine gas emissions from the Romanian chemical combine across the Danube, an organised ecological movement, that would later adopt the name Eco-glasnost, was formed that openly challenged the government's indifference to the destruction of the Bulgarian environment. In various parts of the country other groups were formed to promote human rights, religious freedom, or to revive old political parties.

Zhivkov turned to the measures that had been effective in stamping out dissent in the past. Party members affiliated with dissident groups received sanctions or were expelled from the BCP. Many of them, along with non-party people, were dismissed from their jobs and subjected to vicious slander in the press. In February 1989 Zhivkov met with 'representatives of the intelligentsia', warning them that Bulgaria would not tolerate 'national nihilism' or 'negative attitudes toward our country or toward socialism'. But this time the opposition did not retreat into passivity. Bulgarian dissidents carried on their activities in defiance of these threats and actual persecution. During the year most of the usually submissive cultural unions voted out their old leaders in favour of critics of the regime.

During the spring of 1989 the protest movement also spread among Bulgaria's ethnic Turks, who had been relatively quiet since the brutal assimilation campaign of 1984–5. Hunger strikes escalated to clashes with the authorities that resulted in several deaths. By the end of May demonstrations were reported that included thousands of participants, forcing Zhivkov to go on national television to quell rumours of massive unrest. Denying that Bulgaria had a substantial Turkish minority, he repeated the fiction that most of the ethnic Turks were really Bulgarians who had been forcibly converted to Islam and a Turkish identity during the Ottoman period. He attributed disturbances among Bulgaria's Moslems to an anti-Bulgarian campaign carried on by Turkey, and he challenged the Turkish government to open its borders to Bulgarian Moslems so that it would be revealed how few really were discontented with life in

Bulgaria. When Turkey responded to Zhivkov's challenge by declaring that it would accept refugees from Bulgaria, the authorities launched a broad reign of terror against the ethnic Turks, forcing thousands to cross the border where they were placed in hastily organised camps. Before the Turkish government again closed the border, more than 300,000 ethnic Turks had abandoned or were forced from the country, an exodus that focused worldwide attention on Bulgaria's human rights record and disrupted an already shaky economy.

Prolonged economic stagnation and Zhivkov's increasingly erratic leadership, compounded by his efforts to promote his wastrel son's career, caused an erosion of support among his immediate colleagues. Several versions of the plot against Zhivkov have been given, but the key figures were clearly Petur Mladenov, in charge of foreign affairs since 1971, and General Dobri Dzhurov, the minister of defence.

On 10 November 1989, the day after East Germany opened the Berlin Wall, a meeting of the BCP's politburo and secretariat accepted Zhivkov's 'resignation'. The fiction that Zhivkov had resigned voluntarily lasted only days, and he soon came under intense attack for personal corruption and for establishing a 'totalitarian' regime. His relatives and closest supporters were purged from their posts in the party and state. Many other 'dinosaurs' of his generation quietly went into retirement, and others found themselves the targets of popular demonstrations that began to play an increasingly large role in putting pressure on the leadership to speed the pace of reform.

Mladenov and the rest of the new leadership pledged to welcome and promote the development of pluralism in the country and to respect the rule of law. To this end they halted the persecution of the ethnic Turks and invited those who had fled to return to the country; allowed opposition groups to register as legal entities; and promised to eliminate the domestic role of the State Security forces. Bowing to widespread demonstrations, the party also amended Article One of the constitution, which had recognised the BCP as the guiding force in society.

At an extraordinary congress that began at the end of January 1990, the party carried through a number of structural and personnel changes and took the first steps to separate the party from the state. Petur Mladenov resigned the party leadership while remaining titular head of state. Andrei Lukanov, widely regarded as the party's ablest statesman, became prime minister. And Alexander Lilov, who had a reputation for 'liberalism' and whom Zhivkov had purged from the politburo in 1983, was elected chairman of a restructured BCP Supreme Council. With the slogan of converting the BCP into a 'modern, left-wing party', Lilov and his allies moved to bring forward younger and better educated leaders, denounced the 'totalitarianism' of the past, and conducted a party referendum that changed the name from 'Communist' to 'Socialist'. Some former dissidents responded to these changes with enthusiasm and returned to the party fold, where they would push for changes beyond those acceptable to Lilov. A number of 'factions' appeared, including the Alternative Socialist Party, which later broke away to affiliate with the opposition, and 'Road to Europe' formed to promote more rapid democratisation and to pursue a policy of reconciliation with the West. Its members too would ultimately withdraw from the Bulgarian Socialist Party. On the other hand, at the lower levels of the party in the provinces and industrial management a strong tendency toward conservatism began to crystallise.

In addition to the changes that took place within the party in the wake of Zhivkov's fall, a number of the party's auxiliary organisations also collapsed or ceased to function. The Central Council of Trade Unions declared its independence and elected a new leadership. Some unions dropped out altogether, while alternative unions, especially the independent *Podkrepa*, recruited thousands of new members. The Komsomol exploded at its congress early in the year and was replaced by a new organisation that declared itself independent of party control, and by a number of rival youth organisations, some of which affiliated with the political opposition. The puppet Bulgarian Agrarian National Union (BANU), purged itself of its old leadership, and declared its independence. Party cells in the workplace were disbanded.

From Red to Blue

While the Communist/Socialist Party was dealing with the legacy of the Zhivkov era, opposition political groups were also being organised. The Discussion Clubs transformed themselves into a political party, as did Eco-glasnost, and many of the parties suppressed after the Second World War were revived. The number of parties and movements mushroomed rapidly – approximately fifty were formed – but at the end of 1989 the most important entered into a coalition, the

Union of Democratic Forces (UDF), with Zheliu Zhelev as president.

The UDF, adopting the colour blue for its banners and symbols, quickly proved its ability to stage mass demonstrations in the capital, and its leaders gained the agreement of the BSP to enter into round-table discussions on the future of the country. The roundtable, whose sessions were televised, came to function almost as a substitute parliament, and its decisions were routinely legalised by the BSP-dominated National Assembly.

After dramatic negotiations the roundtable reached agreements that paved the way for fundamental political change. The two sides agreed on the election of a Grand National Assembly (GNA) to be composed of 400 deputies, half elected in single-member districts and half selected by proportional representation. Over a period of eighteen months the GNA would function both as a parliament and as a constitutional assembly to design a new political structure for the country. A politically neutral commission was set up to implement the election agreement.

The agreement on political parties was extremely generous, granting recognition to parties on the basis of little more than an individual declaration. It did, however, ban the formation of parties on an ethnic or religious basis, a measure aimed at preventing the organisation of a separate, and perhaps separatist, party to represent the country's ethnic Turks and Moslems. Despite this provision, the Movement of Rights and Freedoms (MRF), organised by Akhmed Dogan, became *de facto* the 'Turkish party', although its charter proclaimed general goals.

In the face of the BSP's advantages in organisation, material resources, and access to the media, the UDF entered the campaign with a high level of confidence. Assuming that if the populace were given the opportunity to vote freely it would automatically reject the BSP, the UDF sought to make the election a referendum on the past 45 years of Communist rule. Consequently, much of its campaign focused on the past, particularly on the atrocities committed by the BCP during the Stalinist era. Moreover, by its very nature the UDF coalition had difficulty speaking with a single voice or in advancing specific measures to deal with the country's problems. This was particularly evident with regard to the future of the Socialists. Some UDF leaders, particularly Dr Petur Dertliev of the Social Democratic Party, spoke with a degree of sympathy of the BSP's efforts to reform itself, advocated an eventual reconciliation, and opposed the idea of

TABLE 6.1   *Bulgarian election results, June 1990*

Party	Votes	Percent	Seats
BSP	2,886,363	47.15	211
UDF	2,216,127	36.20	144
BANU	491,500	8.03	16
MRF	368,929	6.03	23
Others	158,279	2.59	6
Total	6,121,198	100.00	400

reprisals against BSP officials. In this vein, Zheliu Zhelev and other UDF spokesmen advocated what they called a 'Spanish policy', following the example of Spain's transition from fascism. Others, however, adopted a far more strident tone, frequently referring to the BSP as 'murderers' and a 'mafia', giving the impression that the UDF would conduct a wholesale purge if it won. The UDF economic platform called for 'shock therapy', an immediate and complete transition to a market economy, but did not make clear how this would be effected or how the most vulnerable elements in the population would be protected.

The BSP presented itself as the party of 'responsible, conservative change', stressing the experience of its leaders, their role in dethroning Zhivkov, and minimising policy differences with the UDF. It denied seeking a monopoly of power and called for the formation of a coalition with the opposition either before or after the elections. The BSP also pledged a gradual transition to a market economy in which no one would suffer, and its claim that old-age pensions would be endangered by a UDF victory proved particularly effective. While cultivating a new image designed to appeal particularly to Bulgaria's middle-class, urban voters, the BSP conducted a more traditional campaign in the countryside where local party and government officials put heavy pressure on the village population, whose habits of subordination developed over the past 45 years were not easily broken.

The election results, given in Table 6.1, came as a shocking disappointment to the opposition, whose expectations had been unrealistically high, but they were hardly the 'overwhelming Socialist victory' that was reported in the Western press. The BSP failed to get a majority of the popular vote and some of its leading figures, such as Prime Minister Lukanov, were forced into embarrassing runoffs or, like Defence Minister Dzhurov, actually defeated. The opposition dominated Bulgaria's cities, especially the capital, and enjoyed a commanding level of support from professionals and among the young. And because decisions of the Grand National Assembly required a two-thirds majority, the UDF was in a position to exercise a veto on any Socialist proposals.

The June 1990 elections in fact produced a prolonged political stalemate, as the BSP proved unwilling to enact painful reforms without the approval of the opposition, while the UDF steadfastly refused to be drawn into a coalition. As the economic situation deteriorated, popular feeling moved steadily toward the UDF. On 6 July, President Mladenov resigned, after the broadcast of a videotape of him proposing that tanks be used against an opposition demonstration. When no candidate could garner enough votes in the Assembly to become his successor, the Socialists threw their support behind UDF leader Zheliu Zhelev. Zhelev accepted the office, resigning from the UDF, and quickly acted with great vigour to make the office a focus of power. By the end of the year, polls showed him to be the most popular figure in the country.

The erosion of the BSP's position continued as the party itself threatened to break up, some of its parliamentary deputies declared their independence, and an open dispute broke out between Lukanov and Lilov. Unable to persuade the party leadership to remove Lilov, and faced with a deteriorating economy and growing strike movement, Lukanov resigned as prime minister at the end of November 1990. The National Assembly turned the task of forming a new government over to Dimitur Popov, a non-party jurist who had won general approval for his work on the Central Election Commission that had administered the June elections. On 20 December a cabinet of eighteen ministers was formed, consisting of eight Socialists, three members of the UDF, two Agrarians, and five independents.

The resignations of Mladenov and Lukanov and the disarray in the Socialist camp contributed to a marked swing of public opinion in favour of the opposition. The UDF, however, experienced a sharp setback of its own when Dr Petur Beron, Zhelev's successor as chairman and an eminent zoologist, suddenly resigned following allegations that he had once been an informant for the State Security. He was replaced by Filip Dimitrov, a lawyer and vice-chairman of the Green Party.

During the period of the Popov government, the GNA proceeded to draft a new constitution. This process proved highly controversial, as a significant minority of the UDF opposed any cooperation with the BSP majority and actually undertook a hunger strike in protest against the adoption of the 'Communist Constitution'. Although the majority of the UDF deputies voted to ratify the constitution and the minority later returned to the Assembly to participate in subsequent legislation, the conflict set the stage for the fracturing of the UDF coalition. Before it adjourned, the GNA also adopted legislation providing for the restoration of agricultural land to its former owners and other economic reforms. This legislation, however, proved complex and ineffective, and brought little real change. The GNA also adopted an electoral law to govern new parliamentary elections set for October 1991.

Prior to these elections the UDF formally split. Two issues provoked the break-up of the coalition. The first was the demand of the largest coalition partners, the Social Democratic Party and the BANU-Nikola Petkov, to have a larger voice in the UDF Council and to have a greater number of candidates on the UDF electoral list. When these demands were not satisfied, these two parties, or at least their majority factions, decided to withdraw from the UDF and run as independents. The second issue was the question of relations with the BSP. While some members of the UDF coalition advocated a moderate policy toward the former Communists, hoping to win its more liberal members away from the party, an emerging majority, whose core was the 'dark blue' deputies who had refused to vote for the constitution, supported a more confrontational policy toward the Socialists. Their position prevailed, and their opponents withdrew to form the UDF-Liberals. Calling themselves the UDF-Movement, the hardline majority inherited the coalition's organisation, newspaper, and blue ballot.

The October elections, which were popularly perceived as a struggle between red and blue parties, saw a narrow plurality for the UDF-Movement, a continuing erosion of support for the BSP, and a strong showing for the MRF (see Table 6.2). No other party was able to meet the 4 per cent minimum to qualify for representation in the new National Assembly. This meant that the advocates of moderation towards the BSP were shut out of parliament, which was considerably more polarised than its predecessor had been. Because the UDF-Movement had not been able to gain an absolute majority it formed a partnership with the MRF, and a new government, headed by Filip Dimitrov, took office in November 1991.

Following the parliamentary elections, a congress of the BSP saw a sharp confrontation between reformists and conservatives. When neither side could muster sufficient votes for its candidate for chair-

TABLE 6.2   *Bulgarian National Assembly elections, October 1991*

Party	Votes	Percent	Seats
UDF (Movement)	1,903,567	34.36	110
BSP	1,836,050	33.14	106
MRF	418,168	7.55	24
BANU (United)	214,052	3.86	0
BANU (Nikola Petkov)	190,454	3.54	0
UDF (Centre)	177,295	3.20	0
UDF (Liberals)	155,902	2.81	0
'Kingdom of Bulgaria'	100,883	1.82	0
Business Bloc	73,379	1.32	0
National Radical Party	62,462	1.13	0
Others	408,625	7.27	0
Total	5,540,837	100.00	240

man – Georgi Piriniski for the reformists and incumbent Alexander Lilov for the conservatives – the congress turned to the little-known Zhan Videnov, a 32-year-old economist whose principal experience had been in the Komsomol, as a compromise. Soon after the congress, a group of leading reformists, who had generally failed to be elected to high party posts, announced the formation of an 'Alliance for Social Democracy' to work for change 'within the democratic unity of the party'.

The UDF in Power

The results of the October 1991 elections and the break-up of the original UDF coalition reflected a tendency seen throughout Eastern Europe – the political demise of the idealistic, intellectual dissidents who had formed the core of the opposition while communism was in power and their replacement by more 'pragmatic' politicians with greater popular appeal. The new 'dark blue' UDF majority was openly hostile to its erstwhile colleagues, referring to them as the 'pink blues' and accusing them of being 'soft on communism' if not actual State Security agents.

The deepening hostility between these elements was visible in the lukewarm support given by the UDF to President Zhelev in his bid for popular election in January 1992. Zhelev was forced to accept the UDF's choice as his running mate, the writer Blaga Dimitrova, who belonged to the dark-blue camp, in return for the UDF's endorsement, and UDF support in the election campaign was unenthusiastic.

Zhelev received only 45 per cent of the votes in the first round on 12 January, and in the runoff held a week later achieved a narrow victory with only 53 per cent against the BSP-backed candidate Velko Vulkanov. In the election's aftermath parliament and the cabinet were critical of Zhelev for appointing 'pinks' to positions in the presidency and moved to reduce his office to figurehead status. In May, Defence Minister Dimitur Ludzhev, whom Zhelev once described as his 'only friend in the cabinet', was fired by Prime Minister Dimitrov backed by a majority of the UDF members of parliament. Zhelev was almost certainly fortunate that the presidential elections followed closely on those for the National Assembly. If the UDF had had more time to consolidate its parliamentary victory, he might well have experienced Vaclav Havel's fate. As it was, the limited powers granted to the presidency by the constitution made it impossible for Zhelev to avoid increasing political isolation.

Members of the UDF–MRF coalition in parliament and the new UDF cabinet stated that their highest priority was the complete decommunisation of the country, and the Assembly's first legislative act was the passage of a law providing for the confiscation of the property of the former Communist Party and its satellites: the Trade Union Confederation, Komsomol, and BANU. The successors of these organisations were forced to vacate hundreds of buildings, including the great Party House that dominates downtown Sofia, placing them at the disposal of the government.

Prosecution of some former Communist leaders, including former first secretary Todor Zhivkov, began under the government of Dimitur Popov, but became more numerous after the UDF–MRF coalition came to power. The Dimitrov government appointed a more aggressive chief prosecutor who brought indictments against approximately 50 figures prominent in the Zhivkov and post-Zhivkov BSP governments. These included former prime minister Georgi Atanasov and former economic minister Stoyan Ovcharov. Another former BSP prime minister, Andrei Lukanov, was forbidden to leave the country pending the completion of an investigation directed against him, and his parliamentary immunity was lifted. The National Assembly also voted to deny pensions to retirees whose careers had been in BCP posts or the security organs. Legislation was also introduced that would result in a broad purge of state administration – for example, by barring former members of the BCP or its satellites above a certain rank or by denying the validity of any degrees earned in Soviet educational institutions. The 'Group of Thirty-nine', the former hunger-strikers against the constitution, and their supporters accused the BSP of planning a coup and called for the party to be banned. The BSP accused these opponents of conducting a policy of 'witch-hunts and McCarthyism', while President Zhelev compared their warnings to the rattling of an empty wagon.

In addition to its moves against the BSP, a majority in the National Assembly voted to grant blanket rehabilitation to the thousands of individuals convicted of war crimes by the 'people's courts' after the Second World War, allowing their descendants to file claims to confiscated property. This rehabilitation was extended to the former royal family, and a significant number of ministers and deputies openly advocated the restoration of the monarchy. Several National Assembly leaders, including Assembly president Stefan Savov and MRF leader Akhmed Dogan, visited 'His Majesty' in Spain. For his part, Simeon Sax-Coburg-Gotski, or Simeon II as his supporters prefer, offered himself to the nation. Popular support for the monarchy, all but non-existent when the constitution was adopted, appeared to have grown to approximately 20 per cent by 1992.

By the end of summer 1992, the UDF and the Dimitrov government faced growing difficulties. In addition to internal conflicts over the monarchy, the pace and nature of economic reform, and the personal ambitions of several UDF leaders, there appeared splits with its MRF ally and with President Zhelev. Initially, the MRF was quite circumspect in its political conduct, seeking no direct cabinet participation even at the vice-ministerial level, and working behind the scenes to achieve its goals of Turkish-language instruction in the schools and the restoration of property confiscated during the Zhivkov persecutions. It grew increasingly concerned, however, as the economic downturn struck its rural constituency with great severity. Land reform favoured the former Bulgarian property owners, and the state was slow, or reluctant, to distribute property to the Turkish minority from the state land fund. MRF leader Akhmed Dogan began openly to press for a change of policy, and when no response was forthcoming the MRF parliamentary delegation joined the Socialists in a vote of no confidence on 28 October. President Zhelev had already made his views clear in a press interview at the end of August when he accused the government of trying to strip the presidency of its powers and of taking extremist positions that antagonised the majority of the population.

The Dimitrov cabinet remained in office while negotiations continued to form a new government. The possibilities appeared dim, however, as the MRF insisted on including in the cabinet not only its own representatives, but figures from the political centre that was not represented in parliament. By early 1993, seemed likely that new elections would have to be held to resolve the stalemate.

Economic Reform

Bulgarians endured a harsh winter of 1990–1 as the economy, described by Pctur Mladenov as 'on the verge of a heart attack' when Zhivkov resigned, came near collapse. Andrei Lukanov's Socialist government spent the last of the country's foreign exchange reserves attempting to maintain stability through the June 1990 elections, but then suspended payments on Bulgaria's foreign debts, bringing on a drastic fall of food and energy imports. Lukanov's government and the BSP majority in parliament refused to enact significant economic reform legislation unless the UDF would assume joint responsibility. When the UDF refused to cooperate, Lukanov did nothing until strikes and popular demonstrations forced his resignation in November 1990.

In the new 'government of cohabitation' under Prime Minister Dimitur Popov, the economic ministries were given to the UDF which proceeded to introduce an austerity programme to begin the transition toward a market economy. Prices of most commodities were freed and the *lev* was allowed was allowed to find its market value (moving from approximately 2 to 24 *lev* to the US dollar). This brought over 300 per cent inflation in the first months of 1991, but prices tended to stabilise during the rest of the year. These measures received international approval, and Bulgaria was able to reschedule most of its debts to foreign banks. Moreover, the International Monetary Fund extended a $503 million loan and accepted Bulgaria for full membership.

Fundamental structural reform of the economy was delayed by the BSP majority in the GNA and by divisions within the UDF. Following the October 1991 elections the government carried out a 'small privatisation', putting shops and service outlets in private hands, and revised the law on foreign investment to grant more favourable terms to foreign investors. 'Big privatisation', involving the country's large state-owned industries, moved more slowly. The UDF government insisted first on carrying out a comprehensive restitution of property seized by the Communist government after the

Second World War. This principle was followed in the government's revision of the law on land that required the complete dissolution of all collective farms and the restitution of the land to its former owners or their heirs. Collective farm workers who were not in line to receive land could become renters or were promised land at some future time from property owned by the state.

The decision 'to give back everything that can be given back' created potential legal claims against state-owned property that delayed comprehensive privatisation. It also appeared that Finance Minister Ivan Kostov and Trade and Industry Minister Ivan Pushkarev favoured a gradualist approach to privatisation that was at odds with the views of a number of parliamentary deputies and with the country's labour organisations. In May 1992 the Confederation of Independent Trade Unions and *Podkrepa*, backed by their allies, called for the resignation of the Dimitrov government owing to the slow pace of economic reform. Dimitrov remained in office, but Ivan Pushkarev was fired and his ministry divided into two. Ilko Eskenazi, a critic of Pushkarev, was appointed deputy prime minister with the assignment of coordinating economic policy. This shake-up of the government was expected to lead to a more vigorous approach to the problems of privatisation.

Ethnic Issues

Despite a degree of mutual mistrust and ongoing tension, Bulgarians and the ethnic Turkish minority have so far found peaceful solutions to potential conflicts. The Communist government that succeeded Zhivkov put an immediate end to the violent persecution of the Turkish minority, invited those who had fled or were driven from the country to return, and promised them the restoration of the Turkish names that had been taken from them in the assimilation campaign in 1984. However, as the ethnic Turks turned to the Movement for Rights and Freedoms (MRF), which had its origin in the underground struggle of the Zhivkov years, as the vehicle for their political expression, and as the MRF allied itself with the UDF, the BCP/BSP became increasingly anti-Turkish and in the October 1991 National Assembly elections even formed an alliance with a few small, ultra-nationalist parties that had a strictly anti-Turkish foundation. Following the election, the BSP challenged the legitimacy of the MRF's deputies, charging that the MRF was a party 'founded on a religious or ethnic basis' and thus was in violation of Article 14 of the constitution. A political crisis was averted when the Constitutional Court narrowly rejected the BSP's claim.

The Bulgarian government, particularly since the formation of the UDF–MRF coalition in the National Assembly, has generally satisfied ethnic Turkish demands, including the restoration of property taken during the Zhivkov persecution, the legalisation of a Turkish-language press, and the introduction of Turkish–language instruction in the schools in areas with a high concentration of ethnic Turks. Bulgarian Moslems, like their Christian counterparts, have also begun the process of purging their clerical hierarchy of former State Security agents.

Despite the fears stirred up by some extreme nationalists, Bulgaria's Turkish minority does not appear to show signs of sympathy to any movement of Islamic fundamentalism. The leadership of the MRF is drawn almost entirely from the segment of the population that may be described as secularised and professional – Akhmed Dogan studied in the same faculty as President Zheliu Zhelev.

Another factor that has strongly contributed to the peaceful resolution of potential nationality conflicts is the ethnic warfare taking place in the former Yugoslavia. The deep desire to avoid such bloodletting has made both sides eager to avoid the experience of Bulgaria's western neighbours. The danger, however, that ethnic warfare may spread from Bosnia-Herzegovina through Kosovo to Macedonia, and thus to the Bulgarian border, has become a major fear. Bulgaria recognised the independence of the Macedonian Republic in January 1992, but the failure of Western Europe and the United States to follow suit, combined with their unwillingness to take effective measures to stem Serbian aggression, has created in Bulgaria the not unrealistic fear that the substantial gains made since the Communist regime crumbled may be swept away in a new era of Balkan wars.

7

Yugoslavia and Its Successor States

JIM SEROKA

The most important point to remember about the former Yugoslavia and its contemporary successor states is that the cruelties of the civil war, ethnic cleansing, forced population movements and withering of democratic ideals witnessed in recent years were the result of conscious decisions or non-decisions by the leaders and peoples within Yugoslavia. It is more than misleading to suggest that the whirlwind of destruction that has consumed the former Yugoslav republics was unavoidable, or that the character of the south Slav peoples or the malevolence of Tito and other leaders inevitably pushed the nation on its march towards barbarism.

The Collapse of Tito's Socialist Experiment, 1981–1989

That is not, of course, to suggest we can ignore the legacy of Marshal Josef Broz Tito, who led the partisans during the Nazi occupation and ruled Yogoslavia till his death in 1980, especially in terms of the excessively high expectations which he generated among the citizenry and the absence of any successor to full his major and longstanding role. According to the propaganda machinery, Tito was a world hero; Yugoslavia's achievements were the envy of the world; and Tito single-handedly kept the peace among Yugoslavia's potentially warring factions.

After Tito's death, no one in authority had the legitimacy to

Federal Republic of Yugoslavia
Area: 102,173 square kilometres
Population (1990): 10,471,000
President: Dobrica Cosic (no party affiliation)
Government: Coalition between the Serbian Socialist Party and Serbian Radical Party

Republic of Bosnia-Hercegovina
Area: 51,129 square kilometres
Population (1990): 4,366,000
President: Alija Izetbegovic (SDA)
Government: Coalition of the Party of Democratic Action (SDA) and the Croatian Democratic Community (HDZ)

Republic of Croatia
Area: 56,538 square kilometres
Population (1990): 4,764,000
President: Franjo Tudjman (HDZ)
Government: Croatian Democratic Community (HDZ) is the ruling party

Republic of Macedonia
Area: 25,713 square kilometres
Population (1990): 2,034,000
President: Kiro Gligorov (SDLM)
Government: Coalition of the Social Democratic League of Macedonia (SDLM), Reform Forces – Liberal Party (RFLP), Party for Democratic Prosperity – National Democratic Party (PDP–NDP)

Republic of Slovenia
Area: 20,251 square kilometres
Population (1990): 1,975,000
President: Milan Kucan (SDP)
Government: Multi-party coalition

deviate from Tito's path, and this failure to respond to new circumstances eventually destroyed Tito's three principles of self-management, non-alignment and decentralised Marxism-Leninism. The failure of Tito's successors to maintain the social contract, preserve the authority of the state, and adapt to the collapse of the

Soviet bloc eliminated the justification for repression, discipline, and a one-party state and paved the way for the re-emergence of overt ethnic antagonisms which it had been Tito's great achievement to accommodate.

Collapse of the Social Contract

The decade of the 1980s was an economic and social nightmare for Yugoslavia. In the latter years of the Tito era, the Yugoslav republic had begun to contract an enormous foreign currency debt. By 1981, the debt nearly equalled the gross domestic product of the nation. Compounding the problem was the phenomenon that relatively few of these foreign currency loans were used to build infrastructure or to enhance economic productivity. Most of the loans were applied to subsidies for consumer spending or for prestigious, but unprofitable, projects. To make matters worse, individual republics were able to incur foreign debts that were guaranteed by the Federation, but were underwritten without any prior federal authorisation or knowledge. At times, service on the debt alone exceeded the entire export earnings of the Federation.

During the 1980s, Yugoslavia's antiquated capital plant, low levels of labour productivity, deteriorating infrastructure, burgeoning black market economy and debt pressures combined to place enormous inflationary pressures on the economy. Inflation rose from somewhat over 30 per cent to over 100 per cent by the middle of the decade and 1000 per cent per year by the end of the decade. As the inflation rate climbed, confidence in the government plummeted. Inflation dissolved personal savings, eliminated investment, impoverished pensioners and the elderly and turned white-collar civil servants and the merchant class away from the regime.

For ideological and political reasons, the post-Tito leaders made no attempt to re-examine and reform Tito's cumbersome self-management system. Despite the economic hardships, irrational decision-making processes, and pressures from the world market and lenders, Yugoslavia's leaders remained stubbornly committed to its peculiar form of indirect decision-making – the delegate system.

Throughout the entire fiasco of the 1980s, politicians continued to advocate commercial decentralism, rather than encourage consolidation of weak and struggling enterprises. Local political machines protected their own enterprises, imposed discriminatory regulations on other Yugoslav firms, and worked to inhibit competition. Inter-republic political disputes entered the economic arena when suppliers in one republic were constrained from delivering their products to another republic as contracted. Banks advanced parochial interests and often became captives to the firms with which they conducted their business (Seroka, 1989).

In brief, by the end of the 1980s, Yugoslavia's economy was engaged in a predatory and self-destructive civil war. Serbia, for example, had declared a boycott on Slovenian goods. The movement of capital, goods and services became increasingly restricted to indi-vidual republic borders. The national currency had lost its value, and economic enterprises and firms became pawns of local political inter-ests. Eventually, the economy was held hostage by the political elites and lost its capacity to function autonomously or even to constrain the destructive actions of the political leaders. Most significantly, however, the political fragmentation of the economy led to the abrogation of the social contract, including a break in the promise to provide pension benefits, an adequate salary for workers, a steadily increasing standard of living, guaranteed employment, and eventual inclusion in the economies of Western Europe.

Tito's heirs did not differentiate between criticism and dissent, or between reform and opposition. By refusing to accept criticism or to consider reform, they radically narrowed their base of support, and the end of the decade much of the population was ready to accept radical solutions to the burgeoning problems. The lexicon of self-management socialism had become an empty shell and a vehicle that eventually served to isolate the communists in Yugoslavia.

Compounding the alienation of well-intentioned reform elements and the sterilisation of the social reform movements was the isolation of the younger generation from positions of state power. Tito's compatriots had generally entered government in the 1940s at rela-tively young ages. In later decades, however, the leadership did not rejuvenate itself. By the time of Tito's death, therefore, Yugoslavia and its republics were still dominated by the Partisan generation and the leaders were cut off from the experiences and concerns of those who had not participated in the war (Seroka, 1988).

Adding insult to injury, the post-Tito leadership disparaged the cultural expressions of the younger generation, and spent consider-able effort in attempting to direct youth energies into the traditionally approved channels. Tito's birthday and Youth Day were merged, and large cities celebrated the holiday with Chinese-style, mass choreographed youth displays, cross-republic youth marches, runs, sporting events and poetry competitions. Youth antipathy towards these antiquated political expressions was strongly criticised by officials as 'un-Yugoslav' and 'anti-Socialist'. Counter culture movements were even more severely repressed, with the use of heavy-handed police action and occasional state-sponsored vigilantism.

As if the repression of reform movements and the alienation of younger-generation groups were not enough, the post-Tito leaders helped dig their own grave by providing an alternative ideological framework for the nascent opposition elements. Any opposition or criticism of the regime, its leaders, or governmental policy was characterised and condemned as 'nationalism'. It was this proclivity of the post-Tito leaders to label all resistance or reform as nationalist-inspired that gave a common identity to opponents of the regime. This failure of Tito's heirs to acknowledge societal pluralism and accept criticism inevitably led to the system's collapse. Under pressure from the regime, all reform movements, opposition movements, and social critics came together and united under the nationalist umbrella (Seroka, 1992).

An apt example to illustrate this process was the Yugoslav Army's attempt to punish the editors of a struggling Slovenian youth journal, *Mladina,* which had exposed the corruption of the defence minister. In response, defence ministry officials planted evidence on the editors, arrested them, tried them for betraying state secrets in a military court, conducted the trial in the Serbian language, and excluded Slovenian officials and the public from the deliberations. The resulting outcry throughout Slovenia led to the unification of the numerous divergent opposition factions in the republic under a common nationalist cause, widespread condemnation of the Federal government, and a snowballing anti-military and anti-Yugoslav movement throughout the republic. In 1990, one of these young editors, Janez Jansa, became the minister of defence for the newly independent republic of Slovenia.

Throughout the 1980s, attempts to restore the social contract and to reform society from within failed. With Tito's departure from politics, the central authorities lost their focus and became increasingly irrelevant to society and the nation. The delegate system which was introduced in the 1974 Constitution concentrated political power in the hands of the local political machines. The bosses of these machines always maintained close ties with the local economic enterprises, and controlled the local socio-political organisations plus the

funds and the votes upon which politics was based. They also determined the fortunes of the republic political leaders.

Failures in Leadership and the Collapse of Regime Legitimacy

Tito's successors proved to be too ill-equipped and ill-trained to be
able to arrest the collapse of the social contract and to preserve the
integrity of the regime. As a group, the leaders were disorganised and
lacked unity of purpose. Distrust among them was high and became
institutionalised through the notion of collective leadership. The
economic and cultural elites were alienated from the new leaders and
proffered them little respect. Entry of new individuals into leadership
posts ceased, Party reform efforts were never taken seriously, and
corruption became endemic throughout all strata of society.

In the years following Tito's death, a series of power struggles
erupted between Tito's hand-picked successors and younger, non-
Partisan-generation challengers who had carefully constructed strong
networks of support in the republics. The old-guard leaders in the
Party and government eventually fell like dominoes. Even such
previously untouchable leaders like Serbia's Dragoslav Markovic,
Slovenia's Stane Dolanc and Croatia's Vladimir Bakaric and Milka
Planinc soon faded into political oblivion. The leaders who replaced
them emerged with strong bases and support from local political
machines. They owed little to the federal Party apparatus.

The trend in republic decentralism was most apparent in March
1981 when demonstrations that demanded republic status broke out
among the Albanian majority in Kosovo. Federal authorities, led by
the interior minister Stane Dolanc, could not restore order, and both
Serbs and Albanians repudiated the current Federal approach to the
situation. Serbia demanded and received authority to restore order,
and potently moved to eradicate Kosovo's autonomy, despite the
objections and resistance of the other republics. Thus, in the first test
of the central authorities following Tito's death, the hand-picked
successors proved unable to rise to the challenge and protect the
authority of the Yugoslav federal state.

Yugoslavia's new political leaders, including Croatia's Stipe Suvar
and Serbia's Slobodan Milosevic, owed much more to their control
over republic Party organisations than to the Federation. Each of
these new leaders advocated a policy of autonomy from control by
other republics; each supported the premise of consensual decision-

making; and each exercised its veto powers. None accepted democratic centralism from outside their republic's borders. Over time, therefore, the role of the federal leadership became more and more extraneous to the body politic.

The vacuum of power at the Centre greatly affected the economic and cultural elites in each of the republics. Both groups were forced to look to the republic leaders for support and policy stability, and both abandoned the Federation. Increasingly, in a *quid pro quo* arrangement, republic political leaders championed republic firms at the expense of other Yugoslav firms; and, over time, they introduced independent economic, fiscal, investment, tax and commercial policies in their home republics.

Cultural elites were also co-opted by the new republic leaders. These cultural institutions were able to provide an alternative source of legitimacy to the republic leaders in return for the enhancement of their power and policy influence. In the mid-1980s, the Slovenian Party solicited the support of the Catholic Church. At the same time, Serbia's Slobodan Milosevic eagerly embraced the platform of the nationalist wing of the Serbian Academy of Arts and Sciences. Slovenia and Serbia's courting of their respective cultural institutions were pivotal points of departure for these republics, and their alliances with their cultural institutions were of crucial significance in the decay of the federal Communist Party.

Remarkably, the decade of the 1980s witnessed no concerted reform efforts on the part of the Party to restore its legitimacy and to rehabilitate its guiding role. Virtually no one risked their careers to attempt to salvage the system. In fact, after Najdan Pasic's ill-fated reform effort in 1982, no other cross-republic reform movements ever materialised.

Cessation of the Security Threat

Tito's third prop to justify and legitimise the regime was the international security threat to the integrity of the Yugoslav state. A large standing army, complex and self-sufficient armament capacity, and a relatively extensive network of diplomatic and international ties all contributed to the cohesion of the state. As long as the international environment was hostile, each republic in Yugoslavia was willing to rely upon the Federation to safeguard its independence. In the 1980s, detente, Gorbachev's international restructuring and the cessation of the Cold War knocked out the underpinnings for the nonalignment policy and the maintenance of a strong security apparatus.

The eradication of an immediate security threat to Yugoslavia's borders brought into question several critical policy concerns regarding military affairs. First, Yugoslavia's huge standing army lacked a convincing rationale and became increasingly viewed within the country as just another tool of a repressive state. Second, support of the arms industry transferred considerable resources from the productive sectors of the economy to the underdeveloped regions, and many viewed it as a *de facto* subsidy to the Serbian republic. Third, the Yugoslav army, which was attempting to remain a professional force in a chaotic environment, became identified with Serbia's centralist policies, and it became increasingly difficult for the army to be perceived as a non-political instrument of the nation.

In summary, when we analyse the Yugoslav experience during the 1980s, we find that the degeneration of the Communist regime did not occur overnight. The failure of the regime to enforce the social contract, to retain popular legitimacy, and to adapt to changes in the international world order all contributed to the final outcome. Nothing in the process leading up to the dissolution of Yugoslavia was preordained. The failure of public will, lack of a guiding purpose, and the absence of leadership were all combined in the final tragedy.

Transition to Post-Communism and Current Challenges

The Yugoslav republics did not follow a common pattern or move at a comparable pace or direction in their transitions from one-party Communist rule. Unlike Bulgaria, Romania, Czechoslovakia and the GDR, transition occurred more slowly and spasmodically and at differential rates of change. Slovenia, for example, jettisoned most features of Communist rule through a gradual process beginning in the mid-1980s and concluding with its successful struggle for sovereignty in 1991. Slovenia's transition was nearly a completely autonomous process which most closely paralleled the Hungarian method of gradual evolutionary change and internal Party reform. On the other hand, Croatia's transition during the spring of 1990 occurred virtually overnight and was both unplanned and marked by passive resistance from within the Party.

Contrary to the experience of Poland's Solidarity or Czechoslovakia's experience with Charter 77, Yugoslavia did not have an indigenous anti-Communist alternative movement. No anti-regime group existed on a pan-republic level, and no non-Communist Yugoslav alternative had even tried to build a mass-based social movement. For practical purposes, the concepts of Yugoslavia as a state and socialism as its ideology were inseparably linked.

Throughout the Yugoslav republics, the guiding principle for change and the foundation for the anti-Communist movement was not democracy or pluralism; rather, it was ethnic differentiation. The anti-communist's organising principle was to protect a specific ethnic heritage, and each opposition group formulated a national vision that rejected inter-ethnic cooperation and pluralism. Since the Communists were linked to the pan-Yugoslav idea, and because they had labelled all anti-regime programmes as fundamentally 'nationalist' in character, the most convenient way for the anti-Communist forces to mobilise against Communist rule was through the articulation of a nationalist agenda. Perversely, the inflexibility of the Communists created the very situation that they were trying to avoid (i.e. nationalist separatism).

The advent of nationalism as a guiding political force also generated corresponding ideological developments, including the creation of new national mythologies and the revision of popular history. The 500th anniversary of the Battle at Kosovo Polje in 1989, for example, became a celebration of an expansionary, intolerant, pre-modern Serbian myth. Similar events, albeit not as dramatic, also catalysed nationalist movements in Croatia, Montenegro and Macedonia.

Slovenia: Western Pluralism and Parliamentary Democracy

Slovenia undertook its initial steps to accommodate itself to the Post-Tito era well before the other Yugoslav republics and before the peoples in the East European socialist states separated themselves from Soviet domination. Slovenia's transformation was not orchestrated or planned by a small group of leaders. Rather, this republic's leadership seemed to respond in a pragmatic way to changing circumstances, and only gradually, but with increasing tempo, moved unilaterally towards a democratic future.

Substantively, Slovenia's transformation is a classic case of controlled and gradual system change instigated from below. It began in the mid-1980s with increasingly strident citizen concerns about the environmental damages suffered by the republic. As a small, alpine republic, Slovenia's citizenry, particularly the youth, were cognisant of the destruction which the primitive industrialisation had caused. Acid rain, polluted rivers, soil erosion and foul air had taken its toll. The concern was heightened further by the Chernobyl disaster of 1986 which helped to remind the people of the precarious and delicate environment in their mountain state.

Initially, this burgeoning environmental movement was ignored by the Party, Socialist Alliance and the Trade Union Association. It was, however, adopted as a *cause célèbre* by the republic's youth organisation. Beginning in 1985, they organised marches, 'happenings' and other consciousness-raising events as a way to force the over-aged and out-of-touch leadership to make way for new societal forces.

They initially attempted to put pressure on the federal level and to organise on a pan-Yugoslav basis. They articulated a strong environmental stance and, at the same time, advocated that Yugoslavia's antiquated treatment of youth as political pawns be replaced by a true partnership. The Slovenian Youth League ridiculed the Youth Day celebrations as demeaning and demanded a true partnership with the government. They enraged the army with the suggestion that the compulsory military service be reformed to permit alternative service to the country, and they antagonised the police with the demand that the constitution be amended to guarantee the freedoms of speech and free assembly.

This reform agenda was rejected at the federal level without any serious deliberation. On the republic level, however, the organisation had seized the initiative, defined the political agenda and achieved widespread grass-roots support, particularly in Ljubljana, the capital. Other interest groups were encouraged by the success of the youth, and in an interesting turn of events, the Party courted their support as a counterweight to the growing influence of the Youth League. An example is the formation of an autonomous organisation of Slovenian peasants which condemned governmental agricultural policy and threatened to run candidates in the elections. In a bid to win Church support, the Party even recognised Christmas and Easter as state holidays, and went so far as to send Christmas greetings to the Slovenian citizenry, via the electronic media.

One significant event that fixated Party attention on its eroding base of support was the defeat of the Party's candidate for republic president by the relatively unknown and young economist, Janez Drnovsek, in 1989. This event, along with defeats for the Party's candidates at the local level throughout Slovenia, and the mushrooming of autonomous social groups and political organisations, forced the Slovenian Party to reassess its relationship between the citizens and its fraternal Party organisations in other republics. The Slovenian Party cast its lot in with the reform movement and actively, but futilely, pressured the Federal Party in the direction of reform.

In 1988 and 1989, the Slovenian Party leaders became more aggressive in their defence of Slovenian prerogatives. Not only did they condemn Serbian activities in Kosovo, they actively and vocally supported the Albanian minority in the province. The Slovene Party pushed for constitutional reforms and advocated a confederal system among the republics. They also implemented a republic constitution that gave the republic the right to nullify Federal laws and to restrict the movements of the army within Slovenia's borders. The Party sided with the youth organisation during military trials in 1989–90 and warned about the imminent danger of a Federal military *coup d'état* in Slovenia. Serbia aggravated the situation further and made the Slovenian Communists local heroes by declaring a boycott of Slovenian goods and services, despite the evident unconstitutionality of such a move.

During this tense period, the burgeoning number of *de facto* political organisations compelled the government to call for free and open multi-party elections. A coalition of opposition parties formed under the umbrella designation of DEMOS whose common platform centred around anti-communism and the defence of Slovenia's sovereignty.

Prior to the campaign, the Slovene Party renamed itself the 'Party of Democratic Reform', and it conducted a strong campaign to retain control over the legislature. In March 1990, it garnered less than 20 per cent of the vote, a respectable showing, but insufficient for inclusion in the DEMOS coalition government. In this election, the Party's presidential candidate, Milan Kucan, fared much better and was elected with a majority of the vote. Kucan was seen as a strong proponent of Slovene sovereignty, and his election also provided some continuity within the socialist federation which made direct intervention from Belgrade more difficult.

By June 1990, Slovenia had completed its transformation from a one-party Communist regime to a multi-party parliamentary system. Although not a perfectly functioning parliamentary democracy, Slovenia had successfully embraced pluralism and democratic government. By the summer of 1991, it had achieved independence, with very little bloodshed and virtually no internal resistance.

Since the first multi-party election, the DEMOS coalition has all but collapsed, and the reformed Communist Party has moved to the margins of political life. The government has proved itself to be reasonably tolerant and committed to reducing the state role in economic affairs. The fact that there is no significant minority population has simplified domestic politics and permitted the emergence of a relatively democratic political ethos.

Foreign policy objectives for Slovenia have centred on facilitating inclusion within the European network of associations. It has remained aloof from the civil wars afflicting the other regions in the former Yugoslavia, and the republic has attempted to reorient its trade towards Austria and the EC.

Eventually, Slovenia must discover its role within the former Yugoslavia. Border incidents and impediments to trade with Croatia hurt the economies of both nations and pose a significant challenge in the immediate future. Slovenia must also find an accommodation with the Federal Republic of Yugoslavia and the market which it represents.

From a comparative perspective, the Republic of Slovenia has undergone a successful transition to Western parliamentary democracy and has emerged as a reasonably stable sovereign nation state (Andrejevich, 1992). Challenges exist, but none of these issues threatens either the survival of Western democracy or international peace. Finally, while it is unlikely that Slovenia will enjoy immediate acceptance among the European family of nations, it seems certain that it will eventually join its Western neighbours.

Croatia: Pre-War Political Revival

When compared to Slovenia, Croatia's transition process has been unplanned, unled and unpredictable. Since the repression of the Croatian Spring in 1971, the Croatian Party had lost much of its vigour and creativity. Its role, under such colourless leaders as Bakaric and Planinc, was to preserve the status quo, keep the peace, and to facilitate the expansion of the tourist economy to become the engine of economic growth throughout Yugoslavia. Those seeking reforms and those with initiative considered the Party to be hopelessly conservative, and they generally migrated or turned their attention to the economic and commercial sectors.

In order to retain power, Croatia's party and governmental leaders closely allied themselves with the state sector of the economy and the local or regional economic interests. Increasingly, the remittances from abroad and the earnings from the tourist sector were used to subsidise the non-productive social sector. In the 1980s, Croatian growth slackened, a significant black market economy emerged, and the capacity of the state to monitor and control social groups lessened. During this time, Croatia's leadership became subordinated to the interests of their business patrons. They found themselves without influence in Belgrade, the federal capital, to alter policy and defend Croatia's interest; and, increasingly, their local supporters were drawn heavily from the Serbian minorities in Croatia.

In the latter 1980s, Stipe Suvar, a Zagreb University sociology professor, was elected Party leader after an intense factional and inter-generational struggle. In the past, Suvar had alienated the intellectual elite, young people and the urban middle classes. He was the ideologue behind the purges of the Tripalo wing of the Party in the 1970s: he was the architect of the much resented educational reform movement that abolished the traditional gymnasium and mandated compulsory vocational education; and he facilitated the emasculation of the autonomy of the republic's universities. Suvar's support was limited to the *nomenklatura*; and his selection represented a regime that was essentially undemocratic, unresponsive to citizen concerns, hostile to Croatian ethnic values, and dependent upon Belgrade for support.

Initially, Croatia's leadership attempted to remain neutral in the Serbian Kosovan struggle. In the 1980s they backed a veto system at the federal level, criticised Slovenia's movement towards interest group pluralism, and attempted to block any change that might upset the status quo. Internally, the Party repressed the emergence of a vocal youth movement, facilitated the movement of Serbian capital into the republic, and worked to reassert control over the local political satrapies. The regime remained fixed against change until the collapse of the Berlin Wall, reunification of Germany, and the *de facto* secession of Slovenia made further resistance impossible.

The extent to which the Croatian Party had lost touch with its base was evident during the first multi-party elections held in May 1990. Immediately prior to the campaign, believing itself to be firmly in control, it altered the election rules to favour the party which won a plurality of votes. It was assumed that the primary opposition would come from an *ad hoc* coalition of parties led by the heroes of the

Zagreb Spring, and so the conservative Croatian Democratic Community (HDZ) was disregarded. The Party conducted its campaign based upon gradual reform and continuity. The HDZ, meanwhile, advanced a vision of Croatian independence and support for Croatian traditional values and the free market.

From the perspective of the Croatian Party, the results were devastating. It achieved nearly 25 per cent of the vote, largely from the industrial Rijeka region and from the Serbian minority which did not have time to field its own candidates and organise its own party structure. It lost Zagreb, Split and virtually every other urban centre. The Coalition's strength also proved illusory, and it garnered only per cent. Meanwhile, the victorious HDZ under Franjo Tudman won slightly over 40 per cent of the vote and two-thirds of all legislative seats.

Virtually everyone was unprepared for the scope and speed of the political revolution that embraced Croatia. The Party simply disintegrated as its Serbian minority clientele abandoned it, and the Coalition could never adjust to the new political reality. More ominously, however, the Serbian republic stepped up its campaign against Croatia, and attempted to build a coalition to isolate Croatia within the Federation.

Since Tudjman and the HDZ lacked any significant parliamentary opposition, they were not restrained in their policy initiatives and not predisposed to compromise with the Communist Party or the Federal government. The government undertook a sweeping purge of the civil service and began efforts to construct an independent military force. The Yugoslav People's army threatened intervention and attempted unsuccessfully to disarm the Croatian territorial forces.

At approximately the same time, the Serbian minority conducted a terrorist campaign in order to force armed intervention by the army to its defence. The Croatian Serbs (i.e. Krajina Serbs) also conducted their own referendum, closed roads, seized armouries and expelled all elements of Croatian state authority from their region. Ominously, various paramilitary groups formed and began to conduct a campaign in mixed areas to expel ethnic Croatians.

The pressure imposed by the Serbian-dominated federation had a counterproductive impact in Croatia. Encouraged by Slovenia's moves towards independence and challenged by the Krajina Serbs, Croatia also scheduled a referendum on sovereignty which passed overwhelmingly in the ethnic Croatian areas. In order to avoid a premature armed clash with the federal army, the Croatian government did not lend active support to Slovenia in its struggle with federal authorities, and it reluctantly permitted the federal army to stage its incursions into Slovenia from Croatian territory.

Federal Yugoslavia's humiliating withdrawal from Slovenia in July 1991 further limited room for manoeuvre in both Croatia and in rump Yugoslavia. The Federal army's pride had been wounded by events in Slovenia, and Croatia's assertions of independence were challenged in the Krajina and Slavonia. In a fateful decision, Federal army bases and supplies were allowed to be used to assist the Krajina Serbs. Tudjman responded by demanding the withdrawal of all Federal military forces from Croatian territories, and a number of unauthorised Croatian seizures and sieges of military bases began.

The resulting war in Croatia destroyed the Federation, Croatia's and Serbia's attempts to achieve democracy, civilian control over the military in both republics, and respect for human rights. The war had little to do with territorial claims and demands for independence; it was fought over issues of pride and revenge. Neither the destruction of Vukovar in late 1991, nor the siege of Dubrovnik, had military strategic significance. Both were tests of wills, and both buried any chance of reconciliation or democracy in the region.

Croatia's attempt to build a modern polity died in the civil war. For practical purposes its political culture is frozen in the rhetoric and vision of the early twentieth century. Democracy and a civil society have been sacrificed to the needs of the state. Freedom of the press and assembly are severely curtailed, and prospects for inclusion within Western Europe seem remote, at best. The position of minorities is precarious, and Croatia seems bent on an irredentist policy.

Although the 1992 Croatian elections were reasonably free, the wartime environment did not permit a free exchange of ideas. On the positive side, the extreme right was rejected at the polls with 5 per cent of the vote, and a moderate alternative to Tudjman did achieve some credibility (Bicanic and Dominis, 1992). The economy is directed towards wartime needs, and a free market is still illusory. Compounding matters further, the costs of reconstruction are high, international loans are unavailable, refugees overburden the nation's infrastructure, and armed paramilitary groups threaten to push Croatia over the abyss once again (Moore, 1992). Croatia, in contrast to Slovenia, became a victim and hostage to the nationalism which the breakup of communism released. Prospects for the future appear to be problematic.

Serbia and Montenegro

As of 1993 Serbia and Montenegro are the two republic units which have retained membership within Yugoslavia. Both are primarily ethnic Serbian in character, although there are significant Albanian, Hungarian and Muslim minorities within the territories. Serbia is, by far, the largest unit in the Yugoslav federation; and Serbia's internal politics, particularly with respect to the predominantly ethnic Albanian province of Kosovo, have shaped events in the Federation and in the former Yugoslavia.

Unlike Slovenia and Croatia, the Serb territories were independent prior to the First World War and had a distinctive national history. Also, compared to the Slovenes and Croats, the Serb territories are less modernised and less integrated into the economies and societies of Western Europe. Finally, Serbs have had a historic sense of persecution, and many had viewed the Tito regime and its policies in support of ethnic autonomy as fundamentally anti-Serb in orientation. From a Serbian nationalist perspective, Tito was a Croat and favoured his own ethnic group. Tito's self-managed socialism had benefitted the economies of Croatia and Slovenia; Serbia's ancestral homeland in Kosovo had been surrendered to the Albanians; Bosnia and Macedonia were severed from the Serbian heartland; Serbia had subsidised the other republics; and now Serbia had become impoverished by the Tito regime. Thus, after Tito's death, many Serbs believed that the time had come for a fundamental restructuring of the federal arrangement.

Until the mid-1980s, Serbia's political scene was essentially frozen into the pattern established by Tito. The Serbian Party resisted reform and change, and it endured considerable criticism for its passive stance *vis-à-vis* the Kosovan Albanians and the deterioration in the economy. While the Slovenian mass movements formed, Serbia's population outside Kosovo remained essentially unorganised and apathetic. Its leadership practised the time-honoured formula of musical chairs' rotation of posts and veneration of Tito's name.

In 1986, a moderate reform group and new generation came to the fore. The leadership consisted of Ivan Stambolic, as President of Serbia, Slobodan Milosevic, Serbian Party President, and Dragisa Pavlovic, Belgrade Party President, and this group pushed for an economic reform package to move Serbia from its economic doldrums (Ristic, 1989). The troika also introduced a new more populist style of leadership, with fact-finding trips and hands-on involvement in policy issues.

During a fact-finding tour to Kosovo in 1987, Slobodan Milosevic promised a crowd of Serbian Kosovan residents that the police would never again act against the Serbs. The response was electric, and Milosevic became a hero to the Serbian nationalists in the republic. This speech and the policy which it implied had not been approved by the Central Committee and met with strong criticism from the other members of the Serbian troika. Milosevic, in turn, used the criticism to purge his former compatriots from power and to build a new, aggressive, nationalist Party apparatus.

In 1988, Milosevic and his allies orchestrated an extraordinary series of events, culminating in huge street demonstrations, which resulted in the wholesale replacement of the provincial Party and governmental structures in Vojvodina and Kosovo and, most extraordinarily, the mass resignation of the Party and governmental leadership in Montenegro (Cohen, 1991). These events gave Milosevic control over four of the eight federal units of Yugoslavia and the ability to isolate Slovenia and other pluralised forces within the former Yugoslavia. In a further bid for power, Milosevic attempted to exclude Croatia's Stipe Suvar from the Federal Presidency of the Party, Anton Markovic, a Croat, from the Federal Premiership, and Stipe Mesic, a Croat, from the normal rotation to the Federal Presidency. Adding insult to injury, Serbian nationalists demanded the right to send 500,000 Serbs to Ljubljana to demonstrate against the Slovenian authorities; and, when Slovenia refused, Serbia instituted a unilateral boycott of Slovenian goods and services.

Throughout these crises, Slobodan Milosevic proved unable to compromise with the leadership in other republics or with opposition in Serbia. He remained wedded to the authoritarian politics of the Tito era and the aggressive nationalist populism of nineteenth-century Serbia.

The keystone of Milosevic's policy and approach was the protection of what were considered to be Serbian ethnic interests. With unswerving consistency, the Socialists supported ethnic cleansing in Croatia and in Bosnia. Serbia also appeared poised to pursue ethnic homogeneity in Kosovo and, possibly, Vojvodina.

In 1989, the government strongly aligned itself with the Serbian Orthodox Church, as indicated by the joint Church–State celebration of the 500th anniversary of the Battle of Kosovo. By May 1992, however, the Church unilaterally severed further ties and condemned the human rights abuses of the Milosevic regime (*FBIS*, 11 June 1992). Kosovan Albanians, for their part, have formed a government in exile, conducted elections and have withdrawn from any cooperation or involvement with the Federal or Republic authorities.

The Communist Party of Serbia reorganised itself in 1990. It adopted the name Serbian Socialist Party and expanded its constituency to include former Serbian politicians and intellectuals who had been sidetracked in the past for their nationalist sympathies.

In a brilliant manoeuvre, the Socialist government scheduled multi-party elections in December 1990, and nearly a hundred different parties organised to contest the election. There was no prior agreement between the Socialists and the opposition parties, however, regarding electoral rules, district boundaries, and access to the media. Initially, the opposition parties refused to participate and attempted unsuccessfully to form a united opposition front. Eventually, with less than a month to campaign and organise, most of the opposition parties committed themselves to the process and entered the election without local organisations, programmes, disciplined campaign workers, or public identification.

Thanks to the pre-election manipulations of the Serbian Socialists and the quarrels among the opposition groups, the pattern of electoral defeat for the local Communists that was seen throughout Eastern Europe was not repeated in Serbia. Milosevic's party won slightly over 40 per cent of the vote, but captured over two-thirds of all legislative seats. Albanians in Kosovo had boycotted the elections, thereby allowing the Serbian Socialists to run unopposed in the province. Also, many moderates, frightened of the possibility of nationalist right extremist victory, supported the Socialists in the second round elections. Milosevic himself coasted to an easy victory as President of the Republic.

With the secession of Croatia from the Federation and the ensuing war in 1991, the Federal government of Anton Markovic finally resigned. In March 1991, the first major anti-Milosevic demonstrations erupted in Belgrade and the army chain of command refused to intervene on behalf of the Socialists. The siege of Vukovar further weakened the army which eventually gave up the pretence of protecting the now defunct federation. In the ensuing anarchy Milosevic took control of the remainder of the federal institutions, purged the officer corps of non-Serb remnants, engaged in a protracted battle to control the media, reconstituted the former Socialist

Federal Republic of Yugoslavia as the Federal Republic of Yugoslavia, and withdrew from Bosnia and Macedonia.

Surprisingly, despite the pressures from the war and international boycott and embargo, citizens still retained basic freedoms of speech and assembly. The economy, with the exception of war production, has come to a standstill, and the country is now burdened with enormous numbers of refugees. Serbia, with its extreme nationalistic policies, has become the pariah of the world.

Perhaps the most interesting feature of the new federal government is the role played by the Prime Minister, Milan Panic, and the Federal President, Dobrica Cosic. Both leaders have no party affiliation, but both were selected by Milosevic to support the Socialists' agenda. Perversely, both leaders now have strong popular support, and both are strongly opposed to Milosevic and his policies. In an uncharacteristically poorly planned move, Milosevic proved unable to force the resignation of the Panic government in October 1992 and contributed to unifying the opposition around it prior to the 20 December elections.

Despite the experience of the 1990 debacle, that opposition was still fragmented, poorly organised, poorly led, and had no common programme save opposition to Slobodan Milosevic. Significant components of the opposition forces were more extremist than the Socialists, and few parties within the opposition framework were committed to democratic processes. No consistent attempt was made to include the Albanian or Hungarian minorities within the opposition's voting bloc. No effort was made to resolve the refugee situation, and no significant steps were taken to prevent the government's withdrawal of citizenship to Croats living in Serbia. Although there was much unease about the organisation of the elections and the extent of Milosevic's victory, it was clear that he could count on significant support throughout much of what remained of Yugoslavia.

The prospects for the Federal Republic of Yugoslavia appear dim. Despite huge personal and economic losses, the Serbian struggles against Croats, Muslims, Macedonians and Albanians appear to continue unabated. No one has even attempted to discuss in a serious fashion the reconstruction of the country and the resolution of the refugee problem. Yugoslavia is now isolated from the world community, and its hopes for inclusion within Europe seem an empty dream. Even a new well-intentioned democratic government is unlikely to salvage the situation, because the levels of distrust and personal injury are so high that they cannot be overcome or overlooked in the near future.

Bosnia-Hercegovina

Bosnia's is the most tragic and the least necessary of all the conflicts which emerged from the wreckage of Socialist Yugoslavia. Compared to the other republics, Bosnia-Hercegovina was not dominated by a single ethnic group. It consisted of Muslim, Serb and Croat populations who were quite thoroughly mixed throughout the republic, and with Muslims primarily inhabiting the towns and cities of the republic. From a rational perspective, the separation of the ethnic groups into distinct enclaves made no sense. In fact, prior to the ethnic cleansing and war of 1992–3, it had been assumed that the creation of ethnically homogeneous enclaves would entail such enormous personal, social and economic costs that the thought could be dismissed out of hand.

Prior to 1987, Bosnia's Party leadership could be counted on for its steadfast conservatism and adherence to Tito's path. It was generally agreed among the Bosnian post-Tito leadership that Bosnia's economy and leaders benefited from the Federation and that ethnic conflict or competition would be counterproductive for everyone. It was in Bosnia where the iron triangles consisting of republic Party leaders, local Party leaders and directors of enterprises were most advanced and the 'veza' patronage system most pervasive. Within federal decision-making bodies, Bosnia's leaders tended to maintain the balance of power and to support the status quo. In the early years, Bosnia backed Milosevic and his colleagues against the reformers from Slovenia. In later years, however, Bosnia opposed Milosevic's attempt to depose Suvar as head of the Party; it vigorously opposed Serbia's unilateral boycott against Slovenia; and it reacted adversely to Milosevic's increasingly nationalistic populist style and methods.

Bosnia-Hercegovina had opposed the legalisation of a multiparty system on the grounds that their constitution prohibited the formation of ethnically based social organisations. Ultimately, however, after competitive parties were legalised, ethnic identification proved to be a persuasive organising theme. During the campaign, the political establishment remained loyal to a reformed Party group. Modernists and reformers backed a newly created Federal Party under the leadership of its Prime Minister, Anton Markovic. The local political machines, however, backed Muslim, Serb and Croat parties, depending upon their ethnic identification.

The results of the election in November 1990, particularly the second round, were resounding defeats for the reformed Communist Party and the newly organised Federal Party of Anton Markovic. The ethnic parties received well over two-thirds of all parliamentary seats and immediately formed a coalition government. The winners divided all posts among the ethnic parties and agreed to a system that allowed each ethnic group a veto.

To the dismay of the Serb party, Bosnia declared its neutrality in the Croat–Serb conflict and authorised potential recruits to refuse military service in the Yugoslav People's Army. Despite Bosnia's neutrality, however, the republic was used as a staging ground by the army for incursions into Croatia which significantly strained the multi-ethnic coalition. More ominously, the refusal of Bosnia's Muslim and Croat recruits to report for duty enabled the Yugoslav army units stationed in Bosnia to become an ethnically pure Serbian force. Thus, when the Federation recognised Bosnia's independence in 1992 and decommissioned the Federal units of Bosnian origin, the huge majority of these troops were ethnically Serb and were available to fight for the Bosnian Serb opposition.

The government of Alija Izetbegovic has been increasingly identified with urban, modern elements, particularly centred in the city of Sarajevo. The government has had little support in the rural villages and it had no control or discipline over its coalition partners in the smaller towns. Bosnia's government considered ethnic conflict to be a historical anachronism, and it was frightened about the potential senseless violence which ethnic conflict could cause in the republic. It feared the existence of a secret Milosevic–Tudjman agreement to partition Bosnia between Serbia and Croatia, and it moved quickly to reject any moves that might lend support to cantonisation or partition.

In order to forestall the appearance of a willingness to negotiate partition, the Izetbegovic government decided to move towards independence and international recognition in December 1991. The decision for independence was not taken rashly and seemed politically wise at the time. First, Bosnia's largest ethnic group (i.e. Muslims) would be deprived of influence in a partitioned Bosnia, and their continued support would be vital to any Bosnian government. Second, after the legacy of the Croatian war, the Bosnian Croat minority would not tolerate further membership in the Serb-dominated Federal Yugoslav state. Third, the Izetbegovic government gambled that the Serb-dominated army, exhausted after the Croatian campaign and faced with international condemnation, would not oppose Bosnian independence. Finally, Sarajevo's population, including significant numbers of Serbs and families with mixed parentage, appeared committed to ethnic pluralism and strongly supported the government's independence decision.

The Bosnian government's failures were to refuse to take the recalcitrance of the Serbian minority seriously and to depreciate the preponderance of weaponry and organisation in the hands of the Serbs. From hindsight, it is apparent that the government's decision to press ahead with international recognition, without including the Serbian opposition, was fateful. In addition, the government's support to the Bosnian peace movement and the Sarajevo street demonstrations isolated moderate but anti-government Serbs and eliminated their capacity to influence the Serb extremists.

The cruelties and criminal acts associated with the Bosnian war have made reconciliation and democratic government among the ethnic groups in the near future virtually impossible. More than a million refugees have been created by this conflict, and every city and town has been damaged or destroyed by its violence. Some type of cantonisation or partition is now inevitable, and there seems to be little prospect for recovery or a return to the status quo before the war. The tragedies for Bosnia are that everyone has lost and that the seeds for conflicts in succeeding generations have now been sown throughout the region.

Macedonia

Of all the successor regimes to the former Socialist Yugoslavia, Macedonia is the only republic to be denied recognition by the world community. Possessing approximately two million inhabitants, it is one of the poorest and least developed of all the states in the former republic. It is also the one whose borders are least secure and could be challenged by Bulgaria, Greece and the Federal Republic of Yugoslavia. Approximately three-quarters of the population belong to the Macedonian ethnic group, while the remainder are of Albanian, Bulgarian or Turkish ethnic origins.

Under Tito, the Republic of Macedonia fared relatively well. As a newly created republic under the Tito regime whose existence could be challenged by its neighbours, Macedonian political figures were strong oriented towards preservation of the federal system. In addition, the political leaders under Tito and in the post-Tito periods were generally conservative and averse to change. Local political figures and the republic leadership were closely intertwined, and a strong 'veza' system flourished.

When the disputes between Slovenia and Serbia broke out during the mid-1980s, Macedonia tended to support the federal authorities and, secondarily, the Serbian Milosevic regime. Its basic policy goal, however, was to promote a strong federation, even if that might imply a strong Serbia. Like Serbia, many Macedonians felt threatened by the increase in the Albanian population and gave tacit support to the Serbian attempts to control the situation in Kosovo. Unlike Serbia, however, the Macedonian leadership did not destroy its links with the Albanian leaders in Macedonia and continued to search for reconciliation or a *modus vivendi* with the Albanian population.

Macedonians conducted elections in November 1990 at approximately the same time as the sister republic of Bosnia-Hercegovina. The results, however, were much more mixed and difficult to interpret than in any of the other former Yugoslav republics. The electorate in Macedonia split its support between the reformed Communist party and an ostensibly Macedonian nationalist party. The Albanian minority also participated in the elections and supported their candidates and an ethnic Albanian party. Other minor parties, based on local political machines, also received support and some seats in the parliament.

At the conclusion of the elections, no single ethnic group or ideological cluster was able to dominate the parliament and form a government. After weeks of negotiation, a coalition which included an improbable mix of communists, nationalists and Albanian-oriented parties emerged. In addition, Kiro Gligorov, the Macedonian Communist Party president and the individual who guided Socialist Macedonia during the post-Tito period, was elected president of the republic and head of the government.

During 1991, Macedonia's diverse coalition functioned reasonably well. The government refused to be drawn into the disputes and wars between Slovenia, and later Croatia. It did not arm its citizenry or lay siege to the Yugoslav army forces on its territories. It did not even withdraw from currency union with Yugoslavia, even though it declared its independence on 20 November 1991.

Macedonia had hoped to receive international recognition for its independence declaration at the same time as Slovenia, Croatia and Bosnia. Recognition was considered to be vital in order for Macedonia to preserve the integrity of its borders. The opposition of Greece to the recognition of Macedonia, however, has kept the republic isolated, and it has been under severe economic pressure and boycotts from both the Federal Republic of Yugoslavia and the Greek republic. Despite these pressures, the government coalition of nationalists, former Communists and Albanian ethnic parties has survived (Perry, 1992).

During 1992, the government campaigned strenuously, but unsuccessfully, to receive recognition from the world community. Its economy and banking system have been severely pressed and are on the verge of collapse. The ban on trade with Yugoslavia has affected Macedonian commerce severely, and the prohibition on weapons sales has kept the republic relatively disarmed in a dangerous environment.

Macedonia's future, to a large extent, depends on events beyond its control. If civil disturbances break out in Kosovo, then it is likely that these disturbances could easily cross the border in Macedonia. Greece or Yugoslavia might have secret designs on its territory, and Bulgaria's warm support may prove suffocating. Macedonia, in short, is still engaged in a struggle for survival and its current government seems to recognise and support the notion of ethnic pluralism as the mechanism to enhance chances for its survival.

PART THREE

Patterns of Politics in Post-Communist Eastern Europe

8

Structures of Representation

KRZYSZTOF JASIEWICZ

The Round Tables and the Umbrellas

It is conventional wisdom that the East European revolution was won on the streets of Prague and Leipzig, Timisoara and Bucharest, in the shipyards of Gdansk and steel mills of Cracow. This point of view hardly can be disputed, but it is also true that this revolution was won in voting booths across the region. Street demonstrations and strikes usually initiated the change and often delivered the ultimate blow to the old regimes, but with almost no exception competitive elections were the real turning point in the process of political transition.

Comparative examination of elections in Eastern Europe in the period 1989–92 reveals patterns of remarkable similarity, as well as some local variations. In this chapter we shall focus on elections in Poland, Hungary, the Czech and Slovak republics, Romania, Bulgaria, and Albania, setting aside the cases of the former German Democratic Republic and Yugoslavia. Both are indeed special cases. In the GDR, the issue of the unification of Germany dominated the electoral process in both the March and October 1990 elections. In Yugoslavia, the complex federative structure of the former Yugoslav state, and even more so the recent war in this region, redefine the role of elections there and do not allow us to examine this case within the prescribed size and analytical framework of this chapter. None the less, some of the observations that are presented are also applicable to these two deviant cases (see Chapter 7 for a more detailed discussion of the former Yugoslavia).

In the late 1980s all East European communist regimes faced –

although most of them failed to recognise it – a crisis of legitimation (Rigby and Feher, 1982; Rychard, 1992; Bielasiak, 1992). Since their rise to power after the Second World War, the communists of Eastern Europe legitimised their rule through two mechanisms. The first may be called 'legitimisation through utopia': a promise to create an ideal system of social, political, and economic institutions, guaranteeing all citizens equal rights and equal access to the benefits of a welfare state; a system that would eventually generate an affluent society, free of exploitation and conflict. The second was a legitimisation through 'the Soviet tanks factor': the adoption of the Brezhnev doctrine (well before the very term was invented) to convince the potentially rebellious populations that the Soviet Union would not tolerate other than communist regimes in the region, and that the only alternative to a national communist government and limited sovereignty would be a direct Soviet occupation. The technically democratic procedures, such as elections, sessions of parliaments and nomination of cabinets, served only as a rubber stamp for the legitimisation achieved through the above-mentioned mechanisms. None the less, these rubber stamps were perceived by the communists as very important devices: very seldom would they implement any decisions without subjecting them to a process of such formal legalisation; very often they would prosecute oppositionists for alleged violations of law and 'constitutional order'.

By the late 1980s both mechanisms of legitimisation exhausted their potential. The promise of a better, more just political system and society was never fulfilled, and even the communist leaders occasionally had to admit this. But above all, the countries of Eastern Europe experienced economic crises, or, at the very best, stagnation. The gap between their 'economies of shortage' (Kornai, 1980) and the affluent market economies of Western Europe and North America became wider than ever. The people responded with disbelief to the official statistics on economic growth, which were themselves much less impressive than in the 1950s or 1960s. In recognition of these facts the communist leaderships in Hungary and Poland launched programmes of economic reforms, but the ultimate failure of these programmes contributed to the further delegitimisation of the system.

The election of Mikhail Gorbachev as the Soviet leader originally did not put in question the validity of the Brezhnev doctrine. But in 1987 and 1988 he and his aides began to encourage the communist leaders of Eastern Europe to experiment with their economic and political institutions – within, it should be remembered, the frame-work of a 'socialist state'. These friendly suggestions received a very mixed response from those to whom they were directed. Only the reformist factions of the Polish and Hungarian communist parties understood them as a backing against their own hardliners and pursued cautious policies of liberalisation. None the less, the hardline leaders of Czechoslovakia or the GDR could no longer present their conservative positions as congruent with the Soviet line. The window of opportunity for the opposition and dissatisfied populations had been opened. Still, it was not until the formation of a Solidarity-based government in Poland and the breaking of the Berlin Wall in 1989 that the Brezhnev doctrine could be pronounced dead.

The communist reformers of Poland and Hungary were the first to recognise an urgent need for a renewed legitimisation of their rule. Neither Wojciech Jaruzelski, Mieczyslaw Rakowski, Czeslaw Kiszczak in Poland, nor Karoly Grosz, Imre Pozsgay, Miklos Nemeth in Hungary had planned in 1988 or early 1989 to transfer power to the opposition. They were rather hoping to co-opt moderate opposition groupings to the system and share with them responsibility for the implementation of further economic reforms, which would carry necessary austerity measures, in all likelihood extremely unpopular among the populace. Despite different strength of opposition forces in Hungary and Poland (in Poland the opposition was strong and numerous, since 1980 united in the political movement of Solidarity, and enjoying the backing of the Roman Catholic church; in Hungary dissident groups were weak and isolated from the society), the com-munists of both countries applied very similar strategies. They opened up a process of negotiations, legitimising the opposition but also forcing it to recognise as legitimate the institutions of the system. Among the major items on the negotiation table were the terms for new general elections – elections that would broaden the legitimisa-tion base of the renewed institutions of political representation. The Hungarian and Polish communist reformers were undoubtedly hop-ing to win these elections. With such an outcome, they would have regained unquestioned legitimacy, in exchange for granting the leaders of opposition a limited access to power (which would also mean joint accountability). Neither in Poland nor in Hungary were the communists able to achieve their goals.

In Poland the Jaruzelski/Rakowski government was forced to open negotiations with Solidarity after a series of industrial strikes, which took place in the spring and summer of 1988. They perceived this decision as the only way to overcome a stalemate, or a 'catastrophic balance' of power (Arriagada, 1992, p. 180). Similar perception dominated among the leaders of Solidarity. The formal negotiations began in January 1989 in a palace in Warsaw, with the members of the opposition and the government seated not face-to-face across a long, rectangular table, but around a round one. The symbolism of this spatial arrangement was obvious: 'we meet here not to bargain and struggle against each other, but to jointly work for the benefit of Poland'. The outcome of this effort was the so-called Roundtable Accord of April 1989 (see Chapter 3). According to this contract, 65 per cent of the 460 seats in the forthcoming elections to the Sejm were allocated in advance to the communists (Polish United Workers' Party) and their allies (United Peasant Party, Democratic Party, and pro-communist Catholic groupings). The remaining 35 per cent were subject to an open contest. In addition, the upper chamber of parliament, the Senate, was re-established, with 100 seats to be filled in a free, unrestricted election – the first such election in Eastern Europe for more than 40 years. In the elections, held on 4 and 18 June 1989, Solidarity won all but one of the seats it contested. The communists acquired their allocated seats in the Sejm, but none in the Senate. Moreover, their leaders were humiliated by the failure to obtain 50 per cent of the votes necessary for election from the uncontested national list. Jaruzelski was elected President by the National Assembly (the Sejm and Senate in a joint session), but the communists failed to form a coalition government, after the desertion of Peasant and Democratic parties to the Solidarity camp. Eventually, Tadeusz Mazowiecki, a long-time advisor to Lech Walesa, formed a Solidarity-dominated coalition government.

Less than a year after this historic achievement many Poles felt that they were 'penalized for taking the lead'. The revolutions swept the communists from power across Eastern Europe, but in Poland still there was a communist president and 'only 35 per cent democratic' Sejm. Under pressure from below, Jaruzelski tactfully resigned, and – following a constitutional amendment – an election to the presidency was held in November/December 1990. Solidarity, thus far remarkably united, split into two factions: one supporting Lech Walesa, the other Mazowiecki. The former emerged victorious.

After the presidential election the fragmentation of Solidarity continued. With no common enemy to keep them united any more, various political and ideological orientations emerged from the movement. In 1991, after the Sejm had shortened its term of office, they entered an electoral campaign. The October 1991 elections produced a highly fragmented parliament, with about thirty parties represented in both chambers. Since then Poland has seen two fragile, multi-party coalition governments, but also a surprising continuity in economic and political reforms.

In Hungary (discussed more fully in Chapter 5) the reforms began within the communist party (Hungarian Socialist Workers' Party). At a party conference in May 1988 Janos Kadar was elected to the ceremonial position of party Chairman and replaced as First Secretary by Karoly Grosz, while several reform-minded officials were elected to the Politburo. One of them, Imre Pozsgay, had been instrumental in setting up in 1987 a then semi-oppositionist group, the Hungarian Democratic Forum (HDF). The HDF, along with other dissident groupings (among them the Forum of Free Democrats, and Federation of Young Democrats) organised in March 1988 the Opposition Roundtable – an umbrella organisation, designed to represent the opposition in negotiations with the government. The negotiations lasted from June to September 1989, with the two major partners – the communist government and the opposition – being supplemented by communist-sponsored social organisations (trade unions, Popular Front) as a third party, and neutral observers (among them churches). Hence, the Hungarian negotiations have been known as a Triangular table, while the actual spatial arrangement was a square table, with the government and opposition facing each other. During the course of negotiations there occurred a further transformation of the communist party, with a collective leadership elected in June 1989 (Grosz, Pozsgay, Nemeth, and Rezso Nyers as Chairman). This move strengthened the position of the reformists, but prompted the disintegration of the party, which during its extraordinary congress in October changed its name to Hungarian Socialist Party. A conservative faction, led by Grosz, dissented, and still uses the old party name.

The accord in the tripartite negotiations, providing among other issues for free elections early the following year, was reached in September 1989, but the Free Democrats and Young Democrats refused to sign it. The major controversy concerned the sequence of elections: the communists, with the consent of the HDF, preferred to have the presidential election (by a popular vote) held before the parliamentary one. They had an apparently good candidate for this office, Imre Pozsgay, at that time the most popular politician in the country, while the opposition leaders lacked name recognition. The

Free Democrats and Young Democrats called for a referendum on the sequence of elections, and succeeded in having the order reversed. Eventually, the parliament elected in April 1990 changed the mode of presidential election from a direct one to indirect (by parliament). Arpad Goncz of the Free Democrats was chosen as President, while Pozsgay lost a bid for a direct election to the parliament, and acquired a seat through a party list allocation.

Unlike elsewhere in Eastern Europe, the Hungarian opposition entered the electoral process divided into several parties, but the same was true of the communists, split into a reform-socialist and a hardline faction. This lack of a formidable opponent, along with a relative weakness and isolation of dissidents in the 1980, account for this early, but limited fragmentation of the anti-communist movement. Eventually, six parties surpassed the threshold of 4 per cent and are represented in the parliament: the Hungarian Democratic Forum, Smallholders Party, Christian Democrats (all three in the ruling coalition), Alliance of Free Democrats, Federation of Young Democrats, and Hungarian Socialist Party (post-communist).

While the Polish and Hungarian cases may be described as negotiated transitions in which a reformist wing of the communist party played an active role, in the other East European countries the ruling communists retreated under a rapidly growing pressure from below. In Czechoslovakia (see Chapter 4) a series of mass demonstrations culminated in November 1989. That month, a group of veteran dissidents, led by Vaclav Havel, established in Prague a new organisation – the Civic Forum, which momentarily became the only spokesgroup for all anti-regime forces. A parallel group in Slovakia adopted the name Public against Violence. The communists agreed to negotiate with Civic Forum, and, under constant pressure from below, retreated step by step, until a coalition government under Marian Calfa was formed. Gustav Husak resigned as president, and Havel was elected (unanimously by the still communist-dominated Federal Assembly) to replace him. In the June 1990 elections Civic Forum and Public against Violence mustered a majority in both chambers of the federal parliament, as well as in the national councils in the Czech republic and Slovakia. Havel was re-elected President (for a two-year term). Soon after this victory the process of disintegration of Civic Forum and Public against Violence began. In the course of only two years both organisations practically disappeared from public life. In the elections of June 1992 in the Czech republic the Civic Democratic Party, a splinter group from Civic Forum, emerged as the major force, while in Slovakia a plurality of votes went to the Movement for a Democratic Slovakia – a nationalist-populist group. Their leaders, Vaclav Klaus and Vladimir Meciar, respectively, were committed to separate both parts of the 74-year-old federation, which decision took effect on 1 January 1993.

In Bulgaria on 10 November 1989 a group of more pragmatist communist leaders forced the resignation of Todor Zhivkov, one of the most autocratic and conservative communist rulers in Eastern Europe (see Chapter 6). This move prompted spontaneous anti-communist demonstrations in Sofia and the formation of a Union of Democratic Forces (UDF), which embraced several oppositionist and dissident groupings. In January 1990 this organisation entered roundtable talks with the government. After several setback, these talks led eventually to parliamentary elections in June 1990. The timing came as a compromise between the communists, who insisted on early elections, hoping to win and gain a renewed legitimacy, and the opposition, which preferred a later date, since it needed time to organise and gain momentum. In the elections the communists (now renamed the Bulgarian Socialist Party or BSP) mustered a majority, with 211 seats in the 400-seat Grand National Assembly. The UDF finished second with 144 seats, and the Movement for Rights and Freedoms or MRF (representing the interests of the Turkish minority) came third with 26. The UDF refused to join a coalition government with the BSP, but its leader Zhelyu Zhelev was elected interior president by the Grand National Assembly in August 1990 (his mandate was renewed by a popular vote in January 1992). A BSP-based government of Andrei Lukanov resigned in November 1990 under pressure from the opposition and protesters on the streets, and a caretaker government of Dimitr Popov ruled until the new elections in October 1991. In these elections none of the parties gained a majority. An UDF minority government, supported by the MRF, was formed, but it collapsed in October 1992 after the MRF withdrew its support.

The Bulgarian rhythm of transition was repeated, with about one year's delay and some variations, in Albania. Even in this last bastion of genuine Stalinism in Eastern Europe the pressure from the rapidly changing international environment could be felt, and its leader, Ramiz Alia, began in 1990 a process of very cautious reforms. This only encouraged the desperate population to protest – mostly by trying to seek asylum in foreign embassies in Tirana. Further liberalisation by the regime prompted the emergence of the first oppositionist groupings. As in Bulgaria, the communists decided to have early elections and legitimise their rule in the eyes of the international community and the Albanian population. The opposition threatened a boycott – and the elections were postponed from 10 February to 31 March 1991. None the less, the communists were victorious, by a 2 to 1 margin against the Democratic Party – a loosely organised, urban-based group. Unlike Bulgaria, the opposition originally joined a grand coalition government with the communists, but left it in December 1991, demanding new elections. These were conducted in March 1992 and brought a reversal of fortune: the Democratic Party defeated the Socialist Party (renamed Communists) by a 5 to 2 margin. The leader of the Democratic Party, Sali Berisha, was elected president by the People's Assembly in April 1992.

The course of events in Romania varies significantly from the patterns of developments considered elsewhere in this volume. There was no organised opposition, no reform-minded communist leaders, no roundtable talks; there was violence. The communist party vanished from the Romanian political scene after the December 1989 revolution, but the National Salvation Front (NSF), seemingly an *ad hoc* outcome of this revolt, in many ways substituted for a post-communist party. Allegedly dominated by former communists, the NSF presented itself in 1990 as the only legitimate representation of all Romanians, and intimidated political opponents. It decisively won the May 1990 parliamentary elections, and its leader Ion Iliescu mustered 85 per cent of the popular vote for president. After two years of half-hearted reform policies, the ruling Democratic National Salvation Front (renamed after a split within the old NSF) gained a plurality of seats in the Parliament, while Iliescu was re-elected in the runoff against Emil Constantinescu, the leader of a coalition of opposition forces – the Democratic Convention of Romania. The DCR finished strong second in the elections to both chambers of the parliament.

Looking at the process of regime transition in Eastern Europe from a comparative perspective one can observe that this process has been accomplished in the following stages, or phases:

Phase zero: The communist regimes either resist pressure to reform from a more or less organised opposition, or rule practically uncontested.

Phase one: The communist regimes under pressure from the opposition, the public, and/or international environment open up the process of negotiations. The opposition enters this process represented by an umbrella organization, which covers groupings with various ideological and political orientations. The process of negotiations, usually called the Round table, provides a mutual legitimisation for the opposition (recognised by the regime as a partner) and the institutions of the old regime, in particular the government and parliament. The roundtables as such obviously have exceeded the constitutional framework of a communist state; the state institutions make necessary provisions to legalise the outcome of the negotiations (including adoption of a new electoral law and constitutional amendments). The institutional role of the communist party diminishes during this process (while its leaders still play a significant political role), and in most cases the clause of 'the leading role of the [communist] party' is dropped from the constitution.

Phase two: Both the regime and the opposition claim that they represent the interests of the people, but against each partner of the roundtable negotiations a claim could be made that it represented nobody's but its own interests. These claims had to be weighed through the process of (more or less) contested elections. The elections also provide a broader legitimisation of the roundtable accords, and, ultimately, lead to the creation of indisputably legitimised institutions of political representation. Save for the cases of Hungary and Romania, the opposition enter the electoral process under the protective umbrella of one organisation, with only minor groupings running independently. Also the communist party participates in the elections as a united force (Hungary again is an exception here), often under a changed name.

Phase three: Developments in this phase differ within the region. In the Northern Tier (Poland, Czecho-Slovakia, Hungary) the elections bring about a landslide victory of the opposition. The defeat of the communists leads to a disintegration of this party and/or profound turnover in its leadership. But the victorious former opposition also disintegrates, the umbrella organisations either lose their popular support or simply cease to exist, and the political scene becomes highly fragmented. In Poland (1991) and Czecho-Slovakia (1992) this fragmentation is reflected in the outcome of the second set of general elections, and so is the continuing relative weakness and political isolation of the post-communist parties.

In the Southern Tier the post-communist organisations win the first elections – the opposition is too weak and the population too intimidated to overcome the resistance of communists, entrenched in the state bureaucracy and mass media. But after the elections the opposition – still unified under a protective umbrella, and now a legitimate actor on the political scene – gains momentum and challenges the post-communist governments. In Bulgaria and Albania this challenge leads, within about a year, to new elections, this time won by the opposition. In Romania, an united and better organised (compared with 1990) opposition still loses to the Democratic Front of National Salvation (DFNS) in the 1992 elections, but deprives the DFNS of the majority in parliament and forces Iliescu to a run-off in the presidential vote.

Despite the local variations, the process of political change in all Eastern European countries occurred according to the same general pattern, from polarisation to fragmentation: a united opposition faced the old regime in a stand-off (at a roundtable and/or during elections) and remained united until an apparent defeat of the communists. In Hungary the collapse of the communist party and fragmentation of the opposition preceded the first election. In Poland and Czecho-Slovakia this collapse and fragmentation stemmed from the results of the first elections. In the Southern Tier even after the second set of elections the post-communists remain formidable, forcing their foes (in Bulgaria and Albania the party in power, in Romania still in opposition) to maintain political unity, despite obvious ideological differentiation. While a resurgence of the post-communist parties in the Northern Tier seems unlikely, developments in the southern part of Eastern Europe may unfold in three directions: (i) the Northern variant: the post-communists' influence diminishes, the former opposition undergoes fragmentation; (ii) the Lithuanian variant: the effective resurgence of a post-communist organisation; or (iii) the indigenous variant: the fragmentation of the umbrella organisation occurs despite the continued influence of the post-communists.

It is often stressed (O'Donnell *et al.*, 1986) that the first free elections after a prolonged period of totalitarian or authoritarian rule play the role of 'founding elections': they lead to the establishment of a relatively stable configuration of actors on the political scene (although not necessarily a stable government). In the case of Eastern Europe the definition of founding elections should be extended to encompass the first, the second, and sometimes also the third and perhaps further electoral acts. The first elections were, as a rule, a plebiscite against communism; not until after the defeat of the communists did the party system begin to shape in an unrestricted way.

The Presidents and the Houses

In Eastern Europe and in connection to Eastern Europe, no other citation has appeared more often in the press than the one from Sir Winston Churchill: 'Many forms of Government have been tried and will be tried in this world of sin and woe. No one pretends that democracy is perfect and all-wise. Indeed, it has been said that democracy is the worst form of Government except all those other forms that have been tried from time to time' (Augarde, 1991, p. 55). Indeed, democracy – but what democracy?

The United States, the United Kingdom, France, Italy, all are democracies, but wouldn't it be a waste of time to point out the normative and institutional differences among them? The nations of Eastern Europe have to find their own forms of democracy, and face many actual specific choices – the choice between a presidential or a parliamentary form of government, between a uni- or bi-cameral parliament, and the choice of a voting system. But the first and fundamental question to which these nations had to find an answer has been the one of how much democracy can they afford now.

When in the mid-1980s experts were debating the future of communist regimes, some – predicting a collapse of communism in its orthodox form – believed that a dominant form of regime during the transition from communism to pluralist democracy would be a post-communist or nationalist authoritarianism (Brzezinski, 1990, p. 255). Locally in Eastern Europe there were politicians – communist and anti-communist – who, usually speaking off the record, expressed a desire for such a form of government. Two kinds of arguments have been made in favour of authoritarianism: (i) the people of the region lack democratic traditions and too rapid an introduction of democracy may result in anarchy; (ii) unlike Southern Europe or Latin America, in Eastern Europe the political transition is accompanied, if not dominated, by the economic one: from a command to a market economy. It carries many unpopular measures of austerity, and may be more successfully implemented from above, by an authoritarian state, which derives the unrestricted expression of group interests. These arguments – particularly the second one – deserve serious consideration, and developments in the former USSR and Yugoslavia certainly indicate the viability of authoritarian forms of government (although hardly their superiority to democracy). Also, many public opinion polls have shown quite strong authoritarian sentiments among populations. But by and large Eastern Europe has chosen democracy, and the authoritarian mode of decision-making is widely perceived as an aberration.

The major factor that accounts for these pro-democratic attitudes is the demonstration effect: the totalitarian or quasitotalitarian communist regimes never fulfilled their promises of economic welfare, social justice, and political equality, while the pluralist democracies of the West came much closer to this ideal (or even fully realised it, in the opinion – no matter how naive – of many East Europeans). After four or so decades of first 'popular' and later 'socialist democracy', political pluralism – the 'real' democracy – seemed to both the public and new political elites the only viable alternative. There are many views on the differences between totalitarianism and authoritarianism (see, for instance, Friedrich, 1969; Friedrich and Brzezinski, 1956; Arendt, 1958; Holmes, 1986); authoritarian regimes, unlike totalitarian ones, do not force ideological uniformity and total atomisation of society. But these differences are subtle enough to have been ignored by the people of Eastern Europe: anything that would not be perceived as a government of the people and by the people, even if it were for the people, was by these people *a priori* rejected. For this very reason also the choice between presidential and parliamentary democracy was ruled – in normative theory, though not necessarily in political practice – in favour of the latter.

The political manoeuvring by communist elites in some countries in the period 1988–91 added greatly to these attitudes and decisions. In at least four countries – Poland, Hungary, Bulgaria, and Albania – the communists attempted in the initial phases of transition to establish a pattern of paternalistic rule, in which the reforms would be granted by them from above, and they would issue 'concessions' on particular activities (such as free trade unions or independent newspapers) to selected oppositionist groups. In each case, a post-communist president would have played a critical role in this scheme.

In Poland, the Jaruzelski regime since the imposition of martial law (December 1981) may be viewed as a case of post-communist authoritarianism. Jaruzelski and his associates (Kiszczak, Rakowski) tried in vain to co-opt selected leaders of the opposition, and eventually had to accept the broad formula of roundtable negotiations (basically on Solidarity's terms). The roundtable accord provided for the 'semi-free' elections that have already been outlined, but also re-established the office of president, with an assumption that it would be filled by Jaruzelski. The president, elected in an indirect vote for a six-year term, was given special powers in the areas of national security, defence, and foreign affairs – obviously to serve as guarantor of Soviet interests in Poland. Jaruzelski was elected by the narrowest possible margin, but within a year this whole arrangement became obsolete, and he resigned.

In Hungary, Imre Pozsgay in the late 1980s paternalistically presided over the process of bold political reforms (creation of the Hungarian Democratic Forum, the rehabilitation of Imre Nagy, and reevaluation of the 1956 uprising). If the triangular table agreement between the communists and HDF had been put into effect, he would have had the best chance to win a popular vote for President, but the Free Democrats and the Young Democrats contested this accord and it failed to take effect.

In Bulgaria and Albania the post-communist presidents – Petr Mladenov and Ramiz Alia, respectively – had initiated the process of liberalisation, and Mladenov may be credited with the ouster of Todor Zhivkov. Both seemed to be firmly in control in the first stages of transition, but Mladenov soon was forced to resign, after the opposition proved that he had considered using tanks against demonstrators, and Alia lost office after his defeat in the 1992 parliamentary elections. Both were replaced by the leaders of the opposition: Zhelyu Zhelev (Bulgaria) and Sali Berisha (Albania). Paradoxically, the only case of a surviving post-communist paternalism may be found in the actions of Iliescu and his government in Romania, where there was no personal continuity at the top of the transitional elite.

Probably even without this late communist manoeuvring the new political elites would have opted for parliamentary forms of government. Among Western experts, there is no consensus as far as advantages and disadvantages of presidentialism and parliamentarism are concerned (for a recent discussion, without direct reference to Eastern Europe, see Linz, 1990; Horowitz, Lipset, and Linz, 1990). What seems certain is that the 'winner-take-all' principle of presidential elections may, and in most cases does, exclude significant factions of the polity from effective participation for several years. On the contrary, parliamentary systems tend to be more inclusive: each party that won even a few seats in the parliament will have at least some influence over the decision-making process, and potentially may become a member of a ruling coalition. In a highly fragmented and unstable polity of countries undergoing a fundamental political, economic and social transformation, the obvious strategy for the political elites was to promote parliamentary systems, in order to: (i) secure their own participation in the political process through

TABLE 8.1   *Parliamentary elections in Eastern Europe, 1989–92*

Country	Date	Structure of legislature; no. of seats	Electoral system
Poland	4 and 18 June 1989	Bicameral Sejm: 460 Senate: 100	Majority
Poland	27 October 1991	same	391: PR in districts 69: PR national, 5% threshold
Hungary	25 March and 8 April 1990	Unicameral: 386	176: majority 152: PR in districts, 4% threshold 58: PR national, 4% threshold
Romania	20 May 1990	Bicameral Chamber of Deputies: 396 Senate: 119	PR in districts
Romania	27 September 1992	Bicameral Chamber of Deputies: 341 Senate: 143	PR in districts, 3% threshold
Czecho-Slovakia	8–9 June 1990	Bicameral House of the People: 150 (101 Czech, 49 Slovak) House of Nations: 150 (75 Czech, 75 Slovak)	PR in districts, 5% threshold, in at least one of the republics
Czecho-Slovakia	5–6 June 1992	same	same
Bulgaria	10 and 17 June 1990	Unicameral: 400	200: majority 200: PR in districts, 4% threshold
Bulgaria	13 October 1991	Unicameral: 240	PR in districts, 4% threshold
Albania	31 March 7 and 14 April 1991	Unicameral: 250	Majority
Albania	22 March 1992	Unicameral: 140	PR in districts

representative bodies; and (ii) prevent the development of authoritarian forms (a 'new dictatorship'). As a result, all the countries considered have established parliamentary forms of government, in which the executives – prime ministers and their cabinets – are responsible to parliament, and usually emerge as coalitions of major parties represented in the legislature. Details of the structure of East European parliaments are provided in Table 8.1.

None the less, all these countries also have their presidents, even those – Poland, Hungary, Albania, Bulgaria – where in communist times presidents were replaced by collective heads of state. Three nations elected their present (as of 31 December 1992) presidents by a popular vote: Poland (Lech Walesa in 1990), Bulgaria (Zhelyu Zhelev in 1991), and Romania (Ion Iliescu in 1990 and 1992). In Hungary and Albania presidents were elected by parliaments: Arpad Goncz in 1990, and Sali Berisha in 1992, respectively. In the former Czecho-Slovakia Vaclav Havel was elected interim president by parliament in December 1989, was re-elected in the same manner in 1990 for a two-year term, and failed in his bid for re-election in 1992 (blocked by Slovak deputies). He could have stayed in office until a successor was chosen, but resigned to protest against the forthcoming split in the federation. In January 1993 he was elected the first president of the newly-established Czech Republic, and in February Michal Kovac became the first president of Slovakia.

The actual powers of presidents vary from country to country, but as indicated above they are limited in favour of the parliaments. On the extremes are the cases of Poland and Hungary. In Poland, Lech Walesa stepped into the office, which had been designed for a different incumbent in historically different times. He never felt comfortable with these arrangements, and since his first day in office has been demanding more powers in domestic affairs. He clashed several times over this issue with parliament and government, but some of his requirements have been recently granted. The new provisional constitution (so-called Little Constitution of December 1992) gives the president the upper hand over the Sejm in a very complicated, five-step process of nomination of prime minister and cabinet. In general, this new constitution strengthens the executive branch at the expense of the legislature, but the latter remains the focal point of the policy-making process.

In Hungary, the parliament elected in the 1990 vote designed the office of President of the Republic as a largely ceremonial one. In a conciliatory arrangement, the ruling coalition supported the election of Arpad Goncz, a member of the oppositional Free Democrats. But as a recent conflict over personnel policies in the mass media indicates, even ceremonial presidents are not necessarily lame ducks. Goncz – within his constitutional powers – plays a very active role in Hungarian politics.

Elsewhere in Eastern Europe, the presidents do not confine themselves to toasting foreign guests at state dinners. Political fragmentation and/or polarisation had led to formal arrangements favouring

parliaments, but the same factors impair the efficacy of these institutions. The president quite often has to use his skills and authority to
bring about desired policy outcomes. Also, as happens in many
Western democracies (for instance Finland), personal features of the
incumbents are at least as important as their formal powers. In an age
of television a good communicator may mobilise popular support or
resistance to specific policies. As a rule, the current East European
presidents seem to posses such skills – as well as the ability to be
effective in behind-the-scenes manoeuvreing.

Finally, there is the symbolic role of presidents. They represent the
state and its most general interests in both the international and
domestic arenas. Even when their mandate comes from the electoral
support of a mere plurality (or from an indirect election), most
citizens would be likely to see in them their presidents. In a society
undergoing fundamental change and often torn apart by various
conflicts, the head of state may, as a father figure, provide desired
feelings of stability and continuity. For this potential to be effective,
at least a minimal level of impartiality is necessary on the part of a
president, and even this is not a sufficient condition. Vaclav Havel,
after all, did not prevent Czecho-Slovakia from disintegration. But if
a president fails to present himself as the leader and protector of all
citizens, someone else may wish to try to take over this role. This
possibility is recognised in Eastern Europe, as indicated by the
obstacles that have been raised by the Romanian government against
the return (or even short visits) of the exiled ex-king Michael.

Parliaments may also, under some circumstances, play an important symbolic role. This was the case of Polish Sejm in the 1980s, when
– despite the fact that it was filled by communist nominees – it was
highly regarded by the citizens as a symbol of Polish statehood
(Jasiewicz, 1992). But since the revolution East European parliaments have turned from rubber stamps to working legislatures, with
all the positive and negative consequences of this metamorphosis. To
achieve consensus one needs plenty of time and effort, almost always
at the expense of efficiency. With the former secrecy replaced by
wide publicity (parliamentary sessions are usually televised live), the
representative bodies are the subject of scrutiny by the public, and
the public has grown impatient. The Polish Sejm (and Senate), and
other East European legislatures, now enjoy very unfavourable ratings in opinion polls. Public sympathies rest rather with prime ministers and cabinets. The option in favour of a parliamentary system
may be locally supplemented (if not substituted) by special preroga-

tives given to the executive branch. This concession to the demands of efficiency, in particular when it is temporary, does not have to mean a departure from the principles of democracy.

The Seats and the Votes

When in 1909 universal male suffrage was introduced in Sweden by a Conservative government, the same reform act substituted proportional representation for the existing winner-take-all system. The Conservatives, whose electoral base in the Swedish nobility, spread more or less evenly throughout the country, would suddenly become relatively narrow, wanted to assure for themselves at least a minimal level of representation in parliament (Pontusson, 1992, p. 433). Similar decisions were made at that time elsewhere in continental Europe, leaving Great Britain as the last European bastion of first-past-the-post elections and Westminster-type democracy. Many theorists believe that choosing the proportional representation (PR) voting system was a very unfortunate decision, since plurality voting (first-past-the-post in single member constituencies) is conducive to two-party systems and stable, majoritarian governments, while PR, on the other hand, tends to generate multi-party systems and coalition or even minority governments, vulnerable to challenges and therefore unstable (Duverger, 1963 and 1986; Riker, 1986). This relationship between the type of voting system and political stability has been recently questioned (Lijphart, 1991), and the problem remains open to further inquiries. Eastern Europe provides here several very interesting cases.

The mechanisms of choosing electoral systems in Eastern Europe were in many instances remarkably similar to those in Sweden eighty years before. The East European elections of 1989–92 may indeed be regarded as a case study in the introduction of universal suffrage. True, the people of the region did vote in communist times, and 99.9 per cent turnouts did not come exclusively from the stuffing of electoral boxes. But in reality these people were disfranchised: the act of voting was reduced to a ritual behaviour, with no real political meaning whatsoever. The communist masters had no reason to worry about the outcome of the voting – it had been known even before the elections began.

In 1989–90 this was no longer the case. Just like the Swedish Conservatives, the communists in power, still having the legislative process under their control, opted for solutions they perceived as advantageous. Interestingly, for the first election in a given country their typical choice was a plurality (or rather majority) vote. The communists were hoping to gain in this system of voting because of at least three factors: (i) they were better organised than the opposition; (ii) their local bosses pretended to be still able to intimidate voters, particularly in rural areas; (iii) they had name recognition – the leaders of opposition were in most cases practically unknown to the public. In some instances these calculations were correct; in others they proved fatal.

In the June 1989 elections in Poland, the communists, according to a very peculiar electoral law designed at the Roundtable, were ensured 173 of the 460 seats in the Sejm, with an additional 126 allocated to their allies, and 161 open to contest by anybody else. The constituencies were single-member (so the communists were competing in these elections against other communists, non-affiliated against non-affiliated, etc.), with a majority of the vote required to win. If none of the candidates achieved an overall majority, the two front-runners would qualify for a run-off. Solidarity won all 161 seats it was allowed to contest, 160 of them in the first round (while only one communist candidate achieved a majority in this round). All 100 seats in the Senate were open to unrestricted contest, by majority vote in multi- (2 or 3) member constituencies, and 99 of them were won by Solidarity, of which 92 were divided in the first round. The communists, who under a PR system would have won 25–30 seats in the Senate, were left empty-handed.

Unlike Poland, in Bulgaria and Albania the communists profited from majority voting. In the June 1990 Bulgarian election, according to a compromise solution worked out at the Roundtable, half of the 400 deputies were elected by a two-round majority system in single member constituencies, and the remaining 200 by party list PR, with a 4 per cent threshold. In the PR voting the BSP received 47.1 per cent of the vote and 97 seats, while the UDF received 36.2 per cent of the vote and 75 seats. In the single-member constituencies, however, the BSP won 114 seats (75 of them in the first round), while the UDF won 69 (32 in the first round). The remaining seats went to the Turkish minority and other minor groupings. In the March–April 1991 election in Albania, all 250 seats in the People's Assembly were allocated in single-member constituencies by majority vote (two rounds). The victory of the communists was even more spectacular: they mustered 169 seats (162 of them in the first round).

For the March–April 1990 elections in Hungary, a highly complicated system was adopted – again a compromise between the communists (who insisted on single member constituencies) and the opposition. Of the 386 deputies, 176 were elected in single member constituencies, according to unusually complex rules (at least 50 per cent turnout in the first round and 25 per cent in the run-off required; if nobody gained overall majority in the first round, the three frontrunners or all candidates with at least 15 per cent of the vote would qualify for the run-off). The remaining 210 deputies were elected according to a party list PR system, with a 4 per cent threshold; 152 of them in the districts, and 58 on the national level (for the distribution of these 58 seats another complicated system of allocation of votes unused on the lower levels was adopted). The hopes of the post-communists that they would profit from a plurality or majority vote proved overly optimistic: they won only one seat by majority mode, while the HDF won 114 (three in the first round), the Free Democrats 35, and others and independents 27. By comparison, PR at the district level gave the post-communist Hungarian Socialist Party 10.9 per cent of the vote and 14 seats, while the HDF received 24.7 per cent of the vote and 40 seats, and the Free Democrats 21.4 per cent and 34 seats. After the make-up distribution on the national level, the composition of parliament was as follows: Hungarian Democratic Forum 164 seats, Alliance of Free Democrats 92, Smallholders Party 44, Hungarian Socialist Party 33, Young Democrats 22, Christian Democrats 21, others 10.

In Czecho-Slovakia the communists, wisely, did not object to the Civic Forum Public Against Violence proposal to return in the June 1990 election to the traditional system of proportional representation (with a 5 per cent cutoff). They finished as the second strongest party, with 23 seats in the House of the People, and 24 in the House of the Nations, while Civic Forum/Public against Violence received, respectively, 87 and 83 of the 150 seats in each chamber. The same system was used in the June 1992 election, and the post-communist organisations recorded minimal gains (29 seats in the House of the People, 28 in the House of the Nations). However, more important – due to the eventual 'velvet divorce' of the Czechs and Slovaks – proved to be elections to the representative bodies on the republican level. Despite the disintegration of Civic Forum and PAV, the communists remained in a distant second position to the winners: in the Czech republic the coalition of Civic Democratic Party and Christian Democratic Party obtained 29.7 per cent of the vote, and 76 of the

200 seats; the communist Left Bloc took 14 per cent and 29 seats. In Slovakia the Movement for a Democratic Slovakia took 37.3 per cent of the vote, and 74 of the 150 seats; the post-communist Party of the Democratic Left secured 14.7 per cent of the vote and 29 seats.

Also in Romania, in both the May 1990 and September 1992 elections a PR system was adopted (party lists in districts, in 1990 no threshold, in 1992 a threshold of 3 per cent nationwide). The National Salvation Front won decisively in 1990 (66.3 per cent of the vote, 263 of the 396 seats in the Assembly of Deputies; 67.0 per cent of the vote and 92 of the 119 seats in the Senate). The same organisation, under the name Democratic National Salvation Front, in 1992 won only a plurality of votes and seats (Assembly of Deputies: 27.7 per cent of the vote, 117 of 341 seats; Senate 28.3 per cent of the vote, 49 of 143 seats).

The transition to proportional representation systems in new East European democracies was completed when Poland, Bulgaria, and Albania adopted such systems for the second parliamentary elections in each of these countries. This time the communists, so badly defeated in majority voting in Poland, and losing popular support in Bulgaria and Albania, opted – like the Swedish Conservatives of 1909 – for a PR solution, and because of their strong representation in parliaments were able to secure the desired legislation. They did not face much resistance, however. Their political foes also perceived PR as a fairer system, granting still weak political parties at least a minimum of parliamentary representation.

This factor was of particular importance in Poland, where the movement of Solidarity has fractured into several groupings, and a swarm of other mini-parties has emerged. Some politicians (including Walesa) objected to adopting a PR system, as one that was thought to increase fragmentation, but the vested interests of political parties prevailed. For the October 1991 elections to the Sejm a modified PR system was adopted. The country was divided into 37 districts, with from 7 to 17 seats in each. The allocation of seats in the districts was based on the Hare-Niemeyer system, with no threshold. Of the total 460 seats, 69 were to be awarded on a nationwide base to those parties which: (a) registered their national list (to achieve this a party had to register its list in at least five districts by collecting 5,000 voters signatures in each, and/or collect 50,000 signatures nationwide); (b) surpassed the threshold of 5 per cent nationally and/or managed to have their candidates elected in at least five districts.

Interestingly, the Senate was chosen by a system almost identical with that of 1989, with only one significant difference: the run-off round was abolished, and a mere plurality sufficed for election. Unlike in the first round of the 1989 election, in 1991 only one candidate surpassed the level of 50 per cent of the vote.

But of most interest was the outcome. Two opposite electoral systems produced the same results: deeply fragmented houses of parliament, with 29 parties and organisations represented in each house (since then the numbers have changed, due to mergers and secessions). The frontrunner was the Democratic Union (a post-Solidarity party of former Prime Minister Tadeusz Mazowiecki), with 12.3 per cent of the popular vote, 62 seats in the Sejm and 21 in the Senate, followed by the post-communist Alliance of the Democratic Left (12.0 per cent, 60 and 4), the Polish Peasant Party (9.2 per cent, 50 and 7), the Christian-National Union (9.0 per cent, 50 and 9), the Confederation for an Independent Poland (8.9 per cent, 51 and 4), and others.

Variants of the PR system were also adopted for the October 1991 elections in Bulgaria and the March 1992 elections in Albania. Both countries still experience a high level of polarisation on the political scene, and PR seemed to assist the post-communists in preserving significant influence. In Bulgaria, in the elections to the National Assembly (the new constitution of June 1991 reduced its size to 240 seats), a 4 per cent cutoff helped to reduce the number of parties in parliament to three, but none of them gained a majority: the UDF finished with 110 seats, the BSP mustered 106, and the MRF 24. After the collapse of a UDF minority government, the process of disintegration of both UDF and BSP has intensified, and the support for a new government of Lyuben Berov (approved on 30 December 1992) runs across party lines. In Albania the former opposition now dominates: the Democratic Party mustered 62.1 per cent of the vote and 92 of 140 seats, but the post-communist Socialist Party was still a strong second with 25.7 per cent of the vote and 31 seats.

While the umbrella organisations – although already crumbling, due to increasing factional struggle – are still in place in Romania, Bulgaria, and Albania, elsewhere in Eastern Europe political fragmentation prevails. Is the PR-based electoral law to be blamed? As indicated above, when the electoral regulations were chosen, the effectively available options were very limited: from a certain point onwards the former communists were interested in adopting a PR system, and usually had enough control over the legislature to secure such a regulation. But perhaps more important, they were supported in this bid by many of their foes (for instance in Poland by a strongly anti-communist Christian-National Union): new and renewed small parties, which could not afford the risks associated with a winner-take-all system. Political fragmentation usually preceded adoption of a voting system and elections, not vice versa. This does not mean that a well-designed electoral law would not have curtailed the number of parties represented in the parliament. But it could not prevent or even reduce political factionalism and fragmentation, because their major sources are outside the political and legislative process: in the specificities of the social structure of a society undergoing rapid economic, social, and political change.

The political polarisation of the 1980s and early 1990s reflected sociological features of communist societies: petrified social structures, low levels of social mobility, dichotomised visions of social order – vanguard versus masses, *nomenklatura* versus people, them versus us. The current fragmentation reflects the ongoing change of this order, the disintegration of old structures and the emergence of new ones. The group loyalties and group interests of the past dissolve (some of them die hard, as is true of the provincial *nomenklatura* or workers in the mammoth enterprises of socialist industry). What so far emerges to replace them is not new solid structures, but a state of *anomie* (normlessness), and a fragmented society.

The people are confused as employees (under the old system they were paid poorly, but at least had job security), as consumers (the shortages are gone, but the prices are high as never before), and as citizens and voters. Of two major mechanisms explaining voting behaviour – party identification and rational choice – neither operates in Eastern Europe. Only in the case of post-communist organisations can the voters' identification be traced back to pre-1989 times. The other parties very often still strive to establish name recognition, and it is much too early for stable patterns of party identification. Rational choice theory is also of little value. One can make a more or less rational choice when one knows what options are available and the costs and benefits of each option. But today in Eastern Europe hardly anyone is in this position. The parties are blamed for not articulating group interests – but there are hardly any interests that can be articulated and aggregated, as happens in stable democracies (and economies). The feuds among political elites only add to this confusion, and no wonder that on election day many voters stay home.

Social and political fragmentation poses a serious threat to young democracies. Anomie and fragmentation may be perceived as growing pains, but the process of growth and development of new social and political structures will, without any doubt, last a long time. None the less, one can still see across Eastern Europe (the former Yugoslavia being a tragic exception) a remarkable commitment to democracy and its institutions. Parliaments may rank low in public opinion polls, but thus far they remain focal points in the policy-making process, and there are no institutions that could substitute for them in this role. Even harsh critics of their performance see in them indispensable organs of democracy, and democracy as the only viable form of government. After all, haven't the other forms been tried before and to no avail?

9

Parties and Party Systems in Eastern Europe

JAN AKE DELLENBRANT

There have been three waves of democratisation in Eastern Europe. The first wave occurred after the end of the First World War, when Poland, Czechoslovakia, Hungary, Romania and Bulgaria were all reconstituted as independent states and embarked on the road to democracy. But after only a few years, the wave of democratisation ebbed. As early as 1923, the Bulgarian radical peasant leader Stamboliski was overthrown in a coup by reactionary nationalist forces. In 1926, Marshal Pilsudski carried out his military coup in Poland. Gradually Hungary and Romania slid back onto the road of authoritarianism. Only Czechoslovakia managed to sustain its democracy, until the country was dismembered in 1938 (Fischer-Galati, 1992).

The breakdown of democracy in Eastern Europe in the inter-war period can be explained by both internal and external factors. Many observers have pointed to the political immaturity of the East European societies, the social and ethnic fragmentation, economic backwardness and dislocation which affected all these newly-independent countries in the post-war years. The political culture contained strong elements of paternalism, and religion, whether Catholic or Orthodox, tended to play a deeply conservative role in politics, reinforcing autocratic tendencies. Nationalism was the stron-

This chapter has been revised with the help of Judy Batt, Andrew Lance and Laurence Broyd.

gest ideological force, used by politicians to mobilise and unite the newly-emergent mass publics, but it often degenerated into political intolerance, directed against ethnic minorities which existed in nearly all states. The protracted economic crisis played a large part in exacerbating the weaknesses of democracy in the East European countries. In addition, the external environment, with the rise of Nazism and German expansionism, finally overwhelmed them.

During the second wave of democratisation immediately after the Second World War, political pluralism was restored, at least partially, in the East European countries. Multi-party coalition governments were established, but these were gradually undermined by the activities of the communist parties which existed, with strong Soviet backing, in every country. Eventually, the communists seized power, and by 1947–8 these countries were set on a course of full integration into the Soviet empire.

The third wave of democratisation was unleashed as a result of the radical changes which took place in the Soviet Union under Gorbachev, whose 'new thinking' on international matters finally allowed the East European countries to disengage themselves from Soviet control. This led directly to the collapse of communist rule in Eastern Europe in 1989. The key question is whether this third wave will be allowed to develop fully, or whether it will die out or be diverted into authoritarian channels as happened before. There is no doubt that the external environment is today far more congenial to the development of democracy in Eastern Europe – the predatory dictatorships of Nazi Germany and Stalin's Russia no longer exist to threaten Europe, and West European democracies today are anxious to see the East Europe's transition to democracy succeed. But the legacies of the communist period – social disintegration and atomisation, psychological disorientation, economic crisis and the enormous disruption involved in the transition from centrally-planned socialism to the market economy – all pose enormous challenges to democratisation.

Political parties have a crucial role to play in this. Indeed, in the eyes of many theorists, parties are the prime component in the functioning of modern democracies: they are the vital point of connection between society and government. Parties are vehicles for the expression of the interests and values of different social groups. They filter demands and organise them into more or less coherent policy proposals which form the basis of government programmes. Parties are the essential underpinning of leadership in democracies – parties produce political leaders, and generate the support they need in order to govern.

An obvious feature of any democracy is the existence of more than one party; but party systems – that is, the number of parties and the patterns of competition and coalition among them – vary widely. The variations can be accounted for by the specific history of each country; its social structure (the extent of diversity or homogeneity, polarisation or consensus between its constituent groups); and the political institutions and 'rules of the game', especially the electoral system. Thus we find two-party systems, such as those of the United States and Great Britain; a 'two-and-a-half' party system as in Germany, where a small centre party switches its allegiance between the two major parties; multi-party systems with several evenly balanced parties forming and reforming coalitions in different combinations (Italy); and 'dominant party' systems, where one party is strong enough to rule alone without effective challenge from the opposition parties which are fragmented and ineffective, such as India for most of the time since independence (and, arguably, Britain since 1979).

Obviously it is too early as yet to fit each of the new democracies in Eastern Europe into such models. Their politics is still very fluid and to a large degree unpredictable. Our aim here is limited, first, to describing the types of East European parties which have emerged since 1989, classified mainly by their ideological profile, and second, discussing in a general, comparative way the problems with the formation of stable and coherent party systems, and what this might mean for the prospects for democracy in Eastern Europe.

Types of Parties in Eastern Europe

Giovanni Sartori put forward a simple definition of political parties:

> A party is any political group identified by an official label that presents at elections, and is capable of placing through elections (free or non-free) candidates for public office. (Sartori, 1976, p. 63)

A distinctive feature of the politics of transition from communism was the role played by very loosely-structured groups, drawing in masses of people from all walks of life and many different views. There was a pronounced reluctance to describe these as 'parties': it seemed as if the very word 'party' was tainted in people's minds by their experience of The Party, as the communist parties were usually referred to. So they preferred to describe themselves as 'movements'. Examples of this were Solidarity in Poland, which in many ways was used as a model by the others which sprang up at the point of collapse of communist rule: the Hungarian Democratic Forum, the Civic Forum and Public Against Violence in Czechoslovakia, the National Salvation Front in Romania, the Union of Democratic Forces in Bulgaria.

Obviously, each of these was unique in many ways, according to the circumstances of each country, and they all underwent very rapid evolution and internal differentiation. Most have now split up. But at the height of the crisis, we can identify the peculiar role such movements played as proto-parties, initially uniting the masses of the population against communist rule. At this stage, they took upon themselves some rather unusual functions: Vaclav Havel, the leader of Civic Forum in 1989, saw it as a means of developing the values of citizenship in a hitherto politically intimidated and completely inexperienced public, and as a medium through which people's sense of personal and civic responsibility could be restored. Participation tended to be seen as a good in itself, rather than a means to power. One observer described Solidarity in 1980 as 'a conviction and a state of mind rather than an instrument of collective action' (Touraine *et al.*, 1983). These proto-parties thus seemed more comparable to 'new social movements' in the West (Green movements, feminist movements, etc.) than to political parties.

But as soon as the task changed from bringing down communist rule to that of supplying an alternative government, the pressures to conform more closely to the familiar type of the West European party began to make themselves felt: they needed specific programmes and some set of more or less coherent values, if not an ideology; they needed to build specific social bases; and more effective organisation than before was essential. The parties of Eastern Europe are at present right in the midst of this process of self-reconstruction. The conflicts of opinion generated within the movements over these questions have inevitably provoked splits. The situation is very fluid and sometimes looks chaotic.

It is certainly difficult to construct a typology of the parties which now exist according to the Western models of, for example, Maurice Duverger, who classified parties by type of organisation. Now the special type of 'anti-party', barely organised movement has broken down, most of the many parties which have sprung up still have a long way to go before they achieve the level of organisation found in established democracies. Many are tiny, little more than cliques or groups of followers of individual personalities. Others claim large memberships, but there is little evidence of a developed regional structure or regular communication between leaders and members.

It is also very difficult to identify the social bases of support for different parties. Post-communist societies are characterised by a high level of change and flux. The interests of individuals and groups are changing rapidly as a result of the economic transition. There is thus a high level of volatility in support for the parties. Some old ties remain; for example, industrial workers in large firms which were prestigious in the communist period may still support the communist parties (several of which have, however, undergone radical change, as we shall see below). Peasants are a distinctive social group in Eastern Europe, and peasant parties are important in, for example, Poland. But by no means all peasants vote for these parties, or indeed for any party. The new classes of private entrepreneurs, shopkeepers and so forth are still something of an unknown quantity in political terms.

For these reasons, parties will here be classified by ideology, supplemented, where possible, by some reference to organisational structure and social base. The *left–right spectrum* is the most familiar when classifying parties in Western Europe. There are particular difficulties in trying to fit East European parties into this spectrum. The major points of difference between left and right in Western Europe are attitudes to economic policy, with right-wing parties stressing free enterprise, the unfettered market economy and private property, and left-wing parties stressing social welfare and the role of the state in regulating the economy. These differences rest on under-lying philosophical positions, the right espousing individualistic values, while the left emphasises the collective and social nature of man. In Western Europe, both right and left gravitate towards the centre. Most right-wing parties accept the necessity of state-run systems of social welfare, while most left-wing parties accept that state intervention must be kept within the bounds of compatibility of a functioning market economy.

In Eastern Europe, the left–right ideological distinction is even more blurred and distorted. Firstly, virtually all parties are overtly committed to dismantling state socialism, restoring the market economy, and returning most property to private hands. There is considerable scope for disagreement over the pace of economic transition, and there has been some discussion of different models of capitalism (the Swedish model, the 'Thatcherite' model, the South Korean and Japanese models). But there is more than a touch of artificiality about these disputes, because the task in Eastern Europe is to get *any* sort of market economy working. In practice, the task of transition is unprecedented and models drawn from elsewhere are of little use. The real economic options available are very narrow: the lack of internal resources and dependence on external financial support mean that left-wing parties in government are constrained to adopt basically similar economic policies to right-wing ones, and so their programmes tend to be vague on economic issues, and avoid specific commitments of social welfare.

Another important factor blurring the left–right ideological divide is the importance of *nationalism* in East European political culture. This means that most parties, whether right or left, find it necessary in some way to tap into the appeal of nationalism. Committed nationalists in turn often identify themselves as 'right' and anti-communist, but on economic policy they are often strongly statist and their basic philosophy is collectivist rather than individualist, and thus may have more in common with the left. There is also the *urban–rural cultural divide* which in many contexts is more important than the left–right ideological divide. It is just as difficult to categorise peasant parties as 'right', 'left' or 'centre' as it is nationalist parties.

One Polish commentator put it this way: the basic choice facing voters was not 'right' versus 'left' but 'East' versus 'West', by which he meant the choice between parties which more or less followed the patterns of West European counterparts, whether right or left, and parties which harked back to the past, emphasised the peculiarities of Eastern Europe and the non applicability of Western models, and which tended towards authoritarianism.

Left-wing parties are deeply divided among themselves by the communist legacy. On the one hand, there are the *communist parties* themselves, which have gone through various internal crises and splits since 1989. One can still find traditional Soviet-type or neo-Stalinist parties surviving in some places: for example, in the Communist Party of Bohemia and Moravia, which is still an electoral force. But most hard-line relics, such as the Hungarian Socialist Workers' Party, the Bulgarian Communist Party, are either moribund or already defunct as electoral forces. Many communist parties have undergone extraordinary ideological metamorphoses and rejuvenation of leadership, while retaining much of their old structure and networks more or less intact. The most radical democratic transformation was effected by the majority faction of the Hungarian Socialist Workers' Party, which re-named itself the Hungarian Socialist Party, and is fully committed to West European style social democracy, the market economy and democratic principles. In Poland, the Alliance of the Democratic Left (which in fact comprises several parties, but standing on a common electoral platform and voting together in parliament) represents a rather more traditionally oriented leftist force, overtly sceptical about economic reforms and blocking their implementation.

The National Salvation Front in Romania, which started out as an anti-communist movement, appears to have been rather quickly recaptured by parts of the old communist elite, and in many respects could be described as a reformed ex-communist party with an avowedly 'left of centre' economic orientation. Other former communist parties have turned to nationalism as a means of retaining popular appeal. A moderate case of this is the Party of the Democratic Left in Slovakia, which supported Slovak separatism but has also modernised itself by developing a pragmatic, technocratic image; a less promising case in terms of democratisation is the Bulgarian Socialist Party, which has sought to manipulate popular prejudice against the Turkish minority to win votes. The most notorious case of a communist party turning into an extreme nationalist party is the Socialist Party of Serbia, led by Slobodan Milosevic.

But the left in Eastern Europe also includes various *socialist and social democratic parties* which are hostile to the former communist parties and wary of electoral alliances with them, even though their ideologies may have much in common. For example, in both Hungary and Czechoslovakia, Social Democratic Parties (SDPs) had existed in the inter-war period, but were suppressed by forced merger with the communists in 1947–9, and recalcitrant leaders were persecuted in the Stalinist period. A rather similar case is the Polish Socialist Party. Not surprisingly, when these parties were reconstituted after 1989, their leaders were very hostile towards the communist parties or their successors. But these SDPs also had their own internal problems. The 'generation gap' was a source of conflict: the older generation who had been members of the original SDPs often clung to the inter-war variant of social democratic ideology which was Marxist (but not Stalinist), and have rejected the pragmatic pro-market orientation advocated by the younger generation. Another type of socialist party is the Czechoslovak Socialist Party, a non-communist left-wing party which survived through the communist period in 'alliance' with the Communist Party, but in practice wholly subordinate to it. It was thus compromised by its collaboration and has had to work hard to regain popular credibility.

The *right-wing parties* are equally varied, and most are very different creatures from those found on the right in West European politics, even where they use the same names and or been adopted by Western parties as their recognised counterparts. *Christian Democratic parties* are a case in point. Because of the importance of the Catholic Church in many countries, it was inevitable that Christian democracy would be a major force on the right wing of politics in Eastern Europe. Where Christian democratic parties were founded as resurrections of so-called 'historical' parties (i.e. those which existed in the precommunist period but were suppressed under communism), they often drew on political traditions much more conservative, if not reactionary, in flavour than contemporary West European Christian democratic parties. This applies to the Christian Democratic Movement of Slovakia, and to the Hungarian Christian Democratic People's Party. In Hungary, it is the Hungarian Democratic Forum which is recognised by the West European Christian Democrats as their main interlocutor. This party contains a wide range of views, from far-right nationalist anti-semites to centrist liberals. The party leader tends to describe the party as 'centrist' rather than right wing, and in some ways, the catch-all nature of its appeal harks back to the 'umbrella-movement' type of party mentioned above. But pressures from the nationalist wing threaten to split it in future, as has already happened in the case of the Slovak Christian Democrats.

In Poland, the Centre Alliance is the major Christian democratic party (although now declining in influence), and is affiliated to the Christian Democratic International. But several other small Christian democratic parties exist which keep their distance from the Centre Alliance, and have formed alliances among themselves. For example, the Republican Coalition, which is made up of the Christian Peasant Alliance, the Christian Democratic Party and the Conservative Party, is equal in parliamentary strength to the Centre Alliance, and is now a member of the governing coalition under Prime Minister Suchocka. The main Czech Christian democratic party is the People's Party, which survived under communism by accepting a role as a subordinate 'ally' of the Communist Party. It has since regained some credibility by internal reform, and performed more successfully in elections than its rival, the Christian Democratic Party, led by the long-time dissident activist, Vaclav Benda.

Secular parties to the right of centre tend to be dominated by intellectuals, often former dissidents, and appeal to the urban professional middle classes. In the Czech Republic, the largest party is the Civic Democratic Party, which emerged from a split in the Civic Forum. It has adopted most of the tenets of Western neo-liberalism in its ideology and economic policy, reflecting the personal conviction of its leader, the economist Vaclav Klaus. In terms of its political strategy, it has been quite opportunistic: it is not nationalistic, but it appealed to Czech national feeling when its leader decided that further negotiations with the Slovaks on constitutional reform would be fruitless; it is secular, but it fought the 1992 elections in alliance with the Czech Christian Democratic Party, and has also drawn the People's Party into the governing coalition; it uses anti-communist rhetoric, but at the same time wins votes among many ex-communist professionals and technocrats.

The Democratic Union (DU) in Poland is better described as liberal in the broad sense (which includes support for social policies which have much in common with a social democratic approach) rather than neo-liberal, but it has been the most consistent supporter of radical economic reforms, and in this respect resembles the Civic Democratic Party in the Czech Republic. But in contrast to the latter, the DU leadership contains many of the outstanding figures of the former dissident intellectual opposition in Poland. Some prominent individuals and groups within the DU tend to be overtly antagonistic towards the traditionalist Catholic forces in Polish politics, and are particularly opposed to nationalism, which they see as a primitive, and usually antisemitic ideology. Nevertheless, in the Polish context, no party can afford to be seen as overtly antagonistic towards the Church, and the party has joined in a coalition government with the most traditionalist Catholic party, the Christian National Union.

The Alliance of Free Democrats (AFD) in Hungary shares many of these characteristics: originating from among the Budapest intellectual opposition circles, it has always been one of the strongest advocates in Hungary of radical and rapid economic reform. It is hostile to Hungarian nationalism, and very sensitive to signs of anti-semitism in public life. The Civic Movement (CM) in the Czech Republic is the main repository of former dissident intellectuals. Its ideological position is centrist rather than right wing: although it shares the basic liberal and individualistic values of the secular right wing, on economic policy it rejects the CDP's neo-liberalism as both excessively brutal and too doctrinaire. It would prefer an approach which is more pragmatic and more humane, with more emphasis on social welfare. Such an approach is also emphasised by groups within both the Polish DU and the Hungarian AFD. The fate of the CM may be symptomatic of a more general trend of declining influence of the former dissident intelligentsia – in the 1992 elections, it failed to win enough votes to secure parliamentary representation, and its future place in Czech politics is unclear.

Nationalist parties abound throughout Eastern Europe, although, as we shall see in the following section, they tend to be amongst the smaller parties represented in legislatures, but can be influential where governments, as is generally the case in post-communist Eastern Europe, lack firm majorities. Identifying a 'nationalist' party can be quite difficult where most parties feel impelled to play on the national and patriotic emotions which have come to the fore as demoralised and bewildered societies come to terms with the collapse of the old, communist world and the tasks that face them in building the new world. For example, the Movement for a Democratic Slovakia (MFDS), the major force in Slovak politics after the 1992 election and therefore the party which took Slovakia to national independence, clearly had a strong nationalist component in its programme; but an important part of its political agenda was directed at economic issues: it was against the radical economic transition policy of the federal government, and advocated Slovak self government (not necessarily independence) insofar as that was a precondition of implementing a different economic programme. In many ways, the MFDS looks rather like one of the original 'umbrella-movements'. It contains a wide variety of people, and looks very likely to split now that national independence has been achieved: the task is no longer one of uniting all Slovaks against Prague (in contrast to the way the original movements united people against communism) but one of deciding how to govern an independent Slovakia. The difficult economic situation will generate tension and conflict over economic policy which could lead to a split. Alongside the MFDS there is the Slovak National Party, which is a much more traditional nationalist party, and which claims to be the successor to the pre-communist nationalist Slovak Peoples' Party, which governed the Slovak Republic, a puppet state set backed by Hitler which existed between 1939 and 1945.

In Poland, where nationalism was always such a powerful force in the political culture from the early nineteenth century, which, in the twentieth century sustained the deep popular resistance to communism and Soviet domination, there are many nationalist parties, the major ones being the Christian National Union and the Confederation for an Independent Poland. Romania has two major nationalist parties: the Party for Romanian National Unity, which directs most of its attention at the 'threat' to Romanian identity and the Romanian state alleged to be posed by the Hungarian minority in Transylvania and the Hungarian state; the other, the Greater Romania Party, is more concerned with the reunification of Romania in its 'historic' borders by the re-annexation of the former Soviet republic of Moldova. Extreme nationalist or fascist views can be found within many nationalist parties. The Republican Party in the Czech Republic is a far-right neo-fascist party not dissimilar to those found in Western Europe.

An important type of nationalist party is made up of those parties which represent national or ethnic minorities. Unlike the nationalist parties mentioned above, the basic orientation of these parties is defensive, aiming to preserve their cultural and linguistic identity. Some parties advocate cultural autonomy or even territorial self-government, where minorities are geographically concentrated. But in most cases their leaders avoid making any demands which could be interpreted as secessionist or as advocating changes of borders, as they know this would endanger their domestic position, as well as potentially alienating international support for the cause of minoritly rights. In Romania, the Hungarians of Transylvania have formed the Hungarian Democratic Union of Romania, which has a virtual monopoly of Hungarian votes. In Slovakia, however, four Hungarian parties exist, representing the more differentiated spectrum of views within the Hungarian community there. The major one, 'Coexistence', started out as a movement for uniting the Hungarian, Polish and Ukrainian minorities in Slovakia. Separate gypsy parties also exist. In Bulgaria (where parties overtly based on ethnic identity are banned under the constitution), the Movement for Rights and Freedoms, which is the party mainly representing the Turkish minority, has come to occupy a pivotal position between the two major forces, the former communists in the Bulgarian Socialist Party and the anti-communist Union of Democratic Forces. Another case to mention, which is not, strictly speaking, nationalist but rather regionalist, is the Movement for a Self-Governing Democracy of Moravia and Silesia. This party draws substantial support within these regions for a programme advocating a decentralised constitutional structure for Czechoslovakia, and, since the break-up of Czechoslovakia, for the Czech republic.

Agrarian parties were important in inter-war politics in all East European countries. As a rule, as we have already noted, when attempts have been made to resurrect so-called 'historical' parties, that is, parties which existed in the pre-communist period, these have not been very successful; it is the wholly new parties which seem to be better able to relate to the aspirations of the voters. Bulgaria and Czechoslovakia both had strong agrarian parties in the inter-war period, which have not regained their position in the present period. This is mainly due to the progress of industrialisation in the two countries since the war, but, in the Bulgarian case, is also due to the extreme fragmentation among those agrarian parties which have come into existence. But in Poland, where small-scale peasant agriculture persisted as the major form of agricultural production right through the communist period, peasant parties continue to play an important part in politics. Three parties scored relatively well in the 1991 elections – the Polish Peasant Party and the two-party Peasant Alliance. The former party existed throughout the communist period in an 'alliance' with the PUWP (the Polish communists), thus lending a veneer of respectability to the communist government's claim to be representative. The two parties of alliance grew out of the trade union Rural Solidarity.

The difference in origins of the two parties, as well as personality clashes between the two leaders, makes cooperation between the two difficult, despite the common points in their programmes.

Instability and Fragmentation in the Post-Communist Party Systems

A major tendency in the development of parties, which we have already alluded to in the previous section, is political fragmentation. To some extent, fragmentation was inevitable and necessary: modern societies comprise a multitude of complex and divergent interests, and a properly functioning representative democracy will require several parties if these are to express themselves and be taken into account. But the current state of development of democracy in the East European countries contains the ingredients for possible crisis and breakdown in future. Giovanni Sartori uses the term *polarised pluralism* to contrast the unstable democracies of, for example,

Weimar Germany or Italy in the 1920s and 1930s, with the more stable, peaceful and orderly pattern of inter-party competition seen in the *moderate pluralism* of established democracies. Polarised systems are ones where, among other things, anti-system parties – that is, which reject the basic rules of democratic politics – have a significant following; where conflicts of interest are expressed in mutually irreconcilable terms; where ideological conflict becomes polarised and highly antagonistic, and people see politics in mainly ideological terms and are unwilling to compromise and adopt a pragmatic approach to solving conflict; where opposition parties use their power irresponsibly – for example, to paralyse government by constantly blocking legislation, without being able to offer alternative policies or take over government themselves; where parties compete irresponsibly of outbidding each other to secure electoral support, irrespective of their ability to deliver on their promises (Sartori, 1976). To what extent are these symptons present in Eastern Europe?

The problem of fragmentation is most obvious in the Polish parliament, where the 1991 elections saw candidates from 29 electoral lists winning seats. Some amalgamation subsequently took place, reducing the number of parliamentary groups to 18. There are also numerous other parties which are unrepresented in parliament. In other countries the fragmentation in parliament is not so apparent. But in many cases several parties join together in electoral alliances at election time. These alliances may be unstable and unlikely to last after the election, which means that in practice the number of parties is still in fact quite high. There are often several parties professing allegiance to the same ideology or set of policies, thus competing for the same social constituency. The divisions are produced by personality differences among the leaders, or, in some cases, conflicts between former communists or their allies and newcomers to the political scene who want nothing to do with the taint of the 'old regime'. This is typical of an undeveloped party system, and one can expect some future mergers between parties with basically similar orientations, especially when a new generation of people become active in politics.

It is clear that the electoral systems chosen by the East European countries affect the degree of fragmentation in party politics. Poland's election in 1991 has been regarded as one of extreme proportionalism, which did not favour the larger parties. In many electoral systems, the larger parties are somewhat favoured in the distribution of seats in order to facilitate the formation of majority governments. This means that *part* of the explanation of the Polish fragmentation comes from the electoral system. But Polish society is politically divided, which has also promoted the creation of a large number of parties. In Hungary, a carefully devised, but enormously complex electoral system was used, which was successful in the sense of producing a rather manageable parliament composed of six parties. In Czechoslovakia, no conceivable electoral system could have dealt with the centrifugal forces in the two republics, which led, after the June 1992 election, to the the break-up of the state. But the use of a 5 per cent hurdle which parties have to exceed before they can be allocated seats means that within both republics, political fragmentation is less of a problem than in Poland. But nevertheless, in neither republic is the largest party able to govern alone, and coalitions are necessary. Coalition government, which works well in some established democracies, can be a source of instability, especially where it renders governments vulnerable to pressure from extremist parties, and where politicians are in general inexperienced in the arts of bargaining and compromise.

Nationalist parties can contribute to the instability of the party systems in Eastern Europe where it takes on extreme, chauvinistic forms. Often this extreme nationalism is combined with a strong religious orientation in politics, which can have a very divisive impact. The Czech Republican Party, mentioned above, is numerically rather small, but can have a disproportionate impact: witness, for example, the shambles to which it reduced the session of the Czech Republic's parliament on what should have been a dignified occasion, the election of Vaclav Havel to be the first President of the newly formed Czech Republic in January 1993. The Slovak National Party is important, because the MFDS government depends on its support in the Slovak parliament. The tensions between nationalistic parties representing majority populations and the ethnically-based parties which represent minorities could potentially be dangerous for the whole development towards democracy, and for the stability and security of the whole region. All East European countries, except Poland which is ethnically the most homogeneous country, have ethnically-based parties which support minority rights, and which are usually regarded with a degree of suspicion and mistruct by the majority population or the governments concerned.

Another potential problem from the point of view of democratisation is the strength of the former communist parties. Although these parties are obviously much less powerful now they have lost their monopoly, they can be seen as a threat to the transition insofar as they have not fully rejected their anti-democratic heritage. They have an advantage over the new parties in that they have taken over parts of the old party organisation which still work quite efficiently. They can increase their support by attacking the social effects of the economic transition. In doing so, they undoubtedly articulate widespread popular feeling, but if they came to power and reversed the economic transition, this could serve to resuscitate that political and economic elite created under communism, which still has not been dislodged from many key positions and which also opposes the transition because it threatens its privileges and status. In Romania and Bulgaria, the parties that originated from the communist parties enjoy greater popular support than elsewhere in Eastern Europe. The National Salvation Front and Democratic National Salvation Front (which emerged from a split in 1992) between them occupy about half the seats in parliament. The Bulgarian Socialist Party received more than 40 per cent of seats in the last elections. The 1992 election in Czechoslovakia saw the communists win a place as the second-largest party in the Czech Republic. This party has undergone only the minimum adaptation of its policies since 1989. In Hungary, support for the former communists was 11 per cent in the 1990 election, and the right-wing parties won the dominant position in parliament. There are some recent trends in Hungary, however, that indicate that the Socialist Party in that country is gaining strength. But in the Hungarian case, one can be more confident of the HSP's democratic credentials and commitment to economic reform than in the former cases.

A further worrying trend to be observed in Eastern Europe is the growth of political apathy. After a period of enthusiasm after the 1989 revolutions, the severe downturn in economic conditions and widespread disappointment with politicians and party politics has led to a decline in political participation. Voter turnouts of under 50 per cent of the electorate are not unusual.

Of utmost importance is also the lack of party consolidation. Several parties are centred around one or a few individuals and have no mass political basis. Membership of the political parties is usually low, except for the former communist parties, which still claim quite large numbers of members. Not all parties have regional and local organisations. One scholar has labelled the situation 'democracy without parties' (Kiss, 1991). For a well-functioning democracy, intermediate structures like parties are important for the stability of the system. So far it seems that the political parties in Eastern Europe have only made the first steps in the key tasks of developing contacts with the voters and channelling grass-roots opinion up to the central leaderships.

Many factors, not least within the party systems, point in the direction of polarised pluralism with the corresponding risks of a severe crisis in the process of democratisation. Many of the features noted here (political fragmentation, nationalist intolerance towards minorities, including anti-semitism) were also prevalent in the 1920s. From this point of view, the chances for democracy today look little better than in the inter-war period.

On the positive side, the East European countries today are becoming more integrated into a democratic world community. They have ambitions to join the EC in the future, and also would like to see some West European security arrangement. Support from the West and international cooperation require the existence of a democratic structure in the East European countries. Economic and financial assistance from Western governments and the international financial institutiona is conditional upon sustaining democracy and respecting human rights. Furthermore, even if political apathy is growing, a majority of the populations still support democracy and evince no desire to retreat into a new form of authoritarian dictatorship. All this gives some grounds for optimism about future developments.

But, in conclusion, democracy in Eastern Europe is by no means securely established. The underdevelopment of the parties and party systems is one of the major problem areas. The political cultures of the region are still too much directed towards conflicts over nationalism and ethnicity rather than towards political compromise and consensus. Much has still to be done which only the citizens themselves of the Eastern European countries can do if the future course of democratisation is to be assured. Above all, economic reform has to succeed if political stability is to be restored.

10

Leaderships and Executives

RAY TARAS

The executive branch of government in Eastern Europe has undergone profound transformation since the fall of Communist regimes in 1989. Changes have affected the *process* of choosing political executives, or leaders, but they have also included the *distribution of power* that is vested in the executive branch. Of particular importance in designing the 'architecture' of power has been the manner of controlling the actions of leaders and, connected to this, the relationship between executive and legislative branches of government. For as Robert C. Tucker, a long-time analyst of Soviet politics, has hypothesised, 'we can see the possibility of an authoritarian personality serving as leader in the regime of a constitutional democracy, and, conversely, of a democratic personality serving as the leader in an authoritarian system of rule' (Tucker, 1981, p. 68). It is 'the institutionalized difference between democratic and authoritarian forms of government' which revolves around (i) the possibility or prohibition of active public participation in leadership choice, and (ii) control of or submission to executive prerogatives, that marks the boundary between democratic and undemocratic leadership.

As in such other political spheres as electoral systems and party formation (described in earlier chapters), the nature of leadership in post-communist Eastern Europe is idiosyncratic, often owing more to national preferences and traditions than to any cross-national 'formula' for ensuring democratisation of executive power. There has not been a uniform movement across Eastern Europe to espouse democratic leaders in Harold Lasswell's (1986) sense of the term, and we need to explain why a differing pace of democratisation of executive power has occurred.

A key factor affecting the development of executive power in Eastern Europe has been the Communist experience. Setting aside its non-representative, non-responsive nature, the Communist system was quintessentially elitist, with power concentrated in the hands of a small steering group at the head of a massive political organisation. Whether this group of insiders was united behind the party leader or was internally divided, rule remained oligarchical and unchecked except by episodes of crisis such as societal disturbances. Not surprisingly, in devising new executive structures, the caretaker governments responsible for political transition after 1989 sought to avoid Communist practice by adopting radical alternatives: direct elections of the chief executive and a premium placed on coalition-building skills in multi-party settings as the principal qualifications for selection.

A second influence shaping the emergence of new executive structures has been a country's earlier experience of representative government. The political arrangements of the inter-war period have been particularly important in affecting thinking about new structures. Not in all cases, however, has that experience offered the anti-elitist thrust embodied in the anti-Communist reaction. Thus support for the emergence of a presidential system in Czechoslovakia or Poland is often associated with favourable assessments of dominant inter-war leaders like Masaryk and Pilsudski. But if Masaryk was attentive to the interests advanced by the most significant parliamentary group represented by the *petka*, or five-party coalition, Pilsudski in large measure 'scripted' parliamentary politics both while in retirement, prior to his May 1926 coup, and afterwards as well. The political behaviour of first post-communist Presidents Vaclav Havel of Czechoslovakia and Lech Walesa of Poland was informed by the experience of their inter-war precursors, with the former content to serve in the role of chairman of the board and the latter self-consciously seeking to become an imperial president. Interesting, too, was the cool Slovak response to Havel's presidency, seemingly acting out that nation's earlier lower regard for the Czech Masaryk's rule. However, such comparisons across time have their limitations and we can enquire whether Masaryk or Pilsudski would have given up their political ambitions – to rule over a unified Czech and Slovak state or to establish an all-powerful presidency – as readily as Havel and Walesa did in 1991 when submitting respectively to the 'velvet divorce' and to the 'little constitition' compromise.

In the case of Hungary, no inter-war leader was sufficiently dominant inspire nostalgia. Indeed the succession of undistinguished prime ministers may have, if anything, moulded Hungarian political culture into a less leadership-conscious system than elsewhere in the region, and that appears to hold true after Communism as well. Possibly the pre-First World War Habsburg monarchy has more resonance in Hungary today than any inter-war figure, but it is very circumscribed. Turnout for a referendum in 1990 on the method of electing the country's president was only 14 per cent, indicating Hungarians' seeming diminished concern for leadership compared to other political issues.

In turn, Bulgaria's inter-war experience of illiberal politics and authoritarianism offers largely a negative learning process to contemporary leaders. It may partially explain why the first 'post-communist' government of President Mladenov was so short-lived (see Chapter 6): it was perceived as still too authoritarian and not post-communist enough. In what used to be Yugoslavia, most South Slav nations took advantage of the collapse of monolithic Communism and went on to oppose the return to a Serb-centred federal state. Strong presidencies were created in the former republics of Croatia, Slovenia, and Bosnia-Herzegovina with a mandate to resist Serb encroachment (see Chapter 7).

In addition to the backlash against the Communist legacy and the learning experience of inter-war politics, a third factor at work shaping new executive structures is the self-interest of the architectural team itself. We can agree with Adam Przeworski that 'The decisive step toward democracy is the devolution of power from a group of people to a set of rules' (Przeworski, 1992, p. 14). But taking this step is hardly a purely technical affair, for 'Each political force opts for the institutional framework that will best further its values, projects, or interests' (Przeworski, 1992, p. 80). In practice, then, rules are fashioned by political actors whose own resources and interests differ. Especially in the transitional situation, 'the chances of the particular political forces are very different under alternative institutional arrangements' (Przeworski, 1992, p. 40). Those who favour a strong executive are frequently precisely those politicians who are the strongest candidates for such office; those who prefer collective, cabinet-type government are often party leaders who feel they would do best in a system where parliament determines executive leadership. Where fundamental disagreement about institution-building occurs among roughly evenly matched political forces, a satisficing solution is likely: 'if they know little about their political strength under the eventual democratic institutions, all opt for a maximin solution: institutions that introduce checks and balances and maximize the political influence of minorities, or, equivalently, make policy highly insensitive to fluctuations in public opinion' (Przeworski, 1992, p. 87).

In summary, in the transition period political forces do battle to tailor institutions to their own needs. Hence the different types of executive structures that have emerged in East European states since 1989 reflect the product of bidding and bargaining among interested parties and are not to be seen as outcomes arrived at by disinterested state-builders (though some of these did have input into the choice of executive institutions).

Nature of Executive Government

Simple typologies of political executives – whether they are effective (the US President) or ceremonial (the King of Spain), and individual (the German Chancellor) or collective (the British Cabinet) – are intended to outline the range of alternatives in existence today (Almond and Powell, 1983, p. 106). Institutional arrangements for leadership differ widely, even within a close-knit geopolitical grouping such as the European Community. Executive power also fluctuates longitudinally, as in the case of the US where a 200-year-old constitution has not prevented changes from taking place in the powers of the president. So it should be no surprise that we discover differing approaches to executive power in Eastern Europe today.

When classifying the emergent systems, it is clear that one particular model of executive power is preferred over others. The preference for direct election of presidents means that the Westminster model of parliamentary democracy has been ruled out. Yet the establishment of cabinet government, headed by a prime minister together with a group of ministers responsible for different areas of government, indicates that the US presidential system has also not been adopted. The question then becomes the extent to which parliamentarism – a dominant role in the system for the elected legislature – is allowed.

In many respects, the variation in executive power in East

European states can be visualised in terms of preference for the experience of France under either Third Republic (1870–1940) or Fifth Republic (since 1958). In each of these cases the institutions of the presidency and cabinet government were central. But in the lengthy existence of the Third Republic, and in great measure during the short-lived Fourth Republic (1946–58), the prime minister was ascendant, though he was at the mercy of rapidly shifting coalitions within the popularly elected legislature (called Chamber of Deputies to 1946, since known as the National Assembly). The Fifth Republic created in 1958 by General de Gaulle to suit General de Gaulle transformed France into a strong (but not quite imperial) presidential system. The head of state now nominated the prime minister, subject to ratification by the National Assembly. In conjunction with the prime minister, the president selected cabinet ministers, though formally the president made all appointments. The 'incompatibility' rule of the Fifth Republic further kept the Cabinet and the Assembly off balance: it gave legislative deputies 30 days to resign from parliament if they were to accept a nomination to a Cabinet post – a device quite different from the British parliamentary system. The purpose of the rule was to prevent deputies from voting down one government after another in the expectation that, in this game of musical chairs, their number would turn up. It also ensured that ministers, divorced from the legislature, would have a tough time building a power base in that body.

In the Fifth Republic either the president or the prime minister can chair the cabinet. The most important power the president has over the legislature is the ability to dissolve it and call for new elections. Further, the constitution grants him emergency powers 'when the institutions of the Republic, the independence of the nation, the integrity of its territory are threatened in a grave and immediate manner'. In such cases the president 'shall take measures required by these circumstances'. In keeping with the powers of the office, French presidents such as de Gaulle, Giscard d'Estaing and Mitterrand have affected aloofness in the office. While de Gaulle especially sought to increase his distance from the rest of the body politic by claiming to be above politics, even Socialist President Mitterrand tried to decouple his fortunes from those of his party.

This continental model had obvious attractions to East European states building democracy. But a chief weakness of the system lay in the possibility that parties of the left and right would capture different institutions of power – the presidency and the National Assembly –

thereby bringing on constitutional crisis. While the Fifth Republic survived an uneasy period of 'cohabitation' between a Socialist president and a conservative prime minister and government between 1986–88, it was uncertain what would happen in the more fragile and volatile conditions found in Eastern Europe should such deadlock result.

In addition to struggles between the *ancien régime* and the new, and between competing political parties and movements for representation, the first years of post-communism in Eastern Europe have, then, involved a struggle between rival institutional agendas – in short, between preference for representative and accountable government sensitive to short-term shifts in party fortunes that would be built into a Third Republic-type system, and desire for strong stable visionary leadership rising above partisan parliamentary squabbles promoted by a Fifth Republic-type system.

The general preference for parliamentary as opposed to presidential systems in contemporary Eastern Europe is explained by several considerations. First, a presidential system generates a zero-sum game, with the winning candidate taking all the marbles and the losers receiving nothing. Parliamentary systems, by contrast, increase total payoffs, with many parties and their candidates 'winning' influence. Even clearcut losers in this system have a greater incentive to stay in the parliamentary game with prospects of expanding their representation next time. Paradoxically, then, government instability built into extreme forms of parliamentarism may enhance, at least initially, the stability of the overall democratic regime (as in the Third French Republic). Together with a climate of continued suspicion about elitist politics, it is not surprising to find East European states opting, by and large, for the first variant. On the other hand, at a time of crisis in the future, it should be no less surprising to observe a shift to strong presidential-type, 'strongman' systems.

We have outlined the range of choices available to East European states in designing structures of executive power, and we have pointed to a pattern of preference for Third Republic-type arrangements. There are several reasons why new democracies in this region may remain alike. According to Prezeworski, 'Timing matters. The fact that recent transitions to democracy occurred as a wave also means that they happened under the same ideological and political conditions in the world.' Relatedly, 'contagion plays a role. Cotemporarility induces homogeneity: The new democracies learn from the established ones and from one another' (Przeworski, 1992, pp.

98–9). Finally, 'our cultural repertoire of political institutions is limited. In spite of minute variations, the institutional models of democracy are very few' (Przeworski, 1992, p. 99). Below we begin to disaggregate East European leadership and reveal distinctive patterns that have emerged.

New Leaders in Eastern Europe

Given the institutional choices faced by the polities of contemporary Eastern Europe, how have individual countries chosen their leaders, empowered them, controlled them, and decided upon their qualifications for office? Before turning to a case-by-case analysis of emergent executive power in the region, let us offer a number of generalisations about post-communist leadership.

In many longstanding Western democracies, a frequent criticism made during election campaigns by incumbent leaders about opposition parties is the latter's inexperience with government – a tautological proposition that is also intended to produce a self-fulfilling prophecy. Long-serving Conservative governments in Britain, Christian Democrats in Germany and Italy, Socialists in Spain and Social Democrats in Sweden assail the shadow cabinets of opposition parties (where they even exist) as lacking in experience and offering no name recognition to voters. What, then, are we to make of the qualifications for office of leaders of non-Communist parties in Eastern Europe who could not even function legally until 1989?

Leaders of such parties possess certain advantages, though suffering from shortcomings as well, from their 'newness'. For a start, their very inexperience symbolises the break with Communist politics. As a corollary, not having held decision-making powers before signifies they incurred no responsibility for any of the failures of Communism. Further, some opposition leaders struggled long and hard against corrupt, inefficient, and repressive Communist rule and contributed to its demise.

At first glance it may seem puzzling that relatively few 'old warriors', hardened by years of struggle against Communism, stayed in power for very long in the 1990s. Just as often political leadership was entrusted to individuals with negligible apprenticeship in the anti-Communist struggle but having broader professional experience – in management, private business, law, economics. Since reform of the economy was the most critical issue affecting post-communist societies, it is not surprising that new polities placed high value on such qualifications. In conditions of the enormous power vacuum caused by Communism's sudden collapse, there were numerous aspirants to high office and wild personal ambitions among prospective power-holders; dissidents were not alone in the power game. Ironically, then, while many of the last Communist rulers of the region had spent time in prison during the Stalinist years, not that many post-communist presidents and prime ministers had been imprisoned in the Communist period. Jozsef Antall of Hungary, Vaclav Havel of Czechoslovakia and Lech Walesa of Poland were prominent exceptions.

To be sure, in the Balkan countries a number of new leaders had suffered persecution under the Communist regimes. Paradoxically, this was because they were unorthodox Marxists, not because they had been anti-Communists. In Albania, Bulgaria, Romania, and even Slovenia, new leadership teams have included former Communists who had become dissenting Marxists. This peculiar feature in the career path of some leaders, such as Presidents Zhelyev of Bulgaria and Kucan of Slovenia, owed much to the *sequence* involved in the transition to democracy: Communism had collapsed here in 1990 as a result of contagion from other Soviet-bloc countries, less so due to confrontation between rulers and ruled (sequentially, this happened next). Not having organised opposition groups in existence prior to Communism's collapse meant that Balkan states had to draw from a different pool of alternative leadership candidates than in Czechoslovakia, Hungary, or Poland, where dissident move-ments had been active for some time and where alternative cultures had penetrated the professions. In the latter countries, 'nonconsti-tuted leaders' – in Tucker's words, persons 'advancing a definition of a public situation and a prescriptive for collective action to deal with it' (Tucker, 1981, p. 75) – provided a pool of leadership talent for new political parties. To provide an example, whereas Alexander Dubcek, the embodiment of the Prague Spring of humanist socialism who was overthrown by a Warsaw Pact invasion in 1968, was given a primarily ceremonial function after Czechoslovakia's 'velvet revolu-tion', his reform-minded counterparts in the Balkans (such as Zhelev, Kucan or, for a time, Sylviu Brucan in Romania) secured powerful positions.

Regime transition was in many ways a generational change. Many young professionals in their thirties and forties whose formative years were the halcyon 'goulash communism' period of the 1970s, were

catapulted to executive power as foreign ministers, defence priminis-
ters, and finance ministers. They were free of an obsession with
Communism and were thus well placed to put forward altogether new
agendas. They were largely detached from political storms surrounding release of secret police files naming certain dissidents as past
collaborators with the Communist state.

But the newness of this generation at times created difficulties, too.
They had leapfrogged the embattled dissident generation which had
engineered the overthow of the *ancien régime*. They had fewer
political resources (constituencies, personal followings or party factions) of their own and had, often involuntarily, to work in tandem
with older, more 'legitimate' groups. They had to compete with each
other for political prominence and often appeared overly ambitious
and zealous; some were as dogmatic about the market and as intolerant of dissent as ruling Communists before them; and, increasingly,
they were held accountable by society for the lack of economic
recovery in the region.

In sum, with exceptions like Havel and Walesa, there have been
fewer familiar names in the post-communist administrations of
Eastern Europe than we might have expected. Winning in popular
elections requires different political skills and power resources than
winning out over Communism, and clearly a new set of actors has
emerged endowed with such skills and resources. The question 'What
did *you* do to overthrow Communism?' seems already to have become irrelevant to the choice of power-holders in most of the new
democracies. There can be no better evidence of the transformation
of leadership in Eastern Europe.

If the list of familiar names among East European leaders is short,
it is important to discover the background of the 'obscure leader' –
individuals who are only now beginning to make an impact on the
post-communist political system and remain relatively unknown outside their country. What professional background and career paths
have they exemplified? Are they predominantly young or old, men or
women, free marketeers or state interventionists, liberals or nationalists? While we cannot provide aggregate data across Eastern Europe
about emerging leadership, we can identify the evolution and composition of specific leadership teams, together with the executive structures they occupy, in the individual post-communist states. Our
concluding section offers some generalisations about these obscure
leaders.

Albania

Following the overthrow of the Ceausescu regime in Romania in December 1989, Albania's Communist leaders decided to legalise opposition parties in order to avoid the violence that had occurred in the other Balkan state. In quickly convened elections in March 1991 the Albanian Workers' Party retained power by winning 56 per cent of the vote compared with the opposition Democratic Party's 39 per cent. The result revealed a divided country, with urban areas giving a majority to the opposition, rural regions to the Communists. Recognising the split vote, the Communists patched together a coalition government of five parties, but by December 1991 Prime Minister Ylli Bufi's government had collapsed and the country's first fully-free elections followed in March 1992.

This time the Albanian Democratic Party won a landslide victory over the Albanian Socialist Party (by a margin of 62 to 26 per cent) and put an end to some fifty years of rule by the Communists. President Ramiz Alia, who had ruled the country in the decade following Enver Hoxha's death in 1982, submitted his resignation and was replaced by Dr Salih Berisha, a cardiologist of considerable erudition. Most of his advisors were professionals as well, and his prime minister was the founder of the Democratic Party, Alexander Meksi, an archaeologist, who appointed a cabinet made up largely of young professionals.

As in other post-communist states, however, the break with the Communist regime was incomplete: Berisha himself had at one time been a member of the Communist Party, while the new Defence Minister, the mathematician Safet Zhulali, had also been a former Communist functionary. Gramoz Pashko, head of the Democratic Alliance and former premier who, by 1992, was criticising President Berisha's autocratic methods, had also been a Communist; as such, like in other states of the region, he soon found damaging rumours being circulated about his involvement in the Segurimi (secret police). Pashko was the leader of a group of self-styled technocrats which wanted gradually to introduce economic reforms.

For a country that had often been viewed as Europe's poorest, most backward state, the first post-communist leadership team represented an impressive array of intellectual talent by any European country's standards. Emigré Albanians helped bankroll political contenders so that electoral contests were not as provincial as might have been expected. Berisha's style of leadership seemed to be taking

Albania to an executive-dominant system where checks-and-balances might become insignificant.

Bulgaria

The office of President was created in April 1990, in the wake of other countries setting up this institution, and it was first handed to a Communist, Petar Mladenov, who quickly sought to disassociate himself from the party and resigned from it (see Chapter 6). This action provided him with insufficient immunity, for, by July 1990, he was forced to give up the Presidency as evidence appeared linking him to Communist plans for crushing the democratic opposition with force. The Grand National Assembly, or Parliament, elected Zheliu Zhelev as new President. Zhelev had been a critical Marxist in the previous regime and wrote a study implicitly comparing real socialism to fascism. Initially he was a popular leader who embodied the break with the *ancien régime*, but by the time of the country's first ever direct presidential elections in January 1992 his popular support had declined. Many observers were surprised that, with some 45 per cent of the vote, the incumbent failed to win an absolute majority in the first round. They were further surprised that he garnered just 53 per cent of the vote in the second round.

The January 1992 presidential elections revealed a number of other sobering characteristics of post-communist leaderships. Few women have risen to high office in the new governments, and Zhelev's narrow victory was hardly an enthusiastic endorsement of his running mate, the poet Blaga Dimitrova. The strong opposition to Zhelev was mobilised by nationalist forces teaming up with the Socialists. While the losing candidate, Velko Valkanov, a 64-year-old lawyer, had never been in the old Communist Party, his support came from Socialists, who manipulated social discontent with market reforms, and from nationalists, who fanned anti-Turkish sentiments. Leadership of the Bulgarian Socialist Party (BSP) fell to a 32-year-old economist, Jean Videnov, who represented a new breed of leader whose resumé was strengthened by date of birth and an economics degree.

Another astonishing phenomenon that has occurred in a number of post-communist states is the political appeal of émigré candidates. In the 1992 Bulgarian presidential elections, a ticket headed by such an outsider candidate managed to obtain 17 per cent of the vote. A former basketball player and fencer, 52-year-old 'Georges' Ganchev, who had lived for 25 years in England and the United States and held a US passport, returned in 1990 to take up politics. He claimed he had made a successful career as an actor in the West; not only that, he had married the daughter of the President of Woolworth's. As in some of the other countries of the region, then, a returning émigré boasting, how he had 'made it' in the West attracted a sizeable share of an electorate jaundiced with post-communist home-grown politicians.

Bulgaria's post-communist constitution limits the powers of the state President to security matters and ceremonial functions. The President cannot veto legislation passed by parliament, for example, and governance is effectively in the hands of the National Assembly. Zhelev may have been able to enhance the powers of the office through his ability to broker deals with leaders of the legislature, but he simultaneously suffered from the image of being too pliable. Perhaps trying to rectify this and strengthen the Presidency, he harshly criticised the government party, the Union of Democratic Forces (UDF), in late 1992 for provoking confrontations with a number of state institutions – trade unions, the press and, of course, the Presidency. Cohabition between a President who had been a Marxist and a democratic movement constituting the government quickly produced conflict.

As with the Presidency, the post-communist transition in the legislative branch was marked by a gradual, rather than an abrupt, shift away from Communist leadership. This seemed to have more to do with electoral outcomes than a grand design of gradually stripping Communists of power. In June 1990 Bulgarians freely elected a Communist majority to the Grand National Assembly, although the result could in part be explained by the lack of time for the recently legalised opposition to mobilise. The first Prime Minister was Andrei Lukanov, a member of the Bulgarian Socialist Party (BSP) – the successor to the Communist Party. But by December 1990 an interim coalition government was set up, headed by a new Prime Minister, Dimitar Popov, who was officially not a member of any party but most of whose Cabinet was made up of BSP Ministers. Following the narrow electoral victory of the UDF over the BSP in October 1991 – by a margin of 110 seats to 106 – a minority government was formed under Prime Minister Filip Dimitrov, UDF head. His Cabinet included a number of Ministers who were staunchly anti-Communist and, inevitably, it was brought down in the legislature by the

Socialists. After several candidates nominated for Prime Minister had been rejected, in January 1993 the National Assembly confirmed a 68-year-old economics professor and Zhelev advisor, Lyuben Berov, in the office. The appointment caused a split within the UDF, and the pro-Berov Alternative Social Liberal Party was expelled from the coalition.

A two-party model that had been evolving in Bulgaria had, then, come untracked. The pivotal role of the small Turkish ethnic party – Movement for Rights and Freedoms – in holding the balance of power in the National Assembly, also brought into question the viability of a two-party system. Bulgaria's leadership seemed to be succumbing to the East European rule of political free-for-alls.

Czech Republic and Slovakia

Czechoslovakia's 1989 'velvet revolution' was engineered by the Civic Forum and its Slovak counterpart, the Public Against Violence – both umbrella groups comprising numerous political orientations (see Chapter 4). Predictably, in 1991 the Civic Forum disintegrated and its most successor group became the Civic Democratic Party of Finance Minister Vaclav Klaus. Two other splinter groups were the conservative Civic Democratic Alliance, and the left-of-centre Civic Movement (headed by foreign Minister Jiri Dienstbier). Simultaneously in Slovakia the Public Against Violence split into the nationalist Movement for a Democratic Slovakia of Prime Minister Vladimir Meciar, and the Christian Democratic Movement of Slovakia, at best lukewarm about federalism, headed by Jan Carnogursky. The former Communist Party of Slovakia also metamorphosed into a nationalist group calling itself the Party of the Democratic Left.

By late 1991 a constitutional stalemate had been reached between the President and the Federal Assembly. President Havel sought greater powers for his office, including the right to dissolve the Assembly and call for new elections, but Slovak parties protested such centralisation of power. In January 1992 the Assembly rejected a series of constitutional amendments proposed by Havel. This would have required both Czech and Slovak Parliaments to approve a new constitution and to hold a national referendum in Slovakia on the question of it remaining within a federal Czecho-Slovakia; at that time polls suggested Slovaks might not approve of a breakup of the federation.

Slovak Prime Minister Meciar was opposed to such a referendum since he had read the poll results. At the time, he emerged as the winner of elections to the Slovak regional parliament in June 1992 and, together with his winning counterpart in the Czech regional parliament, Klaus, began the process of separating the country. Havel was correct in concluding that Meciar and Klaus had left him with a *fait accompli* and by summer had resigned as President, claiming 'it is better to split into two states in a peaceful constitutional manner than to descend into legal chaos'. Four rounds of efforts by the Federal Assembly to agree on a successor proved fruitless. By the fifth round the inevitable émigré candidate had surfaced: 40-year-old Jiri Kotas, who had been living in Canada between 1979 and the end of Communism. Notwithstanding the announced candidates, Klaus, by then Czech Prime Minister, seemed to be reserving the office of presidency of an independent Czech republic for Havel.

As Slovakia headed for statehood in January 1993, controversy swirled around Meciar. Some accused him of becoming an ultra-nationalist after he had been ousted as Prime Minister in 1991 by Carnogursky. Others pointed to his autocratic, populist political style. The inevitable accusations of Meciar having once been a Communist secret police agent (alias 'Doctor') also surfaced. While he still appeared to be the most logical candidate to become independent Slovakia's first President, one of his colleagues, Michal Kovac, a one-time Communist expelled from the party in 1970 and the last chairman of the Federal Assembly, also had the appropriate credentials and career path.

If past political culture is any indication, the Czech Republic seemed to be returning towards a Third Republic-type system with effective power residing in Parliament and the party that commanded it. None the less, the enduring popular appeal of Havel might allow him to sculpture a presidency in his own image. In Slovakia, more authoritarian tendencies are being rekindled but the legislature has jealously guarded its powers. In many ways the struggle for power between rival institutions was just beginning in this new state.

Hungary

Legislative elections held in March and April 1990 were won by the right-of-centre Democratic Forum, which had aspirations to becoming a dominant Christian Democratic Party in the country like the CDU in Germany (see Chapter 5). With 43 per cent of the popular vote and slightly larger a proportion of parliamentary seats, the Forum opted for a coalition government with two smaller parties – the Independent Smallholders' Party and the Democratic People's Party. Quickly a dominant role fell to the Prime Minister, Jozsef Antall, a historian, son of an official of the inter-war Horthy regime, and self-styled Hungarian Konrad Adenauer. Having ties with the Hungarian aristocracy, outdoing most of his opponents in his anti-Communism, and being able to invoke his participation in the 1956 insurrection against the Communist regime, Antall's political pedigree was unassailable.

Yet Antall's strong position contributed to problems with coalition partners and with the country's President. Smallholder Party leader Jozsef Torgyan abandoned the coalition while President Arpad Goncz refused to acquiesce in a diminution of his functions. By late 1992, Antall encountered problems within his own party: Democratic Forum vice-chairman Istvan Csurka published a neo-fascist and anti-Semitic manifesto that was an embarrassment in itself, but Antall's failure categorically to condemn it proved as important a political blunder. Antall's leadership was also brought into question when it was reported he had cancer. Polls showed the increasing popularity of the Party of Young Democrats (FIDESZ), perceived by the electorate as above the squabbling of the older politicians and having possibly the only charismatic leader in the country, Viktor Orban.

President Goncz of the opposition Alliance of Free Democrats saw the powers of his office whittled down. The country's influential Constitutional Court ruled that the president had to approve the appointment of candidates for state positions put forward by the government except if democracy was in danger. The president could only give guidelines, rather than orders, to the military; he possessed no veto over legislation but could, at most, request the parliament to reconsider bills. The president was elected by parliament by a two-thirds majority and, subsequently, could only exercise most of his powers with the consent of the prime minister and respective ministries.

Hungary's political leadership has typified that of the emerging democracies of the region. Christian, moderately nationalist, centre-right leaders like Antall represent the conservative spirit of the immediate post-communist period. Cohabitation between president and prime minister aligned with differing parties is tenous and adds to stress on the overall system. Erudite, personable, Westernised political actors exemplified by Foreign Minister Geza Jeszensky, a former Fulbright scholar, have made Hungary the new democracy perceived as most stable by Western observers. The Csurka manifesto should warn us, however, that dark forces remain in the wings in such a progressive democracy.

Poland

The struggle for post-communist power between executive and legislative branches of government has been particularly intense in Poland. The powerful personality and many ambitions of President Lech Walesa is the primary cause of this struggle, but an ineffectual series of governments and bickering among the many parties represented in the country's legislature, the Sejm, which is virtually in continuous session, have contributed to this problem. Walesa himself described this conflict graphically in May 1992 as a 'Bermuda triangle' relationship between himself, the Sejm, and the government. In turn, some cynics in Poland describe Walesa as having established the dictatorship of the proletariat that the Communists had been unable to do; the reference is to Walesa's working-class origins – one of very few post-communist leaders of such social background.

Walesa was elected President in November 1990 after suffering the embarrassment of being forced into a runoff with an unknown émigré politician, 'Stan' Tyminski (see Chapter 3). In turn, Eastern Europe's first post-communist prime minister, Tadeusz Mazowiecki, suffered a greater indignity in not even making it to the second round of presidential elections.

Walesa has arguably proved to be a weak president. He lost to the Sejm on the key issue of the electoral law, which legislators had insisted should be hyper-proportional rather than limiting representation of minor parties as Walesa wanted. He failed to obtain approval from the Sejm for two years for his 'little constitution' project that would re-define the powers of the executive. He was criticised for bringing the dignity of his office into question with populist forays into factories and dairy cooperatives. His response was to assert he had no interest in becoming a champagne-drinking president: instead, 'I pull, I push, I initiate.' Concern about the emergence of a 'political mafia' prompted Walesa to counter the rise of any strong party in parliament, to wage a 'war at the top' within the former Solidarity trade-union leadership, and to purge regularly close associates within the Centre Alliance party with which he identified for a time, and within his own high-profile Office of the President. The fear of any new hegemonic power was Walesa's pretext for dismissing even his closest associates. As he put it, 'That is why I am merciless. My price is losing friends; theirs, losing their posts.'

In late 1992 the Sejm adopted the 'little constitution'. The wording was indicative of the stalemate in Polish politics: 'a presidential-parliamentary system of government' was to exist in the country. The President's powers of forming a government were enhanced and the Sejm was no longer designated as the highest organ of state power. The President could initiate legislation, could veto it (which the Sejm could override with a two-thirds majority), could dissolve the legislature if it could not pass a budget within a three-month period, and could provide stewardship over defence and national security matters. By contrast, the government was now empowered to rule by decree: however, the President could veto a decree, too, in which case it would go to the Sejm for resolution. Further, certain subjects were off-limits for decrees: budget matters, constitutional issues, personal freedoms and, as a concession to left-wing parties, social security measures. The upper chamber, the Senate, stood to lose power to the President, Prime Minister, and Sejm and objected to the constitutional draft. Still, a precarious balance of power was in the making between executive, legislative, and judicial branches of government in order to take the country out of the Bermuda triangle.

Poland had five prime ministers between 1989 and 1992 – possibly the most of any European country. While the President was a former electrician, prime ministers have included people of many other socio-occupational backgrounds – intellectuals, professionals, businessmen, peasants. Mazowiecki, a dissident Catholic journalist in the Communist period, formed a coalition government in August 1989 that included Communists in the key ministries (Defence and Internal Affairs) and a Communist as President (Jaruzelski). He ran for the Presidency the following year and was replaced as prime minister by Jan Krzysztof Bielecki, a private businessman. Walesa chose him over another candidate, Jan Olszewski, because Bielecki agreed to retain Leszek Balcerowicz, a doctrinaire monetarist and architect of market transition, in his government; Olszewski said he would not. In October 1991 parliamentary elections were called again (let us recall the June 1989 elections had guaranteed Communists 65 per cent of all seats and were not fully free) and no strong parties emerged; indeed, 29 electoral lists were now represented in parliament, the largest with barely 13 per cent of the vote. Bielecki's government had ran up an enormous deficit and Walesa turned to Olszewski, a former Solidarity lawyer, to head a new government. Olszewski acted quickly to undermine Walesa's influence, removing the latter's appointee as defence minister – even though the still operative, much-amended 1952 constitution gave the President broad constitutional authority over security and defence policies. The showdown between Olszewski's Ministry of Defence and Walesa's National Security Bureau involved more than a clash over personalities: it brought into question the fundamental matter of who was responsible for what policy.

In February 1992, frustrated by what he saw as an obstructionist parliament and a meddling President, Olszewski asked the Sejm for emergency powers in order to govern by decree but was unable to secure them. In June 1992 a number of sealed envelopes were presented to Walesa by Olszewski's Interior Minister which contained some 60 names of collaborators and agents of the Communist regime. These 'revelations' included Walesa's own alleged loyalty pledges to the Communist secret police after the 1970 political unrest. Olszewski was behind the disclosure of secret police dossiers on prominent officials, though he may have been unaware that some files were actually forgeries. A few days later his government fell.

Waldemar Pawlak, a 33-year-old farmer and head of the peasant party that, in its earlier incarnation, had supported Communist rule, was charged with the task of forming a new government to succeed Olszewski's. But he could not establish a coalition that had majority support in the Sejm. In the summer of 1992 an expanded party coalition agreed on Hanna Suchocka as prime minister. Other than the important fact that she was Poland's first woman prime minister, Suchocka also had a unique career path: she had belonged to the Democratic Party that had been a satelite of the Communist Party before 1989, and had abstained rather than voted against the critical 1981 martial law decree. Predictably, charges of 'recommunisation' policies were levelled at her and at the movement to which she belonged – the Democratic Union (UD), which contained several well-known former Marxist dissidents. Still, her very staying power was welcomed across the political spectrum.

The electoral vote for candidates to the Polish Parliament was so split in the 1991 elections that the largest party, the UD, polled only 13 per cent of the total. The next most 'successful' party was the revamped Communist grouping, the Social Democratic Party (SLD), which was the parliament's most stable: while other parties splintered, it came to serve as an umbrella group of leftist deputies. Interestingly, the two largest parties were formally shunned as partners in the Bielecki and Olszewski coalition governments: the SLD was excluded on principle as a Communist Legatee, the UD for not being on the centre-right. But former dissident Jacek Kuron of the UD had served as a long-time minister and consistently ranked as the public's favourite political leader. Suchocka's UD-based government seemed finally to vindicate the democratic process, which had all too often skewed electoral verdicts once the processes of coalition formation and presidential designation of prime ministerial candidate had been completed.

Romania

Hurried elections were held in May 1990 and the National Salvation Front (NSF) – the organisation that had overthrown Ceausescu – scored a landslide victory against an as yet unorganised opposition. Reformist Prime Minister Petre Roman served until September 1991 when he was replaced by Theodor Stolojan, whose Cabinet was expanded to include members of the democratic opposition such as the National Liberal Party.

In December 1991 a referendum approved a new constitution for the country. It strengthened parliamentary control over the executive and the president but, compared to other post-communist states, the president retained significant powers: he appointed the prime minister, presided over cabinet meetings that concerned defence issues, he was President of the Supreme Council of National Defence and commander-in-chief of the armed forces, and he could even dissolve parliament if it twice failed to give a vote of confidence in the government.

In March 1992 at its third convention the NSF splintered into rival groups headed by Iliu Iliescu – who as president was officially nonpartisan – and former premier Roman. The latter blocked the nomination of Iliescu as NSF presidential candidate, so Iliescu supporters created a breakaway Democratic National Salvation Front (DNSF) that contested the 1992 elections under its own banner. Many former Communists joined the new presidential party.

Controversy surrounded the September 1992 elections when 15 per cent of ballots were declared invalid by the Central Electoral Bureau. Nevertheless Iliescu failed to attain the 50 per cent share needed to avoid a runoff with presidential candidate Emil Constantinescu of the opposition coalition, the Democratic Convention of Romania. Roman's National Salvation Front, now enthusiastic about reform but encumbered with a neo-Communist name and image, lagged far behind. Iliescu's party captured nearly 30 per cent of parliamentary seats (Senate and Chamber of Deputies), the Convention about 20 per cent. The new prime minister was Nicolae Vacaroiu, who was nominally an independent but who presided over a cabinet made up primarily of DNSF members.

Romania was unique in the support expressed for the return of the pre-war monarchy. In 1992 King Michael I returned to his homeland after 45 years of exile and was warmly welcomed. While leading politicians declared how little use a reconstituted monarchical system would prove to Romania, the King himself was less certain that the monarchy had no role to play in a genuinely post-communist Romania. Enough political controversy surrounded his planned Christmas 1992 return that he eventually cancelled the visit.

Political Leadership in Post-Communist Eastern Europe

New leadership is likely, by its very nature, to be obscure, and post-communist Eastern Europe has confirmed this pattern. What the playrights, electricians, economists, and philosophers who rule in Eastern Europe today have in common is career paths different from their Communist predecessors. Most new leaders have emerged from the free professions and from humanistic fields, they remain mostly male but are younger than East Europe's previous ruling generation, and their political careers are likely to resemble the trajectory of a shooting-star more than the movement of a garden snail. To be sure, these leaderships contain an admixture of former lower-order Communist apparatchiks, but this was inevitable and not undesirable where extrication from Communism came as the result of formal or less formal pacts between the old guard and the new. The emergence of a professional class of post-communist politicians is inevitable but also some time away.

In most of the countries surveyed, the architecture of the new executive branch of government has not been finalised. By and large they have adopted constitutional orders that specify the powers of the executive and legislature, but the struggles between the heads of competing institutions have not been fully resolved. State presidents whose powers have been circumscribed in the new order have not passively accepted a relegation of their duties to ceremonial ones, especially as presidents were also figureheads in the preceding Communist regimes. If they have been unable to create Fifth Republic-type institutions and to deprive parliamentary leaders of both executive and legislative powers they currently enjoy (through implementation of the incompatibility rule, for example), new presidents have recourse to other means to strengthen their positions. Ambitious presidents may seek to circumvent restrictions on their prerogatives by creating presidential parties that dominate legislatures. Or they may offer challenges to governments, play off coalition partners against one other, or exploit parliamentary gridlocks whenever they occur. Ultimately it is what presidents and prime ministers make of their offices that will determine their *de facto*, as opposed to *de jure*, powers.

Most of the East European states have tended to adopt parliamentary-dominant systems where elected legislatures can control the actions of the president, the prime minister, and the cabinet. By contrast, Soviet successor states such as the Russian Federation, Georgia, and Kazakhstan have lurched towards strong presidential systems. This is another relic of the difference between Soviet external and internal empires. Let us illustrate the differences within East European executive structures in terms of presidential or parliamentary systems. Further, let us add a second category, the dominant political philosophy (what Marxists would have called ideological superstructure) of leadership. The most important philosophical choice facing rulers in the region today, it seems, is between pursuing a liberal agenda and following a nationalist path. Liberalism is understood here as political and ethnic openness, tolerance, inclusiveness. Nationalism can be juxtaposed with liberalism in its emphasis on political and ethnic boundaries, a prejudicial approach to dissenters, and group exclusiveness.

In general, more countries have adopted parliamentary systems than presidential ones. In addition, parliamentary systems are closely associated with liberal philosophies. Only where nationalist parties dominate the legislature, as may be the case in independent Slovakia, will this association not occur. The closer a country is situated to Western Europe also seems to reinforce the selection of the liberal parliamentary pathway. By contrast, recent secession from a federative state does not appear to tell us which model a country's leadership is opting for.

Presidential-dominant nationalist-oriented leaders are at present found only in the Balkan states. We can thus add to the traditional meaning of Balkanisation – the proliferation of small states with adversarial relations – the notion that nationalist strongmen are preferred over liberal pluralism as the model of choice – for this region at this juncture. This is not to say, of course, that such choice will remain an enduring feature of Balkan politics, nor that it necessarily runs counter to the interests of these societies today. Indeed, Croatia and Slovenia (see Chapter 7) have already parted ways with their neighbours. Further, we should be aware that when a larger non-Balkan state does opt for a nationalist strongman (Germany or Italy in the inter-war period), the dangers to the European order are exponentially greater.

Just as there are inherent dangers in adopting the political philosophy of ultra-nationalism (the centripetal threat) and ultra-liberalism (the centrifugal predicament), so there are shortcomings in choosing one system of rule over another. Sharing electoral spoils among many actors as parliamentary systems do, the danger arises that ineffective government may continue indefinitely. If changes to the constitution are relatively easy to introduce and, with increased maturity, the new democracies come to see advantages of stronger presidential power, then a different equilibrium can be established between the two branches of government and the system has proved flexible. However, if constitutions prove to be sets of rules difficult to change, if a cycle of unstable government occurs, and if economic crises dog the new democracies for some time to come, it is possible that extra-constitutional means, such as protests and political violence, may be employed by disaffected groups intent on buttressing strong executive leadership.

The probabilities of such instability taking place in post-communist Eastern Europe differ from one country to another. Extreme dispersal of power carries with it certain risks, as does empowering executives with too many prerogatives. Holding executives accountable to representative institutions to keep them in check yet freeing them to provide strong leadership, has been an eternal problem of government. It will remain an especially challenging issue in the new democracies for some time.

11

People and Politics

CHRIS CORRIN

The events which rippled or ricochetted throughout East-Central Europe during 1989 and 1990 can indeed be seen to have placed 'the people' firmly back onto the political agenda. This chapter seeks to consider two broad areas: (a) the redefinitions of boundaries between state structures and civil societies including some emerging societal reactions to the development of new political structures; and (b) the developments and activities of several 'new' social movements with particular reference to women's activities and movements towards change.

It will be argued that certain theoretical aspects of 'anti-politics' can help to explain the revolutionary events of 1989–90. Within this, developments concerning new social movements are of interest to understand certain political and social changes and some of the consequences of political developments post-1990.

Political Changes in East-Central Europe

From the dramatic confrontations during 1980–1 in Poland with *Solidarnosc* challenging the party–state establishment, to the activities of the reform communists in Hungary in January 1989, the speed and scope of developments gathered astounding momentum. Perhaps the most visibly dramatic occurrence happened in August and September 1989 when tens of thousands of East Germans made their exit to the west via Hungary and Austria. These events, followed by the tumbling of the Berlin Wall, were watched by television viewers across the region, and elsewhere, and often had a deep impact on people's ideas of 'what was possible'.

German unification on 3 October 1991 was taken by many as a signal for the unification of the 'whole' of Europe – no longer divided east from west, but a 'new' unified Europe. The actual extent of European boundaries remained unclear. Was Russia to be included in 'Europe' and what of the troubled Balkans? No definitive picture emerged as to the direction and scope of change towards this 'new' Europe. In the most general terms, all of the former 'state socialist' countries, including Romania, Bulgaria and later Albania, rejected the rigid systems of party control over state forces and societal structures and relations. With the disintegration of the complex and in certain cases multi-ethnic systems, much change has been at once chaotic, contradictory and in certain cases, notably Romania, Albania and Yugoslavia, violent, in terms of its societal impact. Many women are experiencing quite devastating personal and social changes – such as the oppressive nature of the new legislation passed in Croatia, Poland and Slovakia which has severely restricted or outlawed abortion and restrained women's reproductive rights.

In political terms there has been much talk throughout 1991 and 1992 about how 'democratic' each country is. In Poland the unifying factors of *Solidarnosc* and the Roman Catholic Church were seen as giving expression to the homogeneity of Polish life, yet for many women there is apparent oppression in this linking of Church and state forces. The remarkably fragmented results of the October 1991 elections meant that forming a ruling coalition was very difficult and clear symptoms of 'voter alienation' were apparent. In Hungary voices have been raised against a parliament which involves 'much talk but little action or dialogue'. The emergence of the Charter 91 movement and its impact clearly showed a need for more open political dialogue. The Charter has been described by George Konrad as an intellectual association of democrats (*Magyar Hirlap*, 9 December 1991). Contained within the '17 points' (full text in *East European Reporter*, January–February 1992) are democratic imperatives ranging from respect of Hungary's legal system and democratic institutions and the state withdrawal from the important parts of the economy, to the need for state guarantees of basic social welfare rights to all citizens and active contribution from the state in protection of the rights of minorities. How effective the impetus of this Charter will prove to be within Hungary and elsewhere remains to be seen. The Charter does not mention specific women's rights, yet

given the parliamentary debate in late December 1992 which incor-
poratcd an allowance for women to have abortions only if they are in
a 'crisis' situation, then elements of the Charter could be utilised by
groups pressing for wider democratic rights.

In Czechoslovakia, Civic Forum was deeply divided before it
quietly dissolved in April 1991. The separation of the Czech lands
and Slovakia, whilst apparently 'orderly', is at best a recognition of
deep divisions and something of a failure of cooperation. For Slovak
women, the issue of access to abortion is again an important one. In
the former Yugoslavia the conflict which continues is violent and
brutal and the consequences of 'ethnic cleansing' will be felt for many
years.

State/Societal Relations: Changes under Soviet Direction

Although social class barriers had not entirely been swept away in
East-Central European countries, distinctions had certainly been
blurred. Yet, issues of status remained on the social agenda, with
party members being able to reap rewards from helping to set the
agenda for economically generated change and through direct financial benefits, some corrupt. Within other areas of life being an
'oppositionist' brought with it some status in the form of personal
dignity and self-respect. The recurrent tensions between Soviet forces
and national uprisings in various East-Central European countries
meant that the concept of 'opposition' never fully faded, in that the
possibility of challenging the Soviet domination of these countries
remained on the political agenda.

Yet for many during the communist period, the public political
sphere was devalued to the extent that 'politics' or political involvement, in whatever sense, became something to be avoided. Political
discussion was not only unnecessary but dangerous. People who
joined the Party did so out of career considerations and were often
prepared to sacrifice some of their former social circles in order to
achieve a promising position. Whilst there were certain similar situations apparent *vis-à-vis* party/state and societal relations in terms of
people's everyday willingness to participate in oppositional political
life, there remained obvious differences. In Poland *Solidarnosc* involved very many active citizens whereas opposition groups in
Hungary consisted of a very small percentage of mainly intellectual
activists in Budapest and other major towns. In the Czech lands and

Slovakia artists and writers were prominent in the Charter 77 actions. One similarity for Poland, Hungary and Czechoslovakia was the crossover of certain oppositional groups with western peace movements in the mid- to late.1980s. The consequences of this will be considered in terms of new social movements. In Bulgaria environmental groups were pushing for change, whereas in the much more dictatorial situations in Romania and Albania the dangers of voicing dissent were more obviously and cruelly apparent. In the former Yugoslav republics dissent was freely expressed and since Tito's death in 1980 it was the failure to agree on major republican decisions that appeared to push relations to breaking point.

Party Politics

An important point to bear in mind in terms of state/society relations within East-Central Europe is the particular relationships between the former USSR as a leading power in the region and many of the East-Central European countries. These countries were involved in a complex web of interrelationships including those of the Warsaw Pact and CMEA with many joint ventures directed towards Moscow. Communications between Budapest and Moscow, Warsaw and Moscow, Sofia and Moscow were always much easier and more regular than any communications between various East-Central European countries. Tensions were created throughout the region when the Hungarian revolution erupted in 1956, when the Prague Spring unfolded in 1968 and when the activities of *Solidarnosc* led to martial law being imposed in Poland in 1981. Certain countries, such as Bulgaria and the GDR, were seen to be more loyal to the Soviet model whereas in countries like Poland direct resistance was apparent and in Hungary experiments continued with the new economic mechanism. In Poland activists pushed the boundaries of previous oppositional tactics in direct opposition to state structures. It could be argued that the different historical nature of resistance in each country gave rise to different responses and learning processes. The violence in Hungary in 1956 led to concessions being given in the Kadarist compromise, so that by the late 1960s a New Economic Mechanism could be tried. In Czechoslovakia, twelve years after 1956, the nature of 'normalisation' was such a protracted process in the face of massive peaceful resistance that the Soviet oppression of Czech and Slovak social, political and cultural lives was driven much

People and Politics

deeper by Soviet authorities. This was especially the case in terms of 'changing history' and to some extent the language used, within the educational system and systematically tracing and oppressing opposition activists. In Poland the imposition of martial law in 1981 was another step in the direct practical struggles and negotiations taking place between Polish society and the party/state forces struggling to maintain 'control'. Yet the very imposition of martial law, rather than Soviet intervention, marked an important step away from direct control by force on the part of the Soviet Union. With the external influence of Gorbachev's perestroika, further changes were stimulated in East-Central Europe. The changing nature of these webs of related negotiations between the former Soviet Union and different central and eastern European countries had quite dramatic consequences in terms of rapidly changing political scenes and shattered patterns of trade and economic negotiation.

Consequences of Changes since 1989

Two aspects of the political upheavals were much discussed in 1991. These were connected with aspects of 'civil society in power' and with social and political movements becoming political parties. To take the latter first, it was certainly the case in Hungary that many people were prepared to join the Free Democrats (SzDSz) or the Democratic Forum (MDF) when they were primarily movements for democratising the political system. Many of these people stated that they would leave the movement in which they were involved if it became a political party. The roots of these attitudes are not hard to trace in terms of 'the Party'. Formerly all power and control within political and much economic decision-making had been vested in the Communist Party – be that the Polish United Workers' Party, the Romanian Communist Party, or the Hungarian Socialist Workers' Party. All of these parties bore the hallmarks of rigid hierarchical structures and tightly controlled power relations within them. Essentially, joining the party was often viewed within these societies as a career move, for particular ends, and such party members were then choosing a different life in terms of access to elite structures.

When the political changes came about, in each country at a different pace or depth, it was both problematic yet understandable that many so-called movements became political parties. Yet with huge social movements like *Solidarnosc* and Civic Forum the alliances were too heterogeneous to effectively articulate different interests and develop cohesive strategies and policies. Another problem was the legacy of old identifications with what political parties had come to represent and whether or not they could be truly 'democratic'. Uses of the term 'democratic' differ in various contexts and it often appears in certain East-Central European discussion that 'democratic' is used in the same way that Western analysts use the term 'freedom' – that is, of having unrestricted political liberty and participation. In East-Central Europe it is given a much broader context than in Western discussions which generally associate 'democracy' with a form of government based on the will of the majority of citizens, although there were competing Western conceptions (see Jorgensen, 1992).

Perhaps these broader conceptions of what democracy could involve played a part in the escalating aspirations for widespread political and societal change that many East-Central European citizens seemed to hold in 1991. Many individuals within different societies expressed forms of voter disillusionment. In the local elections in Hungary on 30 September and 14 October of that year there was a relatively low turnout. Of the 3.1 million voters living in rural communities of less than 10,000 the average turnout was 51 per cent, whereas in the larger communities with 4.7 million voters the turnout was around 33 per cent (Vajda, 1991, p. 42). In Poland, the October 1991 elections showed that timing is an important variable in changing political structures. Polish people 'voted with their feet' in that the average turnout was 43.2 per cent and the numbers elected from different parties meant that it was extremely difficult to form a strong coalition government (Corrin, 1992, p. 252)

Anti-Politics

In much of the oppositional writings on politics in Poland, Hungary and Czechoslovakia (e.g. *Samorzadnosc, Beszelo* and *Krytyka*) the sentiments of 'anti-politics' were common. It remained a multifaceted phenomenon, hard to define, but within its boundaries was a critique of the disappearance in East-Central Europe of the relative autonomy of 'politics' and 'economics'. At its broadest anti-politics was a critique of power *per se* and in narrower terms it was a form of tactics. These tactics were different before the advent of Gorbachev to power. One aspect of these anti-political tactics could be seen in

Poland's 'self-limiting revolution' (Staniszkis, 1984). Whereas before Gorbachev's accession to power in 1985 *Solidarnosc* did not aspire to overthrow the state forces or to take state power, by 1989 after the shock of the June elections, *Solidarnosc* intellectuals such as Adam Michnik were proposing to take power, in the form of a *Solidarnosc*-led government. This was a highly controversial development and was very much conceived as power-sharing. There was a mixture during the 1980s anti-politics of theoretical analysis and strategy across the different oppositional groupings in Poland, Hungary and Czechoslovakia. One aspect common to each oppositional movement was that of non-violence. Reasons for this appear to lie in part with the remembrance of the violent 'failure' of the Hungarian Revolution in 1956 and with the early examples from Poland's 'self-limiting revolution' when *Solidarnosc* occupied shipyards and factories thereby limiting violent street confrontations.

Civil Society in Power?

In his opening speech to the founding meeting of the Helsinki Citizens' Assembly in October 1990 in Prague, Vaclav Havel discussed the role of oppositionists under the Communist regime in Czechoslovakia and noted that:

> We always used to say that we did what we did for the sake of the principle; that we did not rely on any outcome; that we were simply forced to wage the struggle by our consciences. And suddenly, the struggle did have an outcome. The circumstances did change. The totalitarian system did crumble. And more than that. Another very strange thing happened: we were elevated to high positions of state.

What did it mean for Czech, Slovak, Hungarian and Polish societies to have the former oppositionists in power? Certainly it left a vacuum in terms of activists within society challenging the state forces – the very social arena of 'civil society' – that is, people and groups actively questioning the actions of the governing authorities. There was definitely a time when these new governments had their 'honeymoon' periods. Yet it is an unbalanced state of affairs for people in a country, especially those involved within a civil society perspective, not to be actively participating in public affairs and not to be able to voice different opinions from those of power-holders. The whole conception of civil society has been that it is a sphere of action distinct from that of the state forces. If suddenly all, or most of, the opposition forces within a society are in power there could be something of a crisis of civil society.

Against those who reasoned that now 'civil society was in power' so all was well, Tomaz Mastnak argued that any such conception represented an uncontrolled and unlimited power such that:

> the unification of civil society and the state in the post-communist polis is the structural destruction of civil society. (Mastnak, 1991, p. 28)

The recognition of the need for civil societies to regain their focal points and develop different identities took time, as the new state powers struggled to claim their own heritage in 'opposition'. It took time to recognise that state structures are no less state structures if those in power had spent a considerable time opposing the former party/state regimes. In Hungary the articulation of a form of civil society protest regarding the democratic nature of the parliamentary government can be seen in the sentiments of those involved in the Charter 91 initiative. In 1992 there were attempts to 'internationalise' the Charter initiative with the Budapest Appeal of 24 October 1992.

One East-Central European initiative proposes to keep a watching brief on 'democracy' in the region. In August 1991 the first meeting of the International Network for Democratic Solidarity was held. An initiative of political activists from Czhechoslovakia, Poland, Hungary, Romania, Russia, Ukraine, Bulgaria and elsewhere, the Network was formed after the coup in Moscow on 26 August 1991. Its essential aims are to bring together politically active people in Central and Eastern Europe to form a common agenda for the region, as 'region specific' not as a general European agenda. Its members aim to try to analyse and influence transition processes, starting with historical trends in the region and the lack of civil society traditions. These activists, the core of whom are former dissidents, wish to evaluate the situation from international standards of democracy, almost like a 'democratic watch' to monitor situations and to transform the legacy of 'the culture of protest' to the new situation. Movements such as *Ecoglasnost* in Bulgaria highlighted individuals such as Dimintrina Petrova who became an MP in the new political climate. In 1991 though, Dimitrina decided not to stand again but to become involved in grass-roots work and take a leading part in the Network for Democratic Solidarity.

'New' Social Movements: Developments and Disintegration

Much has been written recently on 'new' social movements, especially within the Western context (see initially Keane, 1988). A primary difference between traditional citizens' rights groups and 'new' social movements is that newer social movements tend to stress grass-roots involvement against elitist, hierarchical bureaucratic ways of working of political parties. In addition the issues developed within new social movements are interconnected – such as the proliferation of nuclear weapons and environmental destruction. Crucially the newer social movements tend to articulate demands and goals supported by strong moral and ethical convictions and extend the level of debate beyond the Cold War ideological distinctions of left/right, stressing the universal nature and consequences of issues. Within Western social movements the distinctions between 'social' and 'political' were blurred and the feminist viewpoint that 'the social is political' was an important conceptual amendment. Some analysts, including Mary Kaldor in *The Imaginary War*, argue that is was the linkages between the new peace and green movements in Western and Eastern Europe which created some social space for oppositional movements in Central and Eastern Europe in the 1970s. After the intervention in Czechoslovakia in 1968, Kaldor argues, 'the dissident movement developed during the 1970s, especially in Poland, Hungary, Czechoslovakia and the Soviet Union. . . . The combination of a lessened external threat and Western concern about individual dissidents may have provided somewhat more protection' (Kaldor, 1990, pp. 147–8)

In addition, the building-up of pan-European social movements began. The space opened up by dissidents extended the way forward for the development of *Solidarnosc*, which transformed the nature of opposition in Poland and more widely within East-Central Europe. The chilling effect of martial law in Poland at the end of 1981 marked a change in the 1980s away from a tolerance of groups such as 'Dialogue', an Hungarian peace group, and 'Swords into Ploughshares' in the GDR, and towards suppression. This tolerance had withered in the absence of domestic reforms and constraints placed on the East-Central European countries by renewed confrontation between the USA and USSR. Until Gorbachev began to make his policies for change felt in East-Central Europe any bilateral attempts at detente were unable to progress.

Failure or Success of Social Movements?

In viewing social movements as crucial sites of new political forms of expression, as against the hierarchically organised political-party structures, two examples from Hungary illustrate elements of success and failure. One of the movements can be seen to have faded in activity and influence in the 1990s and the other has gone on to become a dynamic force within the new Hungarian political scene. In the 1980s these two movements were of particular political and social significance – the 'Greens' or ecology movement, and the student/ youth movement. The initiatives of the ecology movement were born in the mid-1980s. Whilst there was no integrated ecology 'movement' as such, the biggest citizen's initiative, the political organisation of opponents to the Hungarian–Czech Danube water-power plant at Bos-Nagymaros, was a driving force. Various political groups, including the Danube Circle, The Blues and Friends of the Danube emerged to oppose the ongoing construction. Over time, with political changes, it became clear that the Danube project proved to be one of the major factors in the protests of opposition groupings outside the parliament against the party-state. Yet, with the suspension of the construction works, the limited capacities of mobilisation of the ecology movement became clear. The former activists left the 'umbrella organisation' for other political organisations. A Green Party was established but gained only 0.4 per cent of the votes in the 1990 elections, insufficient to gain parliamentary representation.

Student activism in Hungary had several sources including the movement advocating self-government of the students' hostels, and networks of autonomous initiatives and communities of cultural and political clubs. Opposing them was the Alliance of Young Communists (KISZ) which was harshly criticised within the student movement and in turn developed within it cadres who tried to revitalise its bureaucratic organisation. Over time an intermeshing of these various aspects of youth movements provided a springboard for creating a coalition of reform-minded young people. By spring 1988 students established their alternative youth organisation, the Alliance of Young Democrats (FIDESZ). They fought for their existence against political pressure from the party-state until new laws on assembly and association were passed in Parliament. FIDESZ went on to secure a good proportion of seats in the national elections in March/April 1990 (21 out of 286) and became the second party in the opposition coalition. By 1992 FIDESZ headed several opinion polls as the most popular political party in Hungary.

Why did the ecology movement disappear and the youth movement become a political force? Essentially the different dynamics of the movements led to different developments. Mate Szabo (Szoboszlai, 1991, p. 318) notes three main aspects to this question:

(1) issue orientation: the ecology movement was essentially *single issue* whilst the students succeeded in generalising their political protest goals;
(2) networking and institutionalisation: whilst the student movements built up their networks in the 1980s and created formal political organisations, the ecology movment was divided and could not develop such networks nor a persistent political unity;
(3) social basis and relevance; given the intellectual nature of Hungarian politics and the problems of long working hours after graduation (generally at 25 years), Szabo argues that the social basis of the new social movemments in Hungary is primarily made up of students, and participation within such movements heavily declines after graduation.

Whilst it is apparent from oral testimonies and some scattered records that women played significant parts in both of these movements, with women from FIDESZ taking a leading role in one of the major demonstrations against the Dam in Budapest in 1989, it remains the case that the merits of women's achievements are seldom acknowledged or built upon.

Women and Politics

During 1989 and 1990 women were highly visible on the streets, in demonstrations, organising meetings, electioneering and voting. When the new governments were formed and people began taking their places within the new power structures, women seemed to 'disappear' from view. Why was this so obviously the case across virtually all of these countries? Three factors are of importance here:

(1) All aspects of politics were viewed as 'dirty' by women and

many men. The public political sphere had become so devalued under the Communists that few, at first, were willing to enter it. Since the elections of 1990 and 1991 many more people have entered politics yet have had to withstand the often abusive, personal nature of attacks on their reputations. Women are often not prepared to negotiate their survival in such an atmosphere of personal confrontation.

(2) Many people in East-Central Europe are currently struggling for survival. With rising unemployment and increasing inflation, domestic budgeting, which generally falls to women, is taking up a great deal of time and energy. This includes not just queueing for food but constantly 'shopping around' for affordable prices, cooking alternative meals which use cheaper ingredients and making clothes 'stretch' for another year.

(3) The legacy of chauvinism and patriarchal attitudes remain an important aspect of many post-socialist societies. Women have long been treated as second-class citizens in East-Central Europe both in terms of vertical and horizontal segregation within the workforce and with women generally regarded as having the primary responsibility for domestic work. Domestic work ranges from the drudgery of washing floors (often with headless mops draped with rough cloths) to sophisticated care given to children and elderly people, yet it all tends to fall to women. With few notable exceptions, rather than being involved in the 'important' and well-paid work which some men at least have the opportunity to undertake, most women have to juggle so many responsibilities at once that they feel constantly under pressure.

Attempts at 'equalising' women's situation with men's by 'socialist policy' in terms of work opportunities, involved a dual process of women's entry into the national economy and relative withdrawal from the domestic economy. Experience demonstrates that the burdens of domestic work are not automatically lessened by nationalisation of the means of production. It also confirms that structural changes must be accompanied by some form of cultural revolution aimed at the elimination of gendered power imbalances and the opening-up of domestic opportunities and responsibilities. Within such an imbalanced situation progressive distortions emerge, particularly with regard to women's opportunities, abilities and willingness to develop 'movements' of any sort. Unlike in the USSR in the 1920s when women's political potential was recognised to the degree that 'mobilisation campaigns' were supported, in most East-Central

European countries the encouragement of 'passive' support from women via official party organisations such as the National Women's Councils was the norm. Women, for and of themselves, had few opportunities for active engagement, as women activists. Irene Dolling makes this point specifically with reference to women in the former GDR in terms of their having become used to a strong, protective state and having developed expectations of being 'cared for'. To appreciate other ways of interacting with children, such that caring for children can be a pleasure denied to men, is quite a far step for people emerging from particular forms of 'state paternalism' (Dolling, 1992; similarly Tatur, 1992). Notions of masculinity and femininity were neither extended nor explored.

Women's Formal Political Participation

One obvious feature of the changeover of power from the Communists in East-Central Europe has been the decline in the number of women in the higher levels of the governmental structures. As is generally noted (see Corrin, 1992, p. 250), this participation was often of a token nature and even referred to as 'the milkmaid syndrome' in the former Soviet Union, as rural women were drafted into meetings. Often the women who were included to make up a decent sex ratio were given no political education, did not receive enough information on which to make informed decisions and sometimes were involved for the same careerist reasons that many men joined 'the Party'. In any event, following the free elections in most countries of East-Central Europe the numbers of women standing for office and getting elected as MPs fell quite markedly, as Table 11.1 shows.

The most dramatic drops in the number of women representatives are in the two countries with the cruellest forms of dictatorship and with the lowest standards of living – Romania under Ceausescu and Albania under Hoxha. This could suggest that women in these two countries are more concerned than ever with the everyday struggle for survival and that the 'dirty' and dangerous nature of post-Communist politics in these two countries is most apparent.

But, in comparative perspective the numbers of women now involved at the parliamentary level of politics are at least equal with certain Western democracies such as Britain and France, yet they fall far short of participation rates in Sweden and Iceland. It is apparent

TABLE 11.1   *Percentages of women holding seats in Parliaments 1988–91*

	1 Jan 88	30 Jun 89	30 Jun 91
Albania	28.8	28.8	3.6
Bulgaria	21.0	21.0	8.5
Czechoslovakia	29.5	29.5	8.7
GDR	32.2	32.2	20.4
Hungary	20.9	20.9	7.0
Poland	20.2	13.5	13.5
Romania	34.4	34.4	3.6
USSR	31.1	15.3	15.3

Source: Adapted from Inter-Parliamentary Union, *Women in Parliament*, 1991.

in many parts of East-Central Europe, including Albania and Romania, that women are very active within political life in party offices, writing social policy documents, working in the trade unions and labour offices, and such women are becoming vital activists within 'civil society' contexts. Those women who are actively making decisions on an everyday level in their homes, at their children's schools and in the local housing communities are also key political activists.

Changing Women's Situations

The differences between the regime's rhetoric and women's everyday reality in the state socialist regimes was enormous. Essentially policy-makers were concerned primarily with material provision to allow the introduction of large numbers of women into waged employed. Measures aimed at easing women's paid work, or preventing their exit from the workforce, by providing some contraception and children-care services. Exceptions were the dictatorships in Romania and Albania, where abortion was illegal (until 1990 and 1992 respectively). Yet in all of these countries women still worked hard in paid and unpaid work. Women as paid workers, domestic workers, child-bearers and child-carers are at the heart of social relations. Where decision-making in all of its spheres is concerned, women are seen to have no real part. 'Reform' is not gender neutral and varies in different countries according to national conditions, historical developments and current resources. It is clear that one common factor in these countries is that women's interests are not given any official

TABLE 11.2   *Unemployment (data at the beginning of 1992)*

	Unemployment rate % (total population)	% of women in total unemployment
Albania	20	–
Bulgaria	14	54.3
Czechoslovakia	6.6	54.0
former DDR	17	61.6
Hungary	10	42.0
former USSR	–	75.0
Latvia	1.5	75.0
Poland	13	53.0
Romania	4	61.0
Former Yugoslavia	28	–

Source: Adapted from Eva Eberhardt and Jacqueline Heinen, *Central and Eastern Europe: Women Workers in the Transitional Phase*, May 1992, p. 16.

priority. Women are often in the first place when redundancies are decided. As Table 11.2 shows, women's unemployment is steadily increasing throughout East-Central Europe.

As these figures demonstrate, women are certainly in the forefront of experiencing unemployment. Losing their paid work of course does not necessarily lessen women's burdens, given the apparent continuing need for two wages within all East-Central European countries. Women are having to make difficult domestic decisions regarding budgeting of money and other resources. From Russia to Romania women are trying to find things to sell – small piles of mint leaves on pieces of newspaper, handfuls of wrinkled apples and a multitude of handiworks are evidence that many women are desperately trying to provide the bare minimum for their families. In some contexts, such as that in Albania during 1992, the struggle for survival is primary as there is very little food, heat, or in some towns light, and the fear of chaos is apparent. The new democratic forces had very different beginnings and certainly where dictatorship was strong as in Romania and Albania these societies are now restructuring from very disadvantaged positions.

It is often women from so-called minority groups – such as Romanies or ethnic minority groups within larger national groups – who suffer most, as they tend to be poorer, are less protected by social policy measures and have less access to resources such as health care, education and, of course, jobs. Many women in East-Central Europe are also reeling under the impact of constitutional changes which will radically affect their lives. Having been given or awarded 'paper rights' to abortion by constitutional means under the state socialist authorities, women in several countries including Poland, Croatia, and Slovakia are now having these 'rights' taken away from them by their newly formed democratic governments. The issue is a source of great political controversy in Poland, where the lower house voted for a highly restrictive bill in January 1993, although not one that satisfied the more radical demands of the Catholic fundamentalists. The recent historical lack of women's organisation in defensive or proactive campaigns means that most women are ill-equipped to defend or demand their just desserts or to actively articulate their interests and needs. Yet women throughout East-Central Europe have been actively attempting to change various situations for many years. In Poland, women have been active within trade-union activities since the 1970s and in other countries women have played various roles in oppositional groupings.

Women's Activities towards Change

With the new governments in place there has been an assumption that there is more room for discussion of issues and initiatives within an activated civil society – that is, that women are assumed to be able to enter a civil public space in which they can actively articulate their political and social demands to some effect. Sometimes it is implicitly supposed that in this situation there will automatically be more 'space' for women to be heard, to become active and to participate in broader, differentiated ways. As is apparent in the feminist groupings, which are very much struggling against entrenched beliefs, this is not necessarily true. The coalition of Church and State forces in some countries is generally one that seeks to constrain women's choices. The point has been well made that 'What is now in place is another, perhaps softer form of dictatorship. There is no democracy. Men still make the decisions' (Castle-Kanerova in Corrin, 1992, p. 117). Another argument is that the paternal state oppression of women is being replaced by oppression by the market. Certainly, increased availablity of pornography and sexual advertising is obviously harmful to women's interests.

Ways in which women resist change can be considered in terms of 'passive' and 'active' participation or activity. Choosing not to vote, or not to marry, can be examples of such activity. Choosing to live alone or as lesbians are other examples. In this context the old official women's organisations were important. Women often viewed such institutionalised representation as being carried on within 'paper' organisations, and as such wanted nothing to do with them. The cry 'we have had too much liberation' echoes the oppression women felt from the rhetoric mouthed by such branches of the party as the 'Women Councils'.

Active groups of women are organising in various countries and in pan-European contexts. In Hungary the *Feminista Halozat* (Feminist Network) have been active on various aspects of women's rights in the past two years, lately in defending women's rights to abortion. In Poland much work has been done by women in various groups such as the Polish Feminist Association and the Women's Club, as well as in the mixed group *Neutrom* – the Association for the separation of Church and State. In the Czech lands and Slovakia the number of registered women's groups and parties in 1990 was 37, covering a broad spectrum of beliefs and aspirations. Castle-Kanerova notes two of the most well organised groups are the 'Single Mothers' and a caucus of women within the Social Democratic Party (Corrin, 1992, p. 122). Women organising for themselves in the former GDR are experiencing a unique phenomenon in the unification process with large-scale redundancies demoralising many people. Women in the five new German states appear to be in a vulnerable position currently in terms of defending their rights or articulating their immediate interests. For women in Romania much is still determined by the legacy of attitudes of the former dictatorship in terms of the oppression of individuals. Yet there is growing evidence amongst medical workers that women are suffering more from domestic violence, perhaps as their male partners flex their new-found individual muscles.

In Albania, within the very fragile democratic climate women's groups are the main source of action. Certainly in such groups as those within the Democratic League of Albanian Women, which are represented in many towns throughout Albania, very necessary grass-roots work is taking place. In the former Yugoslavia, though, women are suffering innumerable burdens, not least the violence unleashed by war. In war situations women do not only suffer as soldiers or civilians through bombing and shooting, but they also suffer both from the escalating societal violence through rape and beatings, and the escalating expectations from state forces that women *must produce* children as future soldiers to replace those who are lost. Certain women in 'enemy' groups suffer in an opposite way in terms of not being able to have the children they wish, enduring forced abortions and sterilisations. The recognition of the rape of Bosnian Muslim women as a war crime is evidence of the depth and scale of such gendered acts of war in which women suffer the consequences of rape. For these women it is not just the first impact trauma of rape – personally, culturally and within their religion – but often the difficulties of gaining safe and legal abortions that makes these crimes so devastating. In such a situation women are still bravely organising shelters and refuges for women, trying to represent refugees interests and join international campaigns for peace.

Conclusion

The enormous changes in East-Central Europe have firmly put 'the people' back into political focus, but questions are now being asked about the direction of that focus – who benefits or controls, and where can change be achieved? Certain groups are clearly benefiting from the reforms much more than others. It seems clear that many women's groups are not benefiting to any great degree. Choices of how to work to achieve change are always difficult given limited energy and resources. Yet through citizens' initiatives such as the Helsinki Citizens' Assembly, the European Forum of Left Feminists and other pan-European groups working towards a more 'progressive' and egalitarian democratic future in which gender imbalances are not perpetuated, real changes are being made not only in concrete situations but in how we achieve our politics, and how we work together.

Within feminist groups worldwide participation in formal politics is a hotly debated issue, yet there is a general recognition that without the presence of women in decision-making bodies women's interests cannot be adequately represented. It would seem that in East-Central Europe in the 1990s it is going to be a slow process to undermine the dominant male cultures. It is apparent that many women's lives in Central and Eastern European countries are hard and there have remained areas of prejudice and injustice against women in these societies. Yet it is also the case that most women in these countries, other than very poor women and those in oppressed ethnic groups, are by and large well-educated and view working outside their homes as something in which they expect to be able to engage. Regardless of choices that may be made regarding full-time parenthood, many women will remain active within the labour market and will have expectations instilled from the former period that will give them a drive to fulfil their own desires. This confidence and ability among women will not disappear in the coming years, and it may well become strengthened in the new, more open and democratic conditions.

The violent political climate of the Balkan peninsula will heighten tensions during the early 1990s, and despite a more participatory social and political situation in some countries the reality of nationalism, racism and war radically affects people's lives. In such a situation different groups of women often become fundamentally important as a source of resistance to violent nationalisms and initiators of peace activism. On issues of reproductive rights, violence against women and generally changing women's siutations for the better, women across Europe – east, west, north and south – continue to share communications and activism, which could well become one of the most positive aspects of the next century.

12

The Politics of Economic Transition

JUDY BATT

The collapse of communism in Eastern Europe was in large part a result of economic failure: the failure of the system of central planning to deliver the material abundance promised by the Marxist ideology on which the communist regimes rested their claim to legitimacy. Evidence of intractable economic problems mounted rapidly from the late 1970s with chronic shortages, open inflation, unmanageable levels of external debt, a growing technological lag behind the West, and widescale environmental devastation. Declining economic performance affects the political stability of any regime, but in the case of the East European communist regimes, the problem was particularly acute not only because of the depth of the economic crisis but also because the regimes had been unable to legitimate themselves on the basis of social consent. Communist rule was originally imposed by force when the countries of the region were drawn into the Soviet empire at the end of the Second World War, and was sustained thereafter by a high degree of coercion, if not outright terror, perpetrated by narrow ruling cliques backed by the Soviet Union. Such regimes had obvious difficulties in presenting themselves as genuine representatives and defenders of the national interest. So economic performance came to play a peculiar role as a form of substitute politics: the people were offered high levels of consumption and welfare in exchange, as it were, for the lack of political freedom. No doubt some Marxist materialists expected that in time this 'deal' (sometimes referred to as a form of 'social contract') would lead on to genuine popular support for communism, but in the event economic performance proved woefully inadequate, so the question of whether the promised material welfare could ever in fact have compensated for the lack of democratic legitimacy remains unanswered.

When we come to the politics of the transition from communism, the problematic relationship between economic performance and political legitimacy reappears, but in a different form. What 1989 meant for East Europeans was summed up in the widely expressed longing to 'return to Europe': to be ruled by democratic governments, to work in 'normal' – that is, efficiently functioning – market economies, and to enjoy a West European standard of consumption. But while there was, and still remains, widespread social consensus on the desirability of these goals, the transition period poses enormous problems which are largely unprecedented, and will extend over a much longer time-scale than originally expected. As Ralf Dahrendorf has pointed out, the time-scales of political and economic transition are not compatible: whereas democratic political institutions can be set up in a matter of months, transforming the economic system will take several years. In the intervening period, the passage through the 'valley of tears' of economic upheaval and social dislocation makes extraordinary demands on the political leadership and the new democratic institutions themselves (Dahrendorf, 1990, p. 85). And while the new governments can claim the authority which derives from free, democratic elections, the institutions and mechanisms which sustain political legitimacy over time are as yet very fragile.

In some cases, for example those of Romania and Slovakia, democratic elections have only partially dislodged old communist elites from power. In the rather extreme case of Serbia, old communist elites seem to have been able to manipulate democratic processes by taking on the guise of popular nationalists in order to retain power. The new parties are unstable and fissiparous, with only weak roots in society, and they appear disinclined to offer governments the minimal level of disciplined support normally found in established democracies. The new politicians are inexperienced in the political arts of bargaining and compromise, and they face a daunting task, when it comes to policy implementation, in steering the cumbersome, often recalcitrant administrative apparatuses inherited from the previous regime. In many cases, the fundamental rules of the political game are themselves uncertain, as agreement on revised or completely rewritten constitutions has yet to be reached. In the cases of Yugoslavia and Czechoslovakia, the very existence of the state as a multinational federation has been undermined by intense national conflicts, leading in the first case to a brutal and bloody civil war, and in the second, to a more peaceful and managed dissolution. Thus even where the new regimes enjoy an unquestionable democratic legitimacy which their communist predecessors lacked, it is still not certain that they will be strong enough to lead society through the difficult years of economic transition. Will they bow to popular pressures and allow the economic transition to be slowed down or diverted? Or will they resort to authoritarian methods of rule in the interests of the economy?

The purpose of this chapter is to elaborate upon these dilemmas. First of all, we need to understand why a radical, wholesale transformation of the economic system is necessary, and why previous attempts at economic reform failed. We need to assess the economic legacies of the communist period in order to understand the practical difficulties which now confront the new governments. Major questions which have been vigorously debated by economic experts are the speed of economic transition ('shock therapy' versus gradualist or evolutionary approaches), the role of the state ('hands off' neo-liberalism versus more interventionist approaches), and privatisation. While such questions may appear at first sight to be a technical economic matter, in fact, as we shall see, they are loaded with political implications and are a major source of acute political conflict.

The Communist System: Fusion of Economics and Politics

The communist economic systems of Eastern Europe became established shortly after the end of the Second World War, when communist parties, with Soviet backing, ousted their political opponents and took over a monopoly of power. Thereafter, what had been mixed economies not dissimilar to those found in Western Europe were replaced by the Soviet model of the time, which was proclaimed a universally valid model for the 'construction of socialism'. This model had in fact emerged from the specific conditions of Soviet Russia in the 1930s: it come into being under Stalin's drive to industrialise and modernise the backward, mainly rural Russian economy, and to transform the country in the shortest possible time into a world military superpower capable not only of defending itself from the hostile 'imperialist' powers but also of expanding its reach to bring more and more countries into a bloc of socialist states. The basic features of the model were the virtually complete nationalisation of industrial assets and land, and the replacement of the market by an all-encompassing system of central planning.

Enterprises no longer relied on market signals such as supply-and-demand pricing as a guide to what to produce, with what combination of inputs, and to whom to sell; instead they received compulsory plan targets, directives and norms issued by the planning authorities at five-year, annual or even shorter intervals, covering virtually every aspect of the production process. Instead of being autonomous economic actors, enterprises were transformed into the lowest level of a vast bureaucratic apparatus geared not to profit maximisation (the very meaning of the term 'profit' disappeared once prices were became purely administrative units of measurement with no real economic content), but to meeting the political priorities of the regime. Managers were appointed by and accountable to not share-holders, but government ministries set up to supervise various indus-trial branches, and their salaries and career prospects were determined not by their enterprise's success in meeting customer demands, but by the extent to which they fulfilled the plan set by the central authorities.

The main quality fostered in managers under this system was not entrepreneurial flair, but political conformity with the dictates of their bureaucratic superiors, and unquestioning fulfilment of com-mands, no matter how economically irrational they might be from the point of view of the enterprise or the economy in general. It was assumed that the system of central planning would in fact be more rational than the market economy: 'wasteful' competition would be eliminated by the establishment of vast enterprises with a monopoly of production in their field, and clear priorities for economic develop-ment could be identified from the elevated vantage point of the central authorities and implemented through a disciplined adminis-trative apparatus.

From the point of view of the workers, this system had both disadvantages and advantages. In the Stalinist period, the pace of development was forced by holding down the growth in wages and popular consumption in order to maximise investment. Draconian labour discipline was enforced, and trade unions were transformed into what Stalin liked to refer to as 'transmission belts', and their role as representative of the workers' interests virtually ceased (it was claimed this function was no longer necessary as the whole system, being 'socialist', by definition operated in the workers' interests). Instead, trade unions had the task of mobilising workers to fulfil the Party's policies. But after Stalin's death, labour discipline eased up quite markedly, especially as labour shortages began to make themselves felt. Workers were now in a position to 'bid up' their wages by changing jobs, which they did very frequently. As the economy recovered from Stalinist excesses and the ravages of the Second World War, the standard of living began gradually but steadily to rise. From the late 1950s onwards, workers began to appreciate certain distinctive advantages of the system of 'real socialism'. Jobs were guaranteed for life, unless one chose to move. Along with the job, the enterprise provided many benefits, such as creches for children, subsidised holidays, housing. The government allocated an extraordinary proportion of the budget to subsidies on food, energy, rents, and many consumer goods. Wage distribution was rather egalitarian, and the regime could claim to have realised its basic promises of 'social justice' for the masses.

Thus, in fact, this system was not without its successes in its early days, although economic historians have long debated the enormous costs which accompanied them (Nove, 1964). In particular, the system proved able to mobilise domestic resources by holding down popular consumption and transferring resources from lower priority areas such as agriculture, light and consumer goods industries to high priority areas such as heavy industry and defence production. It worked tolerably well as long as the priorities were rather few and fairly straightforward, for example, more iron, steel, coal and electricity, more basic engineering items, tractors and rockets. This was the case as long as the economy remained at a relatively low level of development and huge untapped reserves of raw materials and fuels were to hand.

But by the 1950s, the Soviet economy had become a more developed, and therefore more complex system. The task was now not more of the same, but the production of a much greater variety of more sophisticated items, requiring a vast range of differentiated inputs. It also began to be recognised that domestic reserves of raw materials and fuels were not infinite, and that wasteful consumption was leading to the prospect of depletion if more economical use of them were not enforced. And at the same time, competition with the West was beginning to put a premium on technological innovation, constant change in products and processes, so that simply producing more of the same would not in future guarantee Soviet pre-eminence. All of these new demands put a burden on central planners, who were faced with an unmanageable problem of data collection and plan coordination. The plan itself ceased to be the motor of change, but increasingly revealed itself as a conservative brake on change. The system was now open to fundamental questioning of its basic premises.

In the late 1940s and early 1950s, when the Soviet Union's East European 'satellites' took over the Stalinist model, there was already some scope for questioning its appropriateness. While there was an arguable case for a system of centralised resource mobilisation in states such as Bulgaria and Romania, which had many of the same problems of underdevelopment that Russia had had, and in others, such as Poland and Hungary, which had suffered from extensive wartime devastation and faced a daunting task of economic recovery, in the cases of Czechoslovakia and East Germany, which were already among the more advanced economies of Europe, the imposition of the Stalinist model represented a 'great leap backward' (Ulc, 1974). Moreover, all of these countries were small, and poor in natural resources, quite the opposite of the Soviet case. Such economies were of their very nature heavily dependent on trade, but the Soviet model had an in-built bias towards self-sufficiency. Adopting the Soviet model implied cutting themselves off from their previous trading links with Western Europe and from the economic impetus that came with it. They became dependent on the Soviet Union for the vast proportion of their raw material and energy inputs, and their firms became geared to meeting the rather less demanding requirements of the Soviet market for their manufactures. The contradiction between the political obligation to follow the Soviet model of socialism and their own national economic needs rapidly became apparent. By the mid-1950s, East European economists were urging reforms of the system to make it more economically efficient and technologically dynamic. But the history of Eastern Europe from that time to the collapse of 1989 was a history of failed reform.

Reform within the Communist System: Politics and Economics in Conflict

What communist economic reformers were trying to do was to introduce elements of the market within the framework of a socialist economy. Enterprises were to be given greater autonomy over their day-to-day management, and were supposed to respond to customer demands, rather than central plan targets. They were meant to be freed from bureaucratic controls to a considerable degree as free pricing was gradually extended to virtually all products, and profit would thus return as the key measure of enterprise performance. Wages and salaries would depend mainly on enterprise profitability. Investment decision-making would be decentralised, as enterprises would retain a much larger share of profits to use according to their own long-range plans, and banks would supply credits on commercial criteria, charging market rates of interest. In other words, it was an attempt to create the same sort of pressures and incentives to economise, cut costs, respond flexibly to changing demand, take risks and launch new products and processes that are found in the capitalist economy.

But the system would still differ from a capitalist economy in certain basic features. The state would continue to draw up long-range plans (but along French-style 'indicative' lines rather than the traditional centralised-directive model), and would continue to steer the economy by controlling the overall pattern of distribution of investment resources, by maintaining a firm prices-and-incomes policy, and by maintaining the state monopoly on foreign trade. Above all, property would remain 'socialist' – enterprises would remain the property of the state, and managers would remain answerable to the state as the representative of the 'social interest', rather than to private shareholders. Thus although this economy would be a 'mixed' economy, combining the strengths of the market with those of planning, it would still not be a mixed economy in the sense that many Western capitalist economies are, where the private sector and the free market remain dominant even where there are extensive nationalised industries and state regulation.

Had it ever been fully put into practice, it seems likely that the socialist mixed economy would have functioned in a different way from a Western-style mixed economy, and probably less efficiently insofar as the degree of state control and protection envisaged was much more extensive, and the scope for genuine entrepreneurship

212　　The Politics of Economic Transition

TABLE 12.1　Economic growth In Eastern Europe

	1981	1982	1983	1984	1985	1986	1987	1988	1989	1990	1991*
Bulgaria	5.0	4.2	3.0	4.6	2.2	5.5	5.1	2.4	-0.4	-11.8	-23.0
Czechoslovakia	-0.1	0.2	2.3	3.5	3.0	3.1	2.1	2.3	0.7	-3.5	-20.2
E. Germany	4.8	2.5	4.6	5.5	5.2	4.3	3.3	2.8	2.0	n.a.	
Hungary	2.5	2.6	0.3	2.5	-1.4	0.9	4.1	0.3			
						0.0	**2.4**	**3.8**	**2.7**	**3.8**	**-4.0**
Poland	-12.0	-5.5	6.0	5.6	3.4	4.9	1.9	4.9	-0.2	-15.8	
						4.2	**2.0**	**4.1**	**0.2**	**-11.6**	**-7.0**
Romania	-0.4	4.0	6.0	6.5	-1.1	3.0	0.7	-2.0	-7.9	-10.5	0.0
						2.1	**0.5**	**-0.3**	**-5.8**	**8.1**	**-15.0**

* 1991 figures are provisional or estimated.

Note: In the communist period, the measure of economic growth was 'net material product', which includes the value-added output of all physical production, transport and distribution. This differs from the normal Western measures, Gross Domestic Product or Gross National Product, in not counting the value of output in 'non-material' sectors such as health, education, administration, defence, banking, hotels and various other personal services. This means that NMP is smaller than the Western GNP or GNP, and the growth rates are likely to differ. The East Europeans are now changing or have already changed over to the Western GDP system as part of their economic transition. Where GDP figures are available, these are given in bold type.

Source: Adapted from Economist Intelligence Unit and United Nations Economic Commission for Europe data.

was much more limited. As it turned out, the socialist mixed economy in most cases was never fully put into practice: in some cases, such as Czechoslovakia in 1968, it was tried but within a short time abandoned; in other cases, such as Hungary and Poland in the 1970s and 1980s, it was implemented inconsistently over a prolonged period. In fact, partial and inconsistent reform proved to be worse in many respects than no reform at all (see Table 12.1): the central authorities relinquished control to powerful monopoly enterprises, and failed to create the stringent competitive environment required to enforce the desired change in enterprise behaviour. Close links between enterprises and ministries continued, and even where, as in Hungary, central plan targets were never reimposed, a plethora of subsidies, tax concessions and other forms of special treatment served to render enterprise autonomy meaningless. A partial liberalisation of trade with the West resulted in mounting hard currency debt as imports rapidly rose to meet the demands of investment-hungry enterprises and impatient consumers, while export performance failed to improve.

The basic reasons for the failure of reform were located in the political sphere: all reforms were circumscribed by Marxist-Leninist ideology, with which it was difficult to reconcile the reintroduction of such quintessentially 'capitalist' concepts as supply-and-demand pricing, profit-oriented production, capital and labour markets. Ideologists were everywhere a powerful contingent of opponents of reform in the communist leaderships, and they found ready supporters among other bureaucratic groups such as the branch ministerial officials, who stood to lose their jobs should a fully-functioning market economy deprive them of their role of supervising enterprises, and the managers of the largest monopoly enterprises, particularly in the traditional high-priority, heavily protected sectors of heavy engineering and defence industries which were ill-placed to maintain their position in the more open and competitive environment the reformers were intending to create.

Such managers could also rely for support on the official trade unions, whose members also faced tougher working conditions, less job security and an end to the previously guaranteed wage irrespective of work performed. The spectre of mass working-class revolt against the social impact of reform was readily raised by bureaucratic opponents of reform to unnerve would-be reformers within the party leadership. Moreover, these groups with a vested interest in obstructing change had an institutionalised power base: they were heavily represented in the communist parties of the region, and in particular, in the parties' Central Committees, the key political decision-making bodies which had effectively supplanted national parliaments. These bodies had a power of veto over all major policy changes, and ultimately were in a position to remove party leaders. Thus where reforming leaderships emerged, they sooner or later found themselves in conflict with the very political-bureaucratic apparatus on which their power depended.

Moreover, would-be reformers also found themselves, during the Brezhnevite 'era of stagnation', in conflict with the Soviet leadership itself, which had the ultimate veto on reforms in Eastern Europe because it was the ultimate guarantor of the survival of the East European communist regimes. The willingness to intervene directly with armed force to reverse reforms that went 'too far' was convincingly demonstrated in Hungary in 1956 and Czechoslovakia in 1968, but more covert but no less compelling political pressure was applied

regularly to keep reforms in Poland and Hungary in check throughout the 1970s and 1980s. The inescapable conclusion was that no
economic reforms would work without a complete dismantling of the
political system which entrenched the power of conservative forces
and strangled all reforms at birth. It was only in 1989, when
Gorbachev himself had came to the same conclusion, that the way
was open for Eastern Europe to set about the task so long recognised
as necessary but so long delayed.

From Economic Reform to Economic Transformation

By this time, however, the definition of the nature of the task itself
had moved on from economic *reform* to economic *transformation*:
the idea of socialist reform had been irredeemably discredited, and
the goal now was the establishment of a Western capitalist market
economy. This was accepted not only by economic experts tuned in to
the international intellectual trend towards economic neo-liberalism,
but by wide sections of the public, exhausted by years of failed
economic experiments and readily persuaded that there was no
'Third Way'. At the same time, the economic conditions inherited by
the new regimes were far more difficult than communist reformers
had ever had to face in the past. The politics of the economic
transition revolve around these factors. On the one hand, the project
itself is more radical and far-reaching than previous reforms, and is
thus likely to cause far more disruption and upheaval; it is also
something of a 'leap in the dark', since there are no precedents for
the transition from socialism back to capitalism. It is thus accompanied by a high degree of uncertainty and mistakes must be accepted
as inevitable. On the other hand, because the general economic
environment has deteriorated so sharply (both as a result of and
independently of the transition itself), there are no virtually no
reserves to cushion the society through the transition.

   The first country to embark on the economic transition was Poland,
whose first post-communist government, headed by Tadeusz
Mazowiecki, had been elected in the summer of 1989. The Finance
Minister was Leszek Balcerowicz, an economic expert with strong
liberal convictions who was ready to work with advisers from the
International Monetary Fund in drawing up a strategy for rapid and
radical change (Sachs and Lipton, 1990). The disastrous East
European experience with partial reforms, combined with the basic

consensus of opinion among Western economic advisers on the functioning of market economies, led to the conviction that a gradual transition was not a feasible option. Market economies comprise a basic set of inextricably linked elements which had to be introduced all together, in a 'Big Bang', as it was frequently referred to.

There were several main components of the programme, which all came into effect on 1 January 1990. First, *macroeconomic stabilisation* was urgently required to halt the accelerating drift into hyperinflation (prices had been rising by over 50 per cent a month in the last quarter of 1989). This meant drastic action to eliminate the ballooning budget deficit by cutting out subsidies to industrial enterprises, imposing a freeze on wages in the state sector and instituting a tight monetary policy. The result of these measures would inevitably make a large proportion of enterprises virtually bankrupt overnight, but it would clearly be undesirable to let them all collapse, since at least some could prove viable once a market economy was established. Without proper market indicators, however, there was no way of telling which enterprises were viable, so *price liberalisation* – the removal of state controls from most prices – was necessary at the same time to sort out which should be allowed to go bankrupt and which were profitable in a market environment and should be preserved. But given the monopolistic organisational structure, there was a clear danger that firms would take advantage of price liberalisation and simply raise prices.

So a further component of the programme had to be the creation of a *competitive environment*. This required the development of the private sector by full legalisation of new private firms and the privatisation of state firms, which would bring about demonopolisation and restructuring according to market demands rather than administrative fiat. But the development of the private sector would take some time, so a further element in ensuring immediate competition was *liberalisation of foreign trade*, which would subject state enterprises to intense competition from foreign imports. This required in turn the establishment of *internal convertibility of the currency*, by which firms would acquire the right freely to buy foreign currency to meet their import needs. The currency was sharply devalued, and a fixed exchange rate was set.

An emergency *social safety net* had to be rapidly put in place to protect the most vulnerable groups in society, such as workers whose firms collapsed under the impact of the 'Big Bang' and pensioners and other groups dependent on welfare payments from the state budget. Other reforms necessary for the full implementation of a market economy would follow over the longer term: a new tax system, new rules for governing the state budget, a whole range of economic legislation, a complete overhaul of the banking system, development of a full system of unemployment insurance, etc. Western economic aid, primarily from the IMF and the World Bank, followed by Western governments, was essential to support the programme. Grants and loans were made available to support the stabilisation policy, the exchange rate and the social safety net, and a massive inflow of advice and expertise was provided. Some of Poland's hard currency debt was written off by Western governments and rescheduling of the remainder was agreed.

The Polish programme became a model for other East European countries in transition, although with different emphases according to local conditions. For example, in Czechoslovakia, the problem of hard currency debt was of quite manageable dimensions, and although inflationary pressures were present, there was no immediate threat of hyperinflation. But a firm approach to curbing the budget deficit and a tight monetary policy were nevertheless found necessary. The problem of monopolies was even more severe than in Poland, however. In Hungary (see Chapter 5), the first post-communist government had won the spring 1990 election on a gradualist programme, arguing that because Hungary's reforms were so much more advanced, having made great strides in the last few years of communist rule, 'shock therapy' was inappropriate. But severe problems remained, particularly with the high budget deficit and associated inflation, and in the highest *per capita* level of hard currency debt in Eastern Europe. Thus elements of the programme were still applicable. But rather than going into detail on each case, let us review in broad terms the results of the first two years of the economic transition, and focus on the problems which have emerged and those which remain to be solved.

What we are particularly interested in here is the way in which the economic successes and failures of the transition have fed into the politics of these new and fragile democracies. The key initial condition for launching the economic transition was popular confidence in the government. Because it was recognised that in the short term the measures would be a shock, with negative effects on virtually every social group, the government had to persuade people that it was absolutely necessary. Apart from the economic arguments, there was also felt to be a significant political argument for the 'Big Bang' approach: it was expected that the major building-blocks of the market economy could be put in place quickly, while popular confidence in the new governments was at its highest, and before coherent interest groups resisting the impact of the changes could form. In the meantime, it was hoped that relatively quickly the programme would begin to show some positive results, thus demonstrating to the public in general that it was working and at the same time creating new interest groups of people who had gained or could expect soon to gain from the new system. This would then provide the political backing for further steps in the programme.

Indeed, in the short term, some positive results were achieved, but the problem turned out to be that the gains were neither as rapid nor as substantial as had been hoped. And worse, unexpectedly severe problems developed which were only in part a consequence of the transition, but in large part also a product of extraneous factors over which the government had little control. Nevertheless, these could be and were blamed on the government and its strategy of transition. On the positive side, after a surge in prices which was only to be expected after price liberalisation, hyperinflation in Poland was very quickly combated in 1991, but all the same, a rather high level of inflation remained, so there was little room for an early easing of monetary policy. In Czechoslovakia, price liberalisation saw a surge in prices by over 70 per cent in the first half of 1991, which was a shock to people far less used to price rises than the Poles, but by the second half year, prices had become virtually stable. Here too, though, the government was aware that the danger of inflation was not over, and had to resist mounting pressures for a relaxation of monetary policy. People were at first impressed, on the other hand, by the sudden appearance of goods, especially imported consumer goods, in the shops, but then they were dispirited by the extraordinarily high prices. It could be argued that overall welfare increased despite the high prices, because shortages and queuing, the bane of East European consumers' lives, disappeared, but this cut little ice where people had grown accustomed over the decades to heavily subsidised consumption.

The key problem centred on the state enterprises. Industrial output has fallen in all countries which have undertaken the first steps in the transition much faster than anticipated, by as much as 30 per cent in the former East Germany (which underwent perhaps the most drastic of all the 'Big Bangs' with its unification in mid-1990 with West Germany), and by over 23 per cent in Czechoslovakia (see Table 12.2). Unemployment correspondingly rose rapidly, although not as

TABLE 12.2 *The impact of economic transition*

	1990	1991	1992*
Hungary			
Annual change in:			
Industrial output	–9.2	–21.5	–15.0
Agriculture	–3.8	2.0	–3.0
Retail prices	28.9	35.0	17.5
Unemployment (as % labour force)	1.7	8.3	11.4(a)
Poland			
Annual change in:			
Industrial output	–24.1	–11.9	0.0
Agriculture	–2.2	–0.1	–13.0
Retail prices	585.0	70.3	46.5
Unemployment (as % labour force)	6.3	11.8	13.8(a)
Czechoslovakia			
Annual change in:			
Industrial output	–3.7	–32.1	–9.0
Agriculture	–3.5	–8.8	–10.0
Retail prices	10.0	53.6	12.0
Unemployment (as % labour force)	0.3	6.6	6.0

* estimate.
(a) September 1992 actual.
Source: Adapted from Economist Intelligence Unit data.

fast as the fall in output, so the prospect of further job losses hangs over workers throughout the region, providing another jarring psychological shock to societies accustomed to guaranteed life employment in their enterprises. A substantial part of the industrial collapse was in fact a result of the break-up of the CMEA (Council for Mutual Economic Assistance), the former communist trading bloc, which led overnight to the transition to hard currency accounting for Soviet and East European trade, severely disrupting trade flows. This was further exacerbated by the crisis in the Soviet economy: oil imports were disrupted, and the Soviet Union was failing to pay for deliveries of East European goods. In effect, East European countries found themselves extending free credit to Soviet enterprises, which they could ill afford, so cutbacks in exports had to be enforced, with serious effects on those industries which had been mainly geared to the Soviet market. In addition, the absorption of the German Democratic Republic, a major purchaser of the exports of manufactures and agricultural products of many East European countries, meant the virtual disappearance of that market too.

But part of the decline in industrial output was indeed a product of the transition programme itself, and in some considerable part a necessary accompaniment to industrial restructuring, which unavoidably involved phasing out outdated and unprofitable industries. Strong pressures from the affected enterprises for a relaxation of credit policy was inevitable, and the arguments were very plausible. Without access to new credits, firms could not invest to modernise and restructure; and potentially good firms were going under because of the government's inflexibility. But the government finds it difficult to move in this situation: it is by no means convinced that the enterprises making the strongest and loudest case for special treatment are indeed the most promising in terms of their long-term economic prospects, and it fears above all that an early loosening of monetary restrictions could undo all that has been achieved in the fight against inflation. The government has to defend the national interest and the long-term perspective against sectoral and short-term interests.

The political problem is, however, that these sectoral and short-term interests are those of large voting constituencies which are difficult for democratic governments to ignore. For example, in Poland, the backbone of the political support for Solidarity had been the industrial workers of large enterprises in traditional industries – notably the shipyards on the Baltic coast. The impact of the 'Big Bang' on these people contributed substantially to the tensions within Solidarity and the eventual split and fragmentation of the movement into supporters of the Mazowiecki government and advocates of a slower, modified version of the programme. These conflicts led to the downfall of the Mazowiecki government, after which the pace of the economic transition slowed down and its direction came into question.

Another example of the intersection of economics and politics is that of Czechoslovakia, where the industrial crisis has been much more severe in Slovakia than in the Czech Republic. This is due to the much greater dependence of Slovak industry than Czech on production of goods for export to the Soviet Union, and in particular defence production, for which the market has virtually disappeared with the collapse of the Warsaw Pact. The Slovak industrial structure is a product of recent decades of communist-style industrialisation, but Slovaks blame their current plight on the new federal government's radical economic transition strategy. Unemployment, which at nearly 12 per cent by the end of 1991 was three times as high as in the Czech Republic, is interpreted as evidence of Prague once again foisting the costs of its policies disproportionately onto Slovaks, and this perception has contributed enormously to the growth in support for nationalist parties calling for either outright separation, or at least a fundamental modification of the economic transition strategy in its application to Slovakia.

The problems are so acute because the private sector has simply not expanded fast enough to absorb the superfluous labour in the state sector. A vast number of new private firms has indeed sprung up, but they are predominantly small family businesses which have not yet accumulated sufficient capital to expand, and which are also held back by the high real interest rates enforced by the tight credit policy. And some of these new firms are highly transitory in nature, comprising unscrupulous individuals out to make a fast buck in a context where legal regulation and consumer protection is still minimal. While in general in Eastern Europe, popular attitudes to capitalism are quite positive and tolerant (in contrast to Russia, where opinion polls show deep popular hostility to private entrepreneurs), the abuses and scandals which have occurred cause deep moral offence and serve to spread scepticism about the government's 'hands off' approach to the private sector. This is particularly the case where the new entrepreneurs are in fact members of the old *nomenklatura* or Communist Party elite, people who amassed sizeable personal fortunes by means of corruption and embezzlement under the old system, and who now can invest that capital in rapidly expanding businesses. Thus the same people turn out on top once again, despite the political revolution. The feeling of having been cheated has a corrosive effect on popular confidence in the whole strategy of transition. The new governments are still far from creating the solid, respectable entrepreneurial middle class which can be relied on to support their liberal economic policies.

Rapid privatisation of the state sector was originally envisaged as the key to breaking enterprise dependence on the state and thus enforcing a rapid change in managerial behaviour towards a more flexible, innovative market orientation (Slay and Tedstrom, 1992). As long as the state sector persists, it is recognised that governments will be under political pressure to intervene and bail out 'lame ducks' (Grosfeld, 1991). The new governments have relatively rapidly organised the auctioning-off of small enterprises, mainly shops, restaurants and workshops in the service sector. But privatisation of the major part of state assets in the form of the large industrial enterprises has proceeded much more slowly than envisaged almost everywhere. The reasons for this are partly connected with the technical complexity of the task. It took the British government ten years to privatise a dozen firms; at the same rate, most East European economies would still be dominated by their state sectors well into the next century. But in Britain and other Western countries, the governments had the benefit of fully established capital markets and the rest of the framework of financial institutions necessary to proceed with privatisation effectively and at a vigorous pace. In Eastern Europe, this framework has yet to be established. It is thus hard to set the right price for firms, many of which at present have very bleak economic prospects and are encumbered with debts. Is the government to write off such debts, and sell national assets at a price below the book value of their capital?

But it is just as hard to find the right buyers for these firms, as there is an acute shortage of domestic capital. What capital is available is frequently in the hands of the old *nomenklatura*, as mentioned above, and sales to such people are politically highly controversial. If domestic capital is not there, the obvious alternative is to search for foreign buyers, but in this case, the government must be realistic about the price that can be offered, and will face strong domestic political criticism for selling out the 'family silver' to foreigners. No government could contemplate the transfer of the major part of national assets into foreign hands, but it is also difficult to set restrictions on foreign acquisitions without putting off foreign investors altogether.

One alternative which has been strongly backed in Poland is the transfer of ownership to the enterprise employees, an idea drawn from the example of Western employee share-ownership schemes and from specific Polish traditions of workers' councils. This option has been resisted, however, despite its political attractiveness as a means of winning worker support, because the government's expert economic advisers are deeply sceptical about the economic efficiency of worker self-managed firms (based on the Yugoslav experience as well as Western case studies). But a further consideration is that of justice: some workers, lucky enough to be in highly profitable firms, would do very well, while others might find themselves landed with virtually worthless shares in firms with very gloomy prospects. In neither case would this inequality necessarily relate to merits of the workers themselves. And what about people who are not employees of state firms – pensioners, administrative workers, or schoolteachers, all of whom have a valid claim of a share in assets which are national property, belonging to everyone?

A more radical approach to the unprecedented task of mass privatisation of the post-communist economies has been the free distribution of shares by means of vouchers which every adult citizen can acquire and use to 'buy' shares in enterprises of his or her choice. This method has been pioneered by the Czechoslovak government (Brada, 1992). It has the merits, it is argued, of transferring really large chunks of state property into private hands relatively quickly, and also ensuring equality of access to shares on social property. But it is a very new, untried and hence risky approach. It is enormously complex and costly to organise and administer, and, unlike the case of direct sales, does not generate any revenue at all for the state budget. Perhaps the most telling criticism is that it seems likely to produce a highly dispersed pattern of share ownership, which means that effective shareholder pressure on enterprise managers will be not be guaranteed. So although it seems socially just, its economic impact is not likely to be as immediate or profound as in the case of direct sales. The Hungarian economist Janos Kornai is a noted opponent of such an approach:

> [This proposal] leaves me with the impression that Daddy state has unexpectedly passed away and left us, his orphaned children, to distribute the patrimony equitably. But the state is alive and well. Its apparatus is obliged to handle the wealth it was entrusted with carefully until a new owner appears who can guaratee a safer and more efficient guardianship. The point now is not to hand out the property, but rather to place it in the hands of a really better owner. (Kornai, 1990, p. 82)

In fact, as time goes on, there is increasing scepticism about the role of privatisation and the priority which it is has hitherto held in the transition strategy. There is a body of expert economic opinion which dissents from the basic underlying assumption that changing the environment of an organisation such as an industrial enterprise will bring about a complete change in its behaviour. There is an inbuilt inertia based on the fact that the knowledge and understanding which shape behaviour are derived from past experience. For example, Peter Murrell argues:

> [O]ne cannot view organizations simply as larger versions of rational economic man, reacting swiftly and accurately to the winds of fortune. Rigidities in economic behaviour must be largely under-

stood in terms of the limits on individual knowledge and the effects of these limits on organizational behaviour. In particular, old organizations, created in a past environment, will behave very differently from new organizations . . . [S]ucessful societies do not rely on existing organizations to undertake fundamentally new activities. Change is accomplished to some great degree by the replacement of the old and by experimentation with, and selection among, new structures: the process of entry and exit. In reforming countries, this can only be accomplished within the new private sector. (Murrell, 1992a, pp. 84–5)

Governments which have become bogged down in the intractabilities of the task of privatising the state sector may *de facto* find themselves presiding over 'dual economies' for some decades, comprising sizeable but economically burdensome state sectors kept going because wholescale privatisation is not possible and wholescale bankruptcy is not politically practicable, alongside burgeoning new private sectors. The key economic policy challenge for government in this situation will be to juggle the competing demands of the two sectors, to ensure that the demands of managing a large state sector are not allowed to throttle the growth of the new private sector. It is clear that in this 'dual economy' scenario, the role of the state in the economy will continue to be much larger than anticipated in some of the over-optimistic neo-liberal concepts of economic transition, and a more explicit industrial policy will evolve as the basis for strategic decision-making in the economy. The warnings of neo-liberals nevertheless should not be forgotten: ambitious, interventionist industrial policies pursued by Western governments have generally been a great (and expensive) disappointment. In the East European context, there is room for even greater scepticism about the likely course of industrial policy in practice: the administrative apparatus is still permeated by culture formed in the decades of communist anti-market etatism, and strong informal, personal links between the staff of government ministries and the directors of large state enterprises persist despite the collapse of the former framework of the *nomenklatura* system. In this context, the political detachment and strict economic objectivity necessary to ensure that industrial policy in fact serves the long-term national interest rather than merely protecting the privileges of politically favoured sectoral groups will be more than usually difficult to achieve.

A further aspect of the economic transition strategy which is undergoing some re-thinking is the basic philosophy of the 'Big Bang' approach. Those measures which were introduced in the 'Big Bang' dealt most successfully with macroeconomic problems, but even here the results were far from decisive, as we have suggested. The problem which has emerged is the rigidity of the micro-economic supply side – firms simply are not responding in the anticipated way to the 'shock therapy' meted out. Change in this respect requires a lengthy process of institution-building, in particular, the development of a fully-fledged financial system, including complete overhaul of the banking system (Ryczynski, 1991, pp. 26–34). It also requires the evolution of a business culture and ethical code to underpin the formal legislative norms (Hare, 1991, p.4). Some Western economists have begun to argue for a more evolutionary approach to the transition altogether, not in the interests of salvaging socialism but on the basis of conservative philosophical principles as derived from Burke and Oakeshott. The most successful societies experience change, they argue, not as the result of the grand designs of intellectuals – this was the fatal flaw of socialism, and it seems, paradoxically, to be being repeated by today's 'Big Bang' theoreticians – but as a gradual process of piece-meal evolution and adaptation to meet specific local requirements. Successful transitions are more likely to be made by means of pragmatic 'muddling through' rather than by 'leaps in the dark' launched on the basis of abstract theoretical knowledge (Murrell, 1992a and b; McMillan and Naughton, 1992).

However, East Europeans have as an unhappy a history of piece-meal reform as they do with grand leaps into utopia. Fascinating as such arguments are to follow as they emerge alongside the practical experience of the East European economic transitions, the evidence is not yet sufficient to make the a convincing case for either the neo-liberal 'Big Bang' approach or the conservative evolutionary approach.

13

Social Change, Social Problems and Social Policy

BOB DEACON

The transition period in Central and Eastern Europe during which the established command economies are giving way, always with the possibility of reversion, to market and probably capitalist economies, is one in which the social structure itself is in transition, giving rise to the complex, confusing and volatile political processes described in earlier chapters. This chapter is concerned firstly with the nature of the as yet uncrystallised new social structure and its shifting pattern of privilege and poverty, power and marginalisation. Some indication will be given of who are the losers and beneficiaries of the process of social change with a particular focus on the social problems of the relatively impoverished in these societies. Secondly the nature of the major issues that a changing social policy is being called upon to address will be examined, both in terms of general issues and in terms of specific recent developments. While a broad brush approach to the whole region will be adopted for the most part, the chapter then continues with a focus on the diversity of social development between countries and argues that in their increasingly diverse futures each society is echoing its own pre-communist historical and cultural legacy. Finally the relationship between the future of social policy in the region and the role of supranational and global agencies that are influencing it will be examined.

From *Nomenklatura* Privilege to Market Inequality

One of the ironies of the period of transition since 1989 is that whereas under the old regimes social statistics were readily available on many (but not all) aspects of society, there is now an absence of data on those aspects of the social transition that should most interest us. Census and other data has hardly begun to shift, for example, from categorising people in terms of their years of schooling to their relationship to property. There are few sociologists systematically counting the new rich and tracing their origins. Longitudinal studies of the new unemployed and their diverse fates hardly exist. Curiously there is much more data on social and political attitudes to the changing pattern of inequality than there is on the pattern itself.

Nevertheless it is possible to sketch a few broad features that capture the social, structural and attitudinal changes that are taking place. We shall call these in turn:

- from *nomenklatura* privilege to market inequality
- from working-class security to post-communist impoverishment
- the *déclassement* of sections of the professional middle class
- the creation of a racialised underclass
- the deteriorating social and political status of women
- the survival in a multiplicity of economies

When the Hungarian sociologist Hankiss presented a paper at a conference of sociologists in Budapest in 1989 suggesting that the process of self-dissolution of the communist party (the Socialist Workers' Party) in Hungary was being accompanied by the hidden transformation of many state enterprises to joint-stock companies owned and controlled by the previous *nomenklatura* managers, few present understood the import of his analysis. Since then evidence has accumulated that in many of the Central and Eastern European countries a section of the newly emergent capitalist class is made up of the former managerial and political elite. A loss of political privilege is being compensated for by newly found economic success. The new rich are constituted not only of this social group but also by those who had come to the successful in the second economy. Where this second economy had been most developed in the interstices of the state system and indeed encouraged by various stages of partial economic liberalisation, such as in Hungary or parts of Yugoslavia, then the chances of this newly emergent bourgeois entrepreneurialism flourishing are greatest. In addition, where the restitution of property rights has been vigorously carried through, as in the Czech republic, a number of the sons and daughters of the old pre-war dispossessed class are reclaiming their economic and social privileges. The winners in the voucher privatisation process are not yet clear, but they are bound to include some from the salaried technocratic class for whom economic reform always held out the prospects of personal gain. Foreign capital is, of course, gaining substantial footholds, especially in the Polish, Czech, Hungarian and Slovenian economies. Alongside and among these new rich are spivs and gangsters, prostitutes and drug-dealers, and organisers of protection rackets. The mafia flourishes in parts of the former Soviet Union and Eastern Europe.

While a small section of Central and East European society is emerging as short-term and possibly long-term beneficiaries of economic reform, the vast majority of society are becoming compared with the past, relatively impoverished. Living standards in real terms have dropped since 1989 by up to one-third. Particularly significant in the general impoverishment are the new poor, the new losers of the post-communist period. These are the people who, under forty years of 'communist' rule, gave up their rural roots and answered the call to be the new working class. Those who came to live in single industry towns or to live in heavily subsidised council flats in urban areas are the new poor of the post-communist period. They have a less diverse set of economies to survive on compared with their rural counterparts. The impoverishment of sections of this part of the population is, of course, contributed to by unemployment or threatened unemployment. Recent data on unemployment trends are indicated in Figure 13.1. These national figures conceal local variation. In some localities 50 per cent of the industrial workforce is unemployed. Those countries like the Bohemian and Moravian parts of Czechoslovakia that have not yet experienced unemployment at high levels are likely to do so when the next phase of large enterprise privatisation takes place. Falling real incomes, increased unemployment, rising rents, and higher food and transport prices consequent upon the reduction of state subsidies have contributed to this impoverishment, and the young, still-to-be-employed suffer the worst consequences of this social change.

This process of deprivileging the once-privileged working class of the 'workers' states is not yet complete and is, in some countries more than others, reversible. The political and cultural freedoms ushered

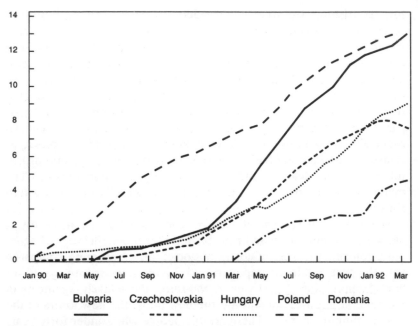

Source: Adapted from Boeri and Sziracki, 1992.

Figure 13.1   *Registered unemployed as a percentage of the labour force*

in since 1989 and enjoyed by the old and newly privileged sections of the population may count less heavily among this threatened and once secure working class than a guaranteed job and a subsidised standard of living, albeit at low levels. Many surveys of the degree of support for privatisation and the withdrawal of state social support have shown a reverse trend recently as the illusions once held about market economies and political democracy fall away.

It is not only the 'communist' working class who are among the short-term losers of the reform process. The once securely employed state technical and intellectual layers are also faced with threats and choices. For some a more secure future with higher rewards either as more highly paid civil servants or as private professionals is possible. For others the prospects of falling out of this social class are real. As budget cuts and cost accounting reach to the heart of government many will be prematurely retired. It is not yet clear whether a large enough range of non-government organisations in the tertiary sector will emerge to absorb this redundant talent. Social reaction may flourish among these downwardly socially mobile elements, as nationalism and chauvinism increase their influence.

The social equality afforded to women in the old regimes was always only formal. The double burden of forced work and care was never challenged. And the signs are that the post-1989 changes have not led to an effective campaign by women to make social equality real and substantive. Rather the tendency is in the opposite direction: part-time forms of employment appear to be emerging and the narrowing-down of enterprise concerns to profit and loss is leading to a closure of creche and other employment-based welfare activities.

The right to return to work without loss of status after several child care years is similarly being eroded. True, there is a new parental leave for three years in Czechoslovakia, but this carries with it no subsequent employment rights and therefore facilitates female unemployment. Liberal abortion provision is under threat in many countries as a result of a Catholic lobby. The 1989 and subsequent elections have led to a reduction in the number of women in positions of political power, as previously reserved seats for women have been abandoned (for a further discussion of these issues, see Chapter 11).

Finally, in this series of six features that I have chosen in order to capture the nature of a social structure in transition, we turn to the mechanism of social survival in this situation of uncertainty. Even in the period of political upheaval, economic crises, rising social intolerance – and in the case of Yugoslavia, open warfare – society goes on. Regardless of a general fall in living standards and the inadequacy of *ad hoc* measures of social compensation (see below), people somehow patch their lives together with resources husbanded from diverse and parallel economies. Some work in the formal sector, some work in the semi-legal second economy, some work on family garden plots, some exchange skills and abilities with neighbours and friends, and large amounts of the uncosted work of women and female children and some reliance on minimal state benefits make life viable. Evidence from Romania suggests some families are active in up to seven such 'economies' (Rose, 1992).

Social Policy and the Problems of Transition

The transformation in Eastern Europe from proletarianised, relatively egalitarian, and undemocratic political and economic systems towards market and pluralist political and economic systems brings into sharp focus the perennial questions of social policy analysis. These are the issues of social justice and of citizenship, to which we now turn. Subsequently we show how, in addition to these perennial issues, social policy-makers in Eastern Europe are faced with a *unique* post-communist problem.

Social Justice and Social Policy

The question of social justice, its meaning, how it is to be achieved, and the part social policy plays in it is perhaps one of the two paramount issues brought into sharp relief by the collapse of the old regimes. Put simply, the old order promulgated an official ideology of egalitarianism tempered only by the need in the socialist phase of development to reward work effort and discourage shirkers. Wage differentials between workers and managers, and between workers and professionals, were in general lower than in capitalist societies. The fact that the *nomenklatura* received hidden privileges in cash and kind did not break this broad official commitment to egalitarianism. But people saw such privileges as not conferring with the conception of justice operating as official ideology, and there was outrage when their extent was 'discovered' in 1989. The question in the new era is whether popular support will be forthcoming for a conception of social justice more appropriate to a phase of capitalist development.

Social policy as an idea and commitment of government and as a set of detailed policies is important for the establishment of a new social contract between rich and poor to replace the old contract between *nomenklatura* and worker. What are the possibilities for cementing such a contract, one that is appropriate to an emerging capitalist society? Two areas may be indicated: government pronoun-cements on social policy, and opinion surveys concerning popular attitudes to emerging inequalities. In terms of the first, the picture is patchy and fluid. Given the identification of social policy with the all-embracing socio-politics of the discredited 'communist' regimes, the initial programmes of most of the first post-communist governments concentrated on economic questions and paid little attention to social policy. There were exceptions, such as Czechoslovakia, which articu-lated a social policy conception designed to provide a social minimum in the transition period and which in practice compensated people for price rises by a universal, now targeted, allowance. Bulgaria and Romania, where the ex-Communists initially retained power under nationalist or social democratic colours, also developed compensation measures to protect those threatened with a fall in living standards. Elsewhere attention to issues of social justice has come later and is only now regarded as an important element in ensuring social and political stability in the transition period.

In terms of opinion surveys, a cross-national study of social justice (Mason, 1992a) together with other single country studies is generating interesting findings. Initially in Poland and elsewhere, evidence pointed to a shift in the late 1980s from egalitarian sentiments to an acceptance of wider inequalities and unemployment as the price to be paid for the transition to capitalism. Increasing degrees of support for a meritocratic system of reward and/or for an equal-opportunity system of social differentiation were found alongside a 'stubborn' residue of people continually attached to substantive egalitarian sentiments.

The most recent evidence from Czechoslovakia however suggests that the tide of opinion is shifting away from the further endorsement of differentiation with an increased harking back to the securities of the shared egalitarianism of relative (by Western standards) impoverishment. Time may be running out for political leaders wishing to cement a new contract based on conceptions of justice relevant to capitalist society.

Citizenship and Social Policy

Of equal importance alongside the issue of social justice is the issue of citizenship. In a sense the development of social justice requires equal citizenship entitlements and the establishment of full citizenship rights for all. In the early rush to enthusiastic comment made by Western social and political analysts about East European developments the twin concepts of citizenship and civil society features strongly (Keane, 1988; Deacon and Szalai, 1990). Events in Eastern Europe seemed to suggest there was a slow ripening of an active civil society underneath the edifices of state power. Once the old order withered and collapsed a new organic society would be ready and waiting to take its place. Furthermore, because the old order had made everybody *déclassé* and there would be no capitalist class – only anonymous state property waiting to be collectively managed – a new type of round-table politics would emerge to reflect this equal active citizenship. And indeed, initially, political life in Czechoslovakia with

Civic Forum, in Bulgaria with the Democratic Forum, in the GDR before the merger, and in Poland with Solidarity's round table, seemed to reflect this vision.

Now, of course, with Civic Forum having split into conventional political parties, as solidarity forms several wings, as Bulgaria is fraught with social and political tension, things look different. The actuality of already existing social inequalities and the emergence of new social inequalities, consequent upon the establishment of a capitalist class, reminds us that the issue of citizenship is precisely whether all or only some of society's members are ready and able – equipped and empowered – to be active agents in the articulation of a meeting of their own welfare and other needs.

Social policy in this situation is called upon to facilitate the achievement of active citizenship by those members of society who, hitherto, had been pacified by paternalistic state bureaucratic procedures and policies. Two recent contributions to the literature by East European sociologists are helpful here. Julia Szalai (1992) argues in the case of Hungary that the peaceful implosion of the old regime in 1989 was a final outcome of organic changes that had been taking place within Hungarian society since 1956. The deal that had subsequently been struck between Kadar and the population was that individual citizens were allowed to build up their own private life in ways which actually subverted the central command economy in return for political quiescence. The second economy, often dependent on the resources of the first, permitted the slow embourgeoisement of a large section of society.

Small-scale agriculture, private house-building and exchange of repair and other skills formed the basis of this new civil society acting in the interstices of the state system. This part of the analysis gives hope for the flourishing of a self-activating and self-motivated civil society in the post-communist era. The other side of the coin are those people who built their lives during the past forty years within the state socialist framework. People of this kind gave up their peasant roots and occupied large urban housing estates built for them. These, Szalai (1992) argues, are now the real victims of 'socialism' who are being 'thrown out of the boat'. A dualisation of society has accordingly come into existence and the task for social policy is to construct means that enable the integration of this lost part of society.

For Poland, Lena Kolarska-Bobinska (1992) has addressed directly the question as to whether a new civil society, once repressed and restricted, will develop fully in the post-communist phase. A very different picture emerges from the Hungarian one, underlining a point to be discussed later concerning the diversity of post-communist developments in Eastern Europe. In Poland, despite the years of oppositional Solidarity activity, a bourgeois civil society did not seem to take such a firm root. The opposition was precisely a confrontational one of worker and intellectual against the state apparatus. There was no quiet growth of a bourgeois class which would be waiting in the wings to inherit the future. Faced with the new situation, there is, argues Kolarska-Bobinska, a sense of anomie and normlessness. People do not choose to vote, and they do not choose to participate.

While the very existence of a civil society capable of managing its own affairs is in question, it might be thought superfluous to discuss the specific citizenship issues of marginalised social groups. But in a situation of normlessness and uncertainty within which strong leadership might be looked to, the existence of outgroups can provide a potent mobilising force. Jews in Poland, however few there are that survived, Slovaks in Czechoslovakia, Hungarians in Slovakia, Hungarians in Romania, Serbs in Croatia, Angolans in former East Germany, Gypsies everywhere, Turks in Bulgaria, Albanians in Serbia – all provide potential fuel for authoritarian, nationalistic and racist political leadership. The opening-up of a space for civil society in Eastern Europe provides the possibility for the first time in forty years for ethnic minorities to articulate their own specific welfare needs. There is clear evidence that this is taking place with demands by Hungarians in Romania and Turks in Bulgaria for mother-tongue teaching. Gypsy communities have won significant small struggles in certain urban settlements in Hungary. Equally the same space can be filled by increased racist sentiment and by the politics of exclusion.

The initial hopes for flourishing civil societies developing a politics of need appropriate to relatively socially undifferentiated societies are now giving way to the uneasy realisation that social differentiation is emerging around ethnicity and locality and this is generating a politics of exclusion and authoritarianism. Civil society may be stillborn in large parts of Eastern Europe.

The Unique Issue of Post-Communist Social Policy

Within the broader framework of establishing a socially just and self-activated civil society, social policy has to tackle very specific social problems bequeathed from the past. The almost impossible task faced by the new social policy-makers in Eastern Europe can be described in the following way. They are presented with a four-fold problem:

(1) a legacy of social problems created by the inadequacy and in-efficiency of the social policies of the 'communist' regimes. These include housing shortages and overcrowding, high mortality rates and underfunded medical care services, a mismatch of edu-cational training and job availability, and the impoverishment of a large section of society who fell outside the work-related social security system (young unemployed, single parents, widows, gyp-sies) and became dependent on inadequate social assistance systems.

(2) a set of popular expectations that the new, more efficient, market economies being built would finally be able to deliver on the promises of the past. Medical care would now be properly funded, houses would become available, jobs appropriate to qualifications obtained would be created and poverty would be alleviated.

(3) a new set of problems that directly flow from the introduction of market mechanisms and the privatisation of parts of the econ-omy. These problems include the creation of large-scale unem-ployment and a fall in living standards of the whole population as the efficiency of East European industry and the value of its products are actually tested on the market place. One dimension of this is the need to move rapidly from a policy of general universal subsidies (low priced housing etc.) to a policy of selec-tive benefits for those least able to cope in the new situation. An infrastructure capable of delivering unemployment benefits, retraining, and selective social benefits has to be constructed.

(4) a reduced government to take actions to solve these past and new problems and to meet popular expectations. The policy of the International Monetary Fund and other Western credit providers has clearly been to make assistance available only where policies are introduced that the government spending in certain areas of social welfare activity.

Given these problems it is not surprising that the concluding com-ments of this chapter are extremely cautious in predicting any major improvements in policy or provision in the short term.

Recent Developments in Social Policy

Although it is possible to analyse systematically, as we have just
done, the general nature of the problems facing social policy-makers
in a period of transition, the nature of actual recent social policy
changes has been far more *ad hoc*, random and hesitant. The immediate measures adopted and policy trends observable after 1989 across
the region may be characterised as follows:

- hurriedly introduced services for the new unemployed and fragile
  systems for compensating social security recipients and employees
  for rapid inflation;
- appeals to philanthropy and voluntary effort to fill gaps left by the
  withdrawal of state services;
- rapid removal of subsidies on many goods and services, including
  housing, with limited anticipation of social consequences;
- limited privatisation of some health and social care services
  (although this may speed up);
- emergence of independent social initiatives in the sphere of social
  care but with evident differential capacity of citizens to participate
  in these;
- desecularisation of education and pluralisation of control over
  schools and colleges;
- erosion of women's rights to some child-care benefits and services
  and free legal abortions (again the final outcome is not clear);
- deconstruction of the state social security system in favour of fully
  funded social insurance funds, often differentiated by categories of
  worker;
- abolition of many health and recreational facilities provided by
  firms for their employees and/or their conversion into local community or private facilities;
- ending of privileged access, by virtue of *nomenklatura* status, of
  the old state-party apparatus to special clinics and services;
- increase of local community control over local social provision, but
  in an impoverished context.

To illustrate the theme of *adhocism* and hesitancy, the case of
unemployment benefit and social assistance provision is useful. Open
unemployment, previously an unknown phenomenon, has been one
of the consequences of the post-1989 economic reforms. In early 1992
registered unemployment rates varied between about 4 per cent in
Romania and 14 per cent in Poland and Bulgaria, with figures of

around 8 per cent for Hungary and Czechoslovakia. Many unemployed are not registered and local unemployment rates can be much higher; figures of 35–40 per cent or even higher are more appropriate for some regions in Poland, Slovakia and elsewhere.

Hurriedly, in all countries, some form of unemployment compensation was introduced (Gotting, 1992). Of importance is the *retreat* in most countries from initial relatively generous income replacement rates and lengths of entitlement to less generous replacement rates and shorter periods of entitlement. These reductions in entitlement are taking place just at the point where more unemployed workers would have been expected to move from the status of initial unemployed to more long-term unemployed. The reality of the tight budget constraints usually imposed by IMF 'negotiated' loan conditions began in 1992 to loom larger than the initial political commitment to reduce the social and personal costs of transition. In all the countries of the region large numbers of unemployed have already or are about to run out of entitlement to benefit and be passed to the mercy of the fledgling social assistance schemes.

The residual social assistance schemes for those who run out of entitlement to unemployment benefit are, in general, devolved to *local* authorities and subject to the budget constraints of impoverished localities. Czechoslovakia provides the best example of a *national* commitment to a social minimum entitlement on a means-tested basis for long-term unemployed and others whose income falls below the prescribed minimum. The legislation gave the responsibility for implementing the scheme to social workers in district offices. They interpreted rather harshly the test of means that applicants are required to pass, undertaking home visits and ordering the selling of hi-fi and video equipment and unnecessary cars. In carrying out this 'relieving officer' role they are contributing to the impoverishment of sectors of the population.

The solution being offered to the long-term unemployed, accordingly, is a combination of a West European-style insurance compensation, which was designed to work in a flourishing economy with short-term unemployment, and a social assistance scheme which, in the context of generally egalitarian and poor societies, actually contributes to the impoverishment of its recipients. This observation, combined with the analysis referred to earlier that many citizens resort to a variety of sources of income to patch their life together, has prompted some commentators (Standing, 1992; Atkinson, 1992) to suggest that post-communist societies would have been better advised to opt for a simple basic income scheme for all employed and unemployed in the transition period. Although costly, it would have encouraged all the unemployed to declare their other sources of income (and hence bring the illegal economy into the taxable formal economy), it would have facilitated labour mobility (rather than leading to trade-union defence of indefensible jobs), and would have reduced the social tension between impoverished tax payers and slightly more impoverished benefit recipients. This 'institutional leap-frogging', whereby part of the former Soviet Union and Eastern Europe move to a basic income system of income maintenance more appropriate to developed post-industrial economies, might yet appear. The greater likelihood is, however, of a further erosion of social assistance entitlement and the further impoverishment of the emerging underclass of post-communism.

Developments in housing, medical care and education policy, while varied between countries also reflect policy borrowing from the more liberal or conservative Western welfare regimes. Policy borrowing from the social democratic Scandinavian welfare states is less evident. As with the mix of insurance and residual assistance in the case of unemployment benefit, it is not necessarily the case that these borrowed policies are most appropriate to the unique period of post-communist transition.

In the case of medical care policy, for example, there is a general move to facilitate private health services – strongly lobbied for by the impoverished medical profession – and accompanying fully-funded health insurance schemes for public services. Detailed examination of legislative proposals in this sphere suggest that in some countries categories of people – especially those working only illegally – will fall outside the insurance net. In the present budget-balancing period severe cuts have taken place in the resources available to some health services. In Poland the health service budget decreased by 42 per cent in 1991), and a quarter of hospital beds were projected to close. Both here and in Russia it is reported that mortality rates, which were already high by European standards, have worsened for certain age groups since 1989 (*Guardian*, 26 September 1992).

In housing, post-communist policy in most countries seems to be stacking up a number of problems for the future. Rent rises and mortgage interest rate rises consequent upon the reduction of subsidy and the move to market lending rates is leading to a rapid rise in the non-payment of rent. On some estates non-payment of rent has risen to 100 per cent. In the present ambiguous period where the security of the past – freedom from eviction – combines with the logic of the future – economic rents which are beyond the means of the poor – the emerging problem is hidden. In some countries the dilemma may be partially solved by the introduction of means-tested housing allowances, but given the constraints on budgets and the underdevelopment of an infrastructure for social assistance administration homelessness is bound to increase. Already there is evidence of this in most large cities across Central and Eastern Europe and as yet there is no adequate provision for them.

International Agencies and East European Social Policy

The concern about whether any of the models of Western welfare capitalism will prevail in Eastern Europe suggests a closer examination might be useful of the role being played by a variety of transnational and supranational agencies in the remaking of social policy in the region.

Before systematically analysing the impact of these agencies, I think we can say that the single most influential factor in the *initial* shaping of post-communist social policy has been the ready acceptance, first by the Polish government and then by most other governments of Eastern Europe, of the extreme *laissez-faire* economic advice proffered by Jeffrey Sachs, the Harvard economist. The popular disenchantment by professionals and some other sections of the population across Central and Eastern Europe with the egalitarianism of poverty, combined with the rise of the myth of the marketplace, allowed self-interested technocratic economic reformers to conspire with the ideologically driven free market proselytisers to reduce the living standards of hundreds of millions of people by one-third in the hope, increasingly not being borne out, that an efficient capitalist phoenix would rise from the ashes (Deacon *et al.*, 1992; Deacon, 1992). Perhaps the tragedy of Central and Eastern Europe in the early 1990s is that its necessary break from the failed command economics of bureaucratic state collectivism took place at the very moment when Keynesian and social reformist economic and social policy ideas were on the wane in the West. That, combined with the fact that the break also coincided with one of capitalism's worst periods of economic slump for decades, means that it now falls to others (social reformists East and West, social movement activists, trade-union members, scholars, intellectuals of other ideological per-

suasions) to repair the damage and re-begin the struggle for intra-
and inter-national social justice both within the East and between
East and West.

An examination of the role of international agencies in this context
suggests that a major ideological struggle is taking place over the
shape and content of the social security and income maintenance
aspects of social policy in the newly emerging democracies of Eastern
Europe. The struggle over what is to replace the social guarantees of
employment for all, whether it be a US-style individualist social
policy, a European-style corporatist or social market policy (with
which social democracy is merging), or a futuristic citizenship entitlement to a guaranteed income regardless of work contribution, is
being articulated and fought every bit as much at the level of supranational agencies as it is being played out within the confines of intra-
state politics. The IMF, the European Parliament and Commission,
and the ILO are as important actors in this connection as local
politicians and local trade-union and social movements. The arena of
social and political struggle over these issues is now a global one; and
it is already clear that the intersection of these competing pressures,
combined with the relative neglect of positive social policies that they
have engendered, may get conspire to derail the transition from
'communism' to market capitalism.

PART FOUR

Eastern Europe and Political Science

14

The Comparative Politics of Eastern Europe

DANIEL N. NELSON

At some point during 1989, as Eastern Europe's communist regimes abdicated power in the face of popular coups, I was asked by a journalist if such changes meant a career change for scholars of communist systems. I answered affirmatively, *if* such scholars had examined these regimes *only* as communist systems; yet, for scholars who had studied politics in the arena of Eastern Europe, I suggest a full and challenging career lay ahead.

Several years after these events, my speculation has given way to certainty; comparative communism as a subfield of political analysis passed away during 1989, while the comparative politics of Eastern Europe was rejuvenated.

In this chapter I intend to review briefly the past efforts at comparative studies of East European politics. I then turn to consider new directions and the principal questions about post-communist transitions that should guide scholarly research into the next decade.

The Birth and Death of Comparative Communism

Within a few years after Mikhail Gorbachev inaugurated changes that he could not control, practitioners of comparative communism were confronted with entirely new conditions for their research and analysis. Notwithstanding the continuation of communist rule in China, Cuba, North Korea and Southeast Asia, the subfield lost its *raison d'être*. But what had comparative communism sought to accomplish? How well did scholars and policy-analysts succeed? Was their any lasting contribution to political studies made by their research?

When communist parties gained power in Eastern Europe, China and North Korea in the late 1940s, a single form of totalitarian government was assumed to have been imposed from Moscow. An iron curtain metaphorically denoted the division of Europe, and the 'Soviet bloc' aggregated all states' and leaders' behaviour within the image of rigid uniformity. Consequently, broadly comparative analyses and rigorous hypothesis testing were unnecessary, while US and Western foreign policy interests, not theoretical concerns, dictated topics for scholarly attention.

That image was shaken by the 1956 revolution in Hungary and widespread, violent protests in Poland that had quickly followed the momentous 20th Party Congress speech of Nikita Khrushchev, admitting and detailing Josef Stalin's egregious violations of party and popular trust. And, despite the additions of other communist regimes in North Vietnam and Cuba in 1954 and 1959, respectively, the emergence of a volatile Sino-Soviet split in the early 1960s strengthened the image of a splintering worldwide communist movement.

Scholars trained in the old schools of Russian and Soviet studies were among the first to advocate comparative methods in order to examine broader questions. H. Gordon Skilling wrote of such a comparative approach in 1960, and later developed it into a text on *The Governments of Communist East Europe* (Skilling, 1960, 1966). Zbigniew Brzezinski's work *The Soviet Bloc*, notwithstanding its title, also recognised that the communist camp is 'neither homogeneous, monolithic nor unchanging'. But it remained for later authors to offer conceptual innovation and empirical analysis.

Discomfort with a constitutional and legal emphasis of political studies, and with the Eurocentric bias of education in 'comparative government', had first been evident in the mid-1950s. Led by then-'Young Turks' such as Roy Macridis, and accelerated by the work of the Committee on Comparative Politics of the US Social Science Council, a field of comparative politics was generated in the late 1950s and early 1960s (see, for instance, Eckstein, 1963; Mavrichs, 1968). Grounded primarily in structural-functional analysis – adapted from the sociological theories of Talcott Parsons and Max Weber – this genesis of comparative politics greatly affected the study of communist states as well.

Students of communist states began to explore the ideological and operational variations of communism, and to juxtapose such characteristics with the Western democracies (see, for instance, Brzezinski and Huntington, 1964). But it was a younger generation, for whom graduate work was completed in the 1960s, that broke entirely with the concepts and models of the early post-Second World War years.

A March 1967 issue of *Slavic Review* conveniently delimits the unequivocal 'birth' of comparative communism. In addition, Frederic J. Fleron's edited volume on *Communist Studies and the Social Sciences* (1969) and Roger E. Kanet's collection, *The Behavioral Revolution and Communist Studies* (1971) both featured younger scholars who emphasised the importance of empirical evidence in the study of Soviet and East European politics. Although some of the articles in both volumes were country-specific, the techniques of analysis and the questions explored – recruitment, policy-making, policy outcomes – stressed universal, 'functional' aspects of political systems.

Comparative communist or socialist studies had become more numerous and diverse by the mid-1970s. Included in these expanded endeavours were efforts to (1) create indicators of socioeconomic and political development applicable to all states ruled by communist systems, (2) classify communist economic systems, (3) gauge political behaviours cross-nationally, (4) compare patterns and methods of liberalisation, and (5) test the strength of association between socio-economic and political changes. With this expansion of topics and methodologies by the 1980s, a 'plurality of approaches had become accepted as legitimate or even desirable in relation to a group of political systems which were increasingly recognized to vary from each other and to contain a level of contradiction and complexity which made any single all-embracing formula more of an obstacle than an aid to understanding' (White, 1986, p. x). Country-specific studies guided by historical and cultural learning were never abandoned, and the coexistence of both research emphases was well established by the early 1970s.

Adherents of this new subfield of political science, most of whom worked in English-speaking advanced democracies, sought to move away from the premises of a monolithic and unchanging communist world, and towards a scientifically-oriented discipline of politics. The former never disappeared, and the relationship between area studies and behavioural social science for those studying communist systems was not always comfortable. But the questions for research and techniques applied were meant to raise the level of discourse to that of politics writ large, rather than to concentrate on the political history of one nation or state.

The Promise and Failure of Comparative Communism

Between a seminal issue of *Slavic Review* in 1967 and the end of 1989, the number of published scholarly articles, books and edited volumes in just three Western languages – English, French or German – that explicitly compared two or more communist states easily exceeded several thousand items, according to a computer search of several principal university libraries. Countless other publications focused on one country only, appeared in other languages, or were non-scholarly or policy-focused.

Although no rigorous consistency existed within such a vast litera-ture, these endeavours connoted an understanding of politics grounded in systemic functions that could be identified everywhere. Or, as Roger Kanet wrote more than two decades ago, these com-parative scholars assumed the presence of uniform political behav iours that '[could] be expressed in generalizations or theories with explanatory or predictive power' (1971, p. 2). Based on such expec-tations, and using standards for validity, reliability and testable prop-ositions, communist states could have become the subject of scientific inquiry.

Implicit to this optimistic premise was a questionable assumption – that the presence of *communist governments*, their highly uniform structures and processes, and their geographic proximity (all within the eastern half of Europe) enabled analysts to 'control' for 'political culture'. At the base of this logic was the epistemology of social science best explicated and argued by Adam Przeworski and Henry Teune in 1970. Written as the methodological treatise for a multi-nation study called 'Values in the Active Community', their volume argued for a *nomothetic* science of politics, rather than a discipline based on idiographic studies. The universality of political behaviour, not its description of each finite variant, was the desideratum of comparative social science. Przeworski and Teune went on to advo-cate specific statistical techniques by which to ensure equivalent measures across cases. Yet, their key contribution was to indict, by implication, studies bound by proper names (e.g., the *Polish* legislature, the *Bulgarian* army, etc.), and to insist on a research design based on 'most different systems'.

Scholarship that went no further than pointing out differences among communist states thus erred not only by focusing on the non-universal, but also by pursuing something akin to a 'most similar systems' research design – i.e., one meant to derive a sample that shared traits, thereby enabling the researcher to hold them 'constant'. Even if the methodological assumptions were not made apparent, research about communist systems often exhibited such tendencies for both pragmatic and intellectual reasons.

On the pragmatic side, Soviet, East European and Asian communist systems were grouped together because US and Western foreign policy denoted such states as adversaries, deserving the same treatment. Universities and analytical organisations brought the USSR and Warsaw Pact countries together because of Soviet hegemony, and languages of the region continued to be taught, more often than not, in 'Slavic' language departments (despite the non-Slavic character of Romanian or Hungarian). Further, Chinese and Russian could sometimes be found in departments of 'non-Western languages' (e.g., of Russian and Eastern studies) and Chinese and Soviet systems were not infrequently grouped in Sino-Soviet institutes.

Most students of states that were ruled by communist parties understood very well the powerful historical and cultural distinctions that drew sharp contrasts between states in Europe's eastern half. Despite the party hierarchies, central economic planning, and rhetorical bows to Marx and Lenin, these elements were never deeply rooted as, for example, Catholicism in Poland, Islam in Kazakhstan, or Confucianism in China. Failure to acknowledge these or other powerful constraints on political behaviour had the effect of denying historical and cultural factors only because they could not be quantified.

Similarities among communist systems that rationalised their comparison should have produced discernible consequences. Yet, the history of comparative communism reflects this lack of a truly unifying characteristic among cases being studied. With relatively few exceptions, edited volumes that pertained to communist states or socialist systems contained more country-specific analyses than cross-national comparisons. And, because data-collection efforts were limited by closed archives, linguistic limitations, or other problems, original sources and empirical resources of the subfield expanded very little until the Gorbachev era.

The limitations inherent to comparative communism were becoming apparent to its adherents by the mid and late 1970s. They acknowledged an 'elusive target' and the 'unfinished revolution' of the subfield, and conceded that paths by which students of such systems could begin to make substantial new progress were unclear (see, for instance, Tokes, 1975; Bunce and Echols, 1979).

'Without general theoretical concepts,' according to Teune, 'the study of Eastern European political systems [will] remain an "area study", a descriptive enterprise apart from mainstream political science' (1984, p. 130). Teune's point was telling about all students of communist politics; mainstream political science and traditional area studies were twains that would not meet. His attitude was clear, and he was probably correct to describe such area studies experts as sceptical about efforts to link broader theories to particular countries because of the distortions invoked.

Significant efforts in the late 1960s to mid-1970s to compare political elites among East European countries were undertaken by Beck, Welsh and others. They sought to test longitudinal and cross-national expectations about political behaviour (Beek, 1970; Welsh, 1973). Others, including John Echols, wrote about budgetary priorities and public policies using comparative expenditure data over time (see, for instance, Echols, 1981). A clear empirical portrait of diverse foreign and defence policies was found by studies of behaviour in the Warsaw Pact and among communist states (Linden, 1981; Nelson, 1977, 1986a).

Studies of communist regimes, however, were often comparative only insofar as the questions they raised were derived from or contributed to large issues that were thought to affect other communist systems. By considering broad issues of parliamentary development and institutional change in authoritarian environments, for example, scholars such as Olson and Simon sought to extend models relevant to many cases, although their work was in Poland (Olsen and Simon, 1982). The Polish case also received attention from Jack Bielasiak in articles about the working class in that country; but the issues raised in his 1980s work was on relationships between variables such as inequality and politicisation (Bielasiak, 1983).

Country-specific studies aimed at theoretical questions nevertheless made contributions to the larger aims that had become widespread in comparative communist scholarship. Uncovering, and where possible, explaining the 'diversity, change, paradox and irony' within the political life of such systems became a leitmotif of the subfield.

Once having surmounted the hold of a totalitarian model for such regimes, practitioners in policy analysis and university-based scholars saw more clearly that these were not nation-states with identical frameworks of government, rules of the game, or political leadership styles. The constancy of totalitarianism gave way to the constancy of dynamic change, even within political environments where opposition was banned and the media controlled.

Attention turned to the effects of new leaders on public policies (Bunce, 1981), on policy initiatives and regime support (Nelson, 1986b), on electoral outcomes (Prarda, 1986), and on the inconsistent and contradictory aspects of regimes once thought to be monolithic and resolute. Wider access to data from internal opinion surveys or budgetary information, or greatly expanded surveys of émigrés (Millar, 1987) also enabled some researchers to do much more in-depth, empirical research within one state.

Efforts made by some scholars to extend the study of communist systems into the mainstream of comparative politics, however, were not characteristic of the entire subfield. The substantial difference between the subfield when it emerged in the 1960s, from its condition a generation later suggests frustration mixed with progress.

An irrefutable empirical record had been established that communist regimes were diverse and dynamic, subjected always to needs for legitimacy, popular support, effective policy-making and implementation, and other requisite elements of political systems. Criteria for merging of political science and comparative politics, however, were never fully achieved.

Remaining an obstacle to further development of the subfield was the core assumption – that states distinguished by virtue of a particular kind of one-party rule warranted separate attention. Unlike studies of underdeveloped states, the nomenclature of communist rule was not amenable to integral or ordinal level 'measurement'; it was unquestionably a nominal variable – communist or not – rather than a value that could be 'scaled'. An idiographic distinction setting this subfield apart from all other parts of political science or companions in comparative politics was always present.

Focusing attention on European communisms may have been a plausible argument for control of cultural variables, were it not for the obvious historical and cultural differences that pervade the continent's eastern half. No one for whom that region is even vaguely familiar could accept the suggestion that methodological concern motivated comparative communism to focus studies on variations within such a region.

Indeed, the traditional organisation of historical and linguistic study plus the political and security-driven organisation of Western studies of Europe's eastern half perpetuated a feature of communist studies that was incompatible with its integration into comparative political science. Instead of, for example, considering leadership recruitment and legitimacy of developing states by including cases such as Romania, Bulgaria and Albania, these countries were incorporated with the quite different environments of Czechoslovakia and Poland. And, instead of considering China's response to revolutionary turmoil in light of other non-European cases, its revolution was juxtaposed with the French, Russian or others in Europe to draw generalisations.

The weight of its own politically derived genesis led to the belaboured breathing of comparative communism. The movement away from a totalitarian model, and the development of some cross-national and empirical components, succeeded in diminishing the distance between an academic field and the socioeconomic and political realities it sought to explore. But in none of the states that had been overtaken by communist party governments were political dynamics controlled by the ideology or apparatus of communist rule. And, paradoxically, the more that study of such systems concentrated on those systems individually, the more those endeavours missed the dynamism that was to culminate in the late 1980s.

Towards a Comparative Politics of Eastern Europe

In the aftermath of 1989–91, scholars of communist systems might be tempted to fold up their tents, elect early retirement, or concentrate on North Korea.

Instead, the end of communist regimes meant the demise of a regime type, not the irrelevance of comparative scholarship on the region. The Poles, Czechs, Romanians, Ukrainians, and all the rest remain and confront intractable problems. Were the significance of the realignment from communist to non-communist taken to the extreme, we might presume that none of the socioeconomic or political knowledge gained while communist regimes were in power would inform us about post-communist transitions. But nothing could be further from the truth.

Several compelling issues militate for attention to the comparative politics of Eastern Europe. All argue strongly for an investment of scholarly energy and policy-maker's attention.

First, the seemingly abrupt demise of communist regimes in 1989 to the end of 1991 (when the Soviet Union collapsed) was not abrupt at all. Many of the same political and socioeconomic dynamics continue today, albeit with greater openness. Contrary to the image of a paroxysm of sudden change, a prolonged process of falling economic performance, rising social malaise, and haemorrhaging political authority plagued Leninist party governments for decades. Public opinion data, economic performance indicators and measures of social unrest suggest that, during the 1970s and 1980s, European communist regimes engaged in a dynamic contest to constrain the widening of political life and 'public legitimation' (see Nelson, 1992). They lost decisively in 1989, but they had been losing for the previous twenty years.

Most important, the processes that led to a wall being torn down, a playwright becoming president, and a tyrant being executed, are *ongoing*. That the communist *nomenklatura* held all important state, economic and military/security posts until 1989 does not necessarily mean that their power had not waned to the point of impotence much earlier. Conversely, seeing non-communists in those roles today means only that popular expectations have now passed to the new politicians and bureaucrats – i.e., erstwhile dissidents. These new leaders, notwithstanding their initial honeymoon, all reached the end of a brief period during which courage and anti-communism had been enough to sustain their governments. But now, in very different circumstances they must make policy that engenders performance, production and progress. The 'genie' of public legitimation, re-born during the last two decades *while communists still ruled*, cannot now be forced back into the bottle.

Scholars who examine widespread and long-term processes of socioeconomic and political change are those who can understand post-communist transitions. By contrast, analysts for whom the Politburo and the queueing at Lenin's mausoleum sufficed as a window on the politics of communist states will have fewer tools with which to engage in the comparative politics of Europe's eastern half. Scholars who have examined the region for some time are precisely those most able, if they have focused on political dynamics rather than on one kind of regime, to see the processes that transcend the communist/post-communist dichotomy.

Second, the wrenching shift from communist to post-communist may be one of the least important for Europe's eastern half. As counter-intuitive as that might sound, the rationale for saying so is compelling. The nominal distinction between communist and non-communist is misleading and superficial. Far more vital for East European populations are ordinal and interval-level distinctions – the *degree* of political legitimacy, the *extent* to which security is achieved, and the *level* of socioeconomic development. These critical issues demand comparative and longitudinal studies, incorporating data from communist and post-communist periods.

Eastern Europe's socio-economic underdevelopment, for example, is more important to the region's populations than is the simplistic communist/non-communist split. They recognise that the climb towards par with Western Europe will be long, steep and uncertain (see Rose, 1992b). But the critical goal is recovery – to return the European corridor from Poland to Bulgaria back to the relative position it enjoyed before the Second World War (i.e., *more* developed or advanced than Spain, Norway, most of Italy, or Greece and, for a region such as the Czech Lands of Bohemia and Moravia, one of the principal manufacturing areas of Europe).

As proto-democratic post-communist governments reveal themselves to suffer from ineptitude, corruption and other ills that populations found objectionable about communist regimes, the significance of free and fair elections, laws that guarantee political rights, and other institutions of democracy will be less relevant. Indeed, in the hands of demagogues, these performance failures can be used as crude tools with which to chip away at public commitment to democracy. Among populations that have known little of free government or free market, it will not take much for them to envisage foreign and domestic peril and to seek scapegoats for their frustration and misery.

Such discouraging scenarios can be avoided only with research that treats these erstwhile communist regimes not as a group of geographically contiguous nation-states or as the universe of post-communist systems. Larger questions about the paths for recovery and re-development can be asked and answered only through broader inquiry of comparative research in which knowledge about nations and states of a region is embedded in theory.

Third, we must be wary of proclamations about East Europe (or any other region) that extrapolate from one country's experience or from a brief period of observation. How one knows something about an ethnically, culturally, and historically diverse region *without* comparative efforts should be questioned. The epistemology of Eastern Europe cannot be based on an accumulation of country-specific knowledge or on quick snapshots garnered from visits of limited duration in the aftermath of 1989. Unlike Latin America, which shares the Spanish language and Roman Catholicism (with the obvious exception of Brazil and indigenous Indian cultures), Eastern Europe contains far more heterogeneity in a smaller area. Yet few Latin Americanists would purport to speak of Argentina's transition from authoritarianism in the same breath as Nicaragua's.

The most profound issues concerning Eastern Europe are not defined by the boundaries of nation-states. The survivability of fledgling democratic institutions in Poland cannot be predicted by observations drawn from the Bulgarian or Hungarian experience. Poland's prognosis, however, can be illuminated by considering the role of occupation, religiosity, education, gender and other factors in electoral support for extremist political candidates from the entire region.

Similarly, our epistemological assumptions about a region such as Eastern Europe will be critical in determining how we interpret experiences in creating a free market. Poland is often cited as the critical 'test case' – as Poland's effort to create a market economy within the briefest possible time (which I call 'cold turkey capitalism') is assessed, its success or failure will be diffused among all of post-communist Europe. But to what degree, if any, can the Polish experience instruct, guide or serve as a model for other East European states? Here the relationships between politics and market (to be discussed further below) enter into the equation, with the limits of applicability for the Polish model being drawn not only because of 'economic' differences (e.g., the existence of private agriculture even during the communist period) but also because of political factors.

How we come to *know* anything about 'macro-issues' such as the creation of a market economy and the applicability of one model requires, then, a capacity to compare across countries and over time. In this regard, little that matters will be known unless the comparative politics of Eastern Europe is energised and extended.

New Directions for Analysis and Research

The Politics of Transition

Implicit to the foregoing discussion are tasks for the comparative politics of Eastern Europe. Put succinctly, the eastern half of Europe faces three tasks of immense proportions – democracy, market and security. Democratic structures, processes and the norms of their operation must be institutionalised. An economy based on the largely unfettered exchange of resources for goods and services must be put into operation. And, most important, new bases for security must be found and solidified.

Unfortunately for the nations and states of Europe's eastern half, all three must be pursued simultaneously. The multiple transitions required in post-communist Europe are dramatically and dangerously unlike other late-twentieth-century European democratic transitions such as Portugal and Spain. In contrast to misleading comparisons offered by many cursory observers, the Iberian transitions and those of Eastern and post-Soviet Europe have little in common.

Both Spain and Portugal, during the period of Franco and Salazar dictatorships, respectively, had moved from outright corporatist economies to expanding market-based economies. Foreign investment had grown rapidly in both countries during the decade prior to the end of dictatorship, with Spain's phenomenal development along the Mediterranean coast leading the way. It was in 1962 that the World Bank had given a favourable report on Spain and a Development Plan Commissariat was formed – the report of which was issued in 1964 laying the groundwork for private and government investments over the next decade. In the years that followed, Spain's economy grew more rapidly than most of Western Europe, with an average annual industrial expansion of 15 per cent between the early 1960s and early 1970s. And, in the mid-1960s, some limited opening of media and politics began to occur, such that a 'constitutional appearance' was created via the 1966 State Organic Law and other steps.

Portugal's transition from dictatorship began because of the painful cost of colonial wars in Africa. When Salazar died in 1970 the dictatorship struggled on, with right-wing senior commanders insisting that the colonial wars continue, otherwise Prime Minister Caetano would face a coup. But these wars had turned middle-ranking officers to the left, and their Armed Forces Movement (MFA) grew as the weight of anti-guerilla combat fell on their ranks.

A *coup d'état* by these younger officers in April 1974, coordinated by Major Otelo Saraiva de Carvalho, led to a turbulent two years in which the far left came close to gaining power. But the confrontational behaviour of Portuguese Communists led by Alvaro Cunhal, the rupture of the political left's alliance with the military, and the mobilisation of Catholics and other forces to oppose communists changed the tide. After an early threat of a leftist coup in Portugal, communists were pushed to the periphery by the end of 1975, a constitution promulgated in 1976, and the Socialists of Mario Soares and centrists held sway in elections of 1979. Key to the Portuguese democratic transition were numerous internal and idiosyncratic factors. Yet Portugal's difficulties were not exacerbated by imminent external threat (Lisbon was a charter member of NATO) or by a rigidly planned economy devoid of private ownership or entrepreneurial skills; it did not have to confront simultaneous transitions in market and security arenas while it was fighting for democracy (see Maxwell, 1986).

In Spain, Socialist Prime Minister Gonzalez became the dominant political figure in 1982 elections by soundly defeating Adolfo Suarez and his coalition of moderate parties. Only a half-decade after the end of Franco's regime, during the midst of considerable public angst about economic performance and the reliability of democratic institutions, Gonzalez won a vote which, by its decisiveness and turnout, 'introduced a triple injection of legitimacy, autonomy and efficiency' into the nascent Spanish democracy (Maravall and Santamaria, 1986). Between 1976 and 1982, Basque and Falangist (fascist) terror, and inflation that rose to 30 per cent and unemployment above 15 per cent by 1981, all had fostered doubts about the survivability of Spanish democracy. The semi-comic occupation of the Cortes by disgruntled officers as part of an attempted military coup in February 1981 occurred at the height of such self-doubt. But the 1982 election underscored Spaniards' desire to give democracy a real chance with a resounding vote against extremism and for one political direction.

In both cases, however, strong support from Western political parties and governments (including covert assistance to anti-leftist parties and politicians), economies that had already made much of the transition away from state-centred direction during the 1960s and early 1970s, and an ample mix of other stabilising institutions (the Church, a business community committed to a democratic transition, etc.) aided the transformation.

By contrast, Eastern Europe reached 1989 with 45 years of centralised, state-owned economies and widespread threats, implied or actual. Portugal and Spain had 'only' to institutionalise democracy, which was no easy task for either country during the late 1970s. Had they been trying simultaneously to tear down a clumsy and inefficient state-owned economy while desperately searching for bilateral or multilateral ways to balance threats with capacities, democracy would have taken a back seat to other crises. Further, had Spaniards and Portuguese regarded external threat as high, the luxury of moving towards an open and competitive system would have seemed less justifiable to many. As it was, both countries had to confront and overcome anti-democratic parties, inflation and unemployment brought on by a global recession, and other debilitating problems. But Portuguese and Spanish democrats did not have to defend the 'affordability' of democratic values such as pluralism, tolerance and rule of law. In a milieu of international security, and where substantial foreign investment was already providing capital for growth in the private sector, extremists of the left and right had fewer opportunities to marshal popular fears to their side.

The interwoven and conflictual ties and dependencies among goals of democracy, market and security ought to be at the core of comparative analyses of Eastern Europe. In all three directions, only comparative analyses provide grounds for explaining progress or lack thereof. The three universal goals of post-communist transitions offer guideposts for future research emphases within the comparative politics of Eastern Europe.

Democracy

Eastern Europe now consists of proto-democracies. These are political systems in which one sees parliaments, parties and elections, and the rudiments of representative governance such as free and fair elections, due process in the judicial procedure, openness in public discourse via independent media, and other tenets of democracy. Yet, these are simultaneously systems in which neither public attitudes nor the making of public policy mirror the norms of equal opportunity, tolerance, or public accountability that citizenry within democracies have come to expect. This is not to say that the Czech Republic's progress towards a smoothly functioning democracy can be equated with Bulgaria's – but, rather, that one continuum exists along which post-communist states are moving at different speeds having begun at different points.

To develop an operational definition of democracy is far beyond the scope of this chapter. Nevertheless, comparative studies of proto-democracies within Eastern Europe cannot avoid judgements about, or measure of, movement along the democratic continuum.

Adam Przeworski denotes democracy simply and usefully as a particular political arrangement characterised by its system of processing and terminating intergroup conflicts. Democracy, in Przeworski's view, institutionalises continual conflicts by subjecting the interests of all groups to uncertainty (Przeworski, 1986). Authoritarians abhor uncertainty, argues Przeworski, and consequently exert control over outcomes of conflicts among interests by using intimidation by the secret police, the threat of military force, and party discipline. These tools of absolute control are denied in democratic systems. Przeworski's core theme – that democracy institutionalises uncertainty – is not far from the notion of institutionalising accommodation found in Arend Lijphart's concept of consociationalism in plural societies (Lijphart, 1977). In these and other modern renditions of democratic theorising, managing conflicting interests rather than repressing them is the essence of democracy.

The comparative politics of Eastern Europe ought to direct substantial effort to testing this and other notions regarding core indices of post-authoritarian transitions. Decreasing concentration of control over outcomes should thus be evident in democratising systems; over time, changing patterns of resource allocation, shifting coalitions in legislative votes, and less dominance of one institution, group or party in prounouncements about or deriving benefits from public policies are among the indicators one might utilise.

Regardless of one's specific research design, the paths being taken after 1989 require explanation. If, as we might expect, a Przeworski-like approach reveals differential levels and rates of decreasing control over outcomes (or increasing uncertainty over outcomes), then comparative politics of Eastern Europe must ask 'why?'.

Part of an explanation may have already been suggested by Alfred Stepan when he pointed to the 'independent weight' and 'distinctive contribution' to the re-democratisation process made by the actual route taken toward that goal. It makes a big difference, Stepan implies, when authoritarianism ends in one case because of internal restoration after external conquest, versus, for example, a society-led regime termination, a party pact, or an organised violent revolt. How re-democratisation starts will affect how it ends (Stepan, 1986).

Yet the comparative politics of Eastern Europe should engage in much broader and all-inclusive analyses. We do not have, unless we were to subscribe to a deterministic interpretation of world history, a parsimonious explanation for 1989 events: the poor performance of communist systems, the mounting public antipathy towards communist party elites, Mikhail Gorbachev's abandonment of the Brezhnev Doctrine of limited sovereignty, the Reagan Administration's military buildup that added to the Soviet/East European military burden, and a host of other factors. Even participants in the events that led communists to retreat from power noted 'centrifugal forces of the economy, international developments and social contradictions' behind systemic changes that brought an end to the German Democratic Republic (Neubert, 1990, p. 209). Empirical and longitudinal studies may reveal that the demise of authoritarian communist regimes had similar undercurrents in all of communist Europe, and that re-democratisation began in much the same way across the region (albeit with nuances in timing and degree of violence). If I am correct, then we would have to look further and deeper to explain variation in levels and rates of reduced outcome-control (i.e. dominance of resource allocation).

That further effort ought to start by considering the relationships among democracy, market and security.

Market

'Free market democracy' rolls off the lips of many policy-makers as if it were one word. In fact, the post-communist goals of democracy and market *are* intertwined, but conflictually so.

Outcroppings of that conflict are not hard to see. Poland's 1990 economic miracle did not occur, and less than one year after Prime Minister Mazowiecki launched a sudden and dramatic shift towards ending his country's Stalinist economic system he had suffered a dramatic political defeat, unable to even gain enough votes in the presidential election to reach the run-off ballot against Lech Walesa (see Chapter 3). Two years later, despite some modest good news about the Polish economy, citizens were more convinced than ever that the future was bleak, and that their new leaders are just as culpable as the old communists. After 1991 parliamentary elections, the Polish legislature was splintered badly into 29 parties, and unstable parliamentary conditions, mixed with presidential threats to assert emergency powers, have characterised Poland through 1992. Despite the growth of a substantial entrepreneurial class, many of whom were the former *nomenklatura* of Poland, strong pressure for slowing the economic transition and for retreating from the original Balcerowicz plan of January 1990 has been felt.

The Polish case is cited merely to provide a tangible sense of the disjuncture between democracy and market. Creating a free market economy suddenly, as opposed to the two centuries since the Industrial Revolution that Western Europe and North America have used to fine-tune the relationship between private ownership and government regulation, has no blueprint. Everyone engaged in this effort is flying blindly.

But it takes no great insight to recognise that the rapid abandonment of a state-controlled economy, including freeing prices, selling state-owned property, making the currency convertible and other steps, sends waves of dislocation throughout the economy. Public support for the general notion of a free market economy quickly begins to break down when the individual costs of that shift are made known.

The transformation of East European economies towards a free market is thus fully intertwined with the maturation of a democratic system, and significantly in conflict with it. The Chinese Communist Party has seen this conflict and has rejected political liberalisation. One cannot imagine, however, a self-sustaining free market economy that is denied, in perpetuity, the expression of self-interest in the political sphere. An interest and need to affect policy outcomes follows closely from entrepreneurial activity, and this linkage between economic and political change seems impossible to contain.

The comparative politics of Eastern Europe must address such a reciprocal relationship. Is progress along the continuum of democracy associated with measures of free market economic activity? As private economic transactions increase, and as unemployment, inflation and other indices fluctuate, do cross-national and longitudinal indices of democracy suggest a strong association in post-communist Europe? Conversely, if political systems exhibit greater competition (i.e., less control over outcomes as Przeworski implied), are steps towards a market economy accelerated, broader, or more effective in creating growth? Because the number of cases is so small, these analyses might best be undertaken at subnational levels – comparable units of local government, for example.

For the comparative politics of Eastern Europe, then, 'politics and markets' is a theme of enormous importance in the next decade or more. Much as Charles E. Lindblom meant in his pioneering work in the late 1970s, the fundamental questions about politics and market systems lie in the relationships between these domains. The functions of government, Lindblom correctly observed (as did Marx), depend substantially on the role of the market. At a time when the relationships between free government and free market are developing and conflictual, the fulcrum of Eastern Europe's future lies in the orderly transfer of economic control from the state to the market (see Lindblom, 1977).

Security

Democracy, a free market, and new bases for security are everywhere the principal goals of post-communist transitions. In some areas, from what was Yugoslavia and the Caucasus, it seems a foregone conclusion that none of these aims will be achieved. Necessary for the achievement of any of these goals, however, is a secure environment. Without security, fledgling systems cannot devote resources to the arduous tasks of building a new polity and economy from the rubble of communist rule. Where there is no security, democracy and market will not long survive. Paradoxically, where there is no democracy or free market, resources with which to create and maintain security are too little and too undependable.

These assertions imply the reciprocal relationships that, once again, must be the focal points for comparative politics in the East European arena. Countries that are democratic are very likely to be those in which economic strengths, social cohesion and political consensus have been adequate to balance threats, thereby ensuring physical and material requisites of security. Democratic principles may enhance such capacities, but democracy itself cannot be nurtured in an insecure environment.

If democracy and market are 'security dependent', then the cost of insecurity is a weakened prognosis for both democracy and a free market. This is a fragile nexus, but a vital one. External peril and internal demagoguery can both displace free markets and free governments unless security has been assured.

The comparative politics of Eastern Europe needs to confront these dependencies. Measures of insecurity depend on the level of analysis (individual, group, locale, nation). Yet, this concept is not confined to a simple dichotomy (secure versus insecure). Through public surveys, military imbalances, indicators for social unrest and economic distress, a gauge of insecurity is plausible. As such systemic vulnerability rises and falls, we need to assess the association with both tenets of democracy and free market economic activity.

Democratisation and privatisation, the buzz-words of Western policy-makers when articulating their desires for Eastern Europe, fail to acknowledge the linkage to security. On individual levels, perceptions of threat appear to be associated with intolerance and authoritarian tendencies. Were that tie demonstrated throughout Europe's eastern half, then the association between market and democracy so often observed becomes a matter for further empirical research, with the degree of systemic security being a determining environmental factor. If political democracy cannot be decoupled from the market, might it not be because the resources of the market enable a system to secure itself? These kinds of multifaceted questions lie ahead for our studies of proto-democracies in Eastern Europe.

Conclusion

The demands that will be placed on students of post-communist Europe are extraordinary. Broad and imposing questions, rapid and interrelated changes, and minimal prior theorising about the region make the social scientists' task daunting.

Comparative communism was a subfield of short duration and truncated accomplishments. Yet its practitioners laid the groundwork for what must now be attempted. This is not the time for minute, configurative descriptions of every variation among each system, old and new, in Europe's eastern half. Change is too rapid, and issues are too urgent, to fail to address the most vital concerns.

And, as discussed above, the most urgent concern is the relationship between democracy, market and security. Post-communist proto-democracies are not like other transitions from authoritarianism since they must pursue all three goals at once. Theirs is a more devilishly complex, and decidedly more dangerous passage.

Comparative studies of the region's politics, dedicated to discovering these relationships, and using findings to build explanations of such transitions, can play a critical role. As a worthy successor to a generation which sought to advance comparative scholarship within the former communist world, the emerging subfield can make far more generalisable contributions to the study of politics than their predecessors could ever have believed possible.

15

History, Europe and the Politics of the East

PAUL G. LEWIS

The End of History?

Since the events of 1989, East European politics as they have been understood for the past few decades have not so much undergone transformation and profound change as simply passed from the contemporary world stage and, in many ways, entered the realm of history. This statement may be understood to refer to both parts of the expression. For the great bulk of the post-Second World War period 'Eastern Europe' was made up of the territories that lay between Western Europe, for the most part closely tied in with the North Atlantic community and its gradually strengthening internal relations of economic and political cooperation, and the Soviet Union, whose specific principles of political activity and economic organisation were carefully applied to the region it then controlled in the intention of developing a rival international community distinct from and largely antagonistic to that of the West. These mechanisms of regional control were, it transpired, no longer operative in 1989 while the very basis of the regional power structure, the Soviet Union, itself collapsed in 1991.

If, then, post-war 'Eastern Europe' in this sense has now passed from the scene, superseded by a unified Germany, renewed conceptions of Central Europe, notions of a Baltic community and the more traditionally oriented Balkans, so have its specific forms of political life been dismantled and characteristic activities overtaken by new modes of behaviour. Party-based bureaucratic rule has been replaced by a varying mix of parliamentarism, presidential authority and constitutional governance. Dominant communist organisations have been disbanded and just some of their formerly numerous followers regrouped into unconvincing social democracies and rump (though by no means insignificant) leftist conservatives. While post-communist structures may remain quite fluid and their institutions only partly formed, all public manifestations of communist rule have been swiftly dismantled and once-awesome seats of authority like Central Committee buildings dedicated to other purposes – like that of exchanging stocks and fostering incipient capitalist activity. Both the Eastern Europe that emerged from the battlefields of the Second World War and the Soviet-derived form of politics it saw develop, then, are in this sense now things of the past.

This rather simple perspective, however, by no means exhausts the range of views on the historical status of developments in Eastern Europe and their implications for more general processes of political change. While discussion of the changes in East European politics has been permeated by an awareness of 'history' and the way in which the demise of communism might relate to its course of development there has, nevertheless, been no consensus about what this might imply in more concrete terms. One view was that 1989 saw the removal of externally imposed limits to change and a 'rebirth of history' which opened the way to the democratic development of East Europe (Glenny, 1993). Another, based on rather different premises, was that the late 1980s had seen the 'end of history' and that for this reason the supremacy of liberal democracy was now assured (Fukuyama, 1989). Both interpretations, it should be noted, refer not just to the historical context and broad implications of the changes in East Europe but also to their intimate relationship with the spread of democracy. In this respect, Glenny's view is straightforward and does not require any lengthy explication. His argument was that the stability of post-war Eastern Europe had been bought at the expense of the democratic development of the area, and that the removal of the structures that had maintained its stability opened the way to the resumption of democratic development.

Fukuyama's argument, however, was a little more complicated and repays further investigation. Why, for example, should the collapse of communism be equated with the end of history – which, in other repects, one might have thought would gain in impetus and acceler-ation from changes like those seen in East Europe? The basis of the answer he offers lies in the very specific understanding of history and historical processes he employs. Attempting to go beyond the commonplace statements of journalists in early 1989 which merely noted the apparent waning of the Cold War, Fukuyama aimed to establish a broader conceptual framework within which it would be possible to distinguish 'what was essential and what was contingent or accidental in world history'. It was based on the philosophical ideas of Hegel and his conclusion that it was the principles of liberal democracy that provided the basis for the ultimate form of the modern state. Later challenges to this ideological dominance in the form of fascism and communism, he now claimed, had now been seen off, enabling liberal democracy once more to present itself as the only viable form of government for the modern world.

While situated on a higher intellectual plane than 'everyday journalism', it could well be argued that Fukuyama's ideas were no less contingent than those of other observers and that his transposition of Hegel's ideas to the late twentieth century was itself arbitrary and unhistorical. Hegel was, after all, more concerned with the trajectory of the 'world spirit' and its incarnation in the Prussian state than with modern political ideology. And it is by no means clear how or why liberal democracy is the necessary outcome of a dialectical process that leads to that specific political conclusion – even though this may have appeared a reasonable enough conclusion in the late 1980s and early 1990s (Adams, 1991). It is by no means clear, too, what precisely is the liberal democracy to which Fukuyama refers. The idea of liberalism spans diverse traditions and involves contrasting conceptions of political order. Liberalism itself cannot really be presented as a unity, while the balance between any form of 'liberalism' and 'democracy' also remains uncertain (Held, 1992, p. 23). It might, as Miliband suggests, be more straightforward and less confusing in this context to refer simply to capitalist rather than liberal democracy; if the final victory of liberalism and democracy remains open to substantial doubt, that of capitalism at least seemed more assured under contemporary conditions (Miliband, 1992, p. 108).

The supremacy of any kind of democracy is, further, hardly a certainty in post-communist Eastern Europe. Ideas both of a rebirth of history and of an end to history are linked to a resurgence of political democracy – but in practical terms this remains very much a question to be examined rather than a conclusion to be assumed. The historical basis for any idea of a return to democracy is, for example, a tenuous one. Only in Czechoslovakia, a country itself destined for a short post-communist existence, could any claim be made for a pre-Second World War democratic tradition – and even that was open to challenge from the Slovak population. Unlike some of the recent Southern European transitions to democracy, those in Eastern Europe could hardly be placed in the context of redemocratisation (Lewis, 1990, p. 247). Any idea of a 'return to democracy' is, then, more of an ambition (and one which involves a considerable amount of hopeful travelling) than a fixed itinerary. More realistic guidance in terms of historical perspective has been offered by Joseph Rothschild (1989) in his account, conceived some time before the major events of the communist collapse, of a *Return to Diversity*.

1989 might have seen an 'end to history' in the sense suggested by Fukuyama – that of the disappearance of the Marxist-Leninist challenge to liberal democracy as an alternative model of social development. But in more concrete terms it meant a return to history for the countries of Eastern Europe in the context of their enhanced national independence, and greater leeway in the exercise of political and social choice. After the Stalinist period East Central Europe's traditional diversities, historical peculiarities and sovereign orientations were gradually able, although at an irregular tempo, to reassert themselves. While growing in strength and importance, these tendencies nevertheless remained submerged and controlled by an ossifying, Soviet-dominated political superstructure until the events of 1989. Far from having ended, then, history appears to have been a living presence in the political life of Eastern Europe for some time. The important question is, of course, which or whose history. Fukuyama's Hegelian claim on behalf of liberal democracy is one thing; Glenny's somewhat general idea of a return to an interrupted course of democratic development is another. But more recent history has also made a significant comeback in contemporary East European politics. The appeal of pre-communist models of social models of development during the latter years of communist rule was hardly surprising, and they provide an obvious point of reference with the ending of the Cold War. Somewhat more striking has been the highlighting of recent communist experience as a positive reference point in countries like Poland, whose movement away from orthodox communism began at an early stage and placed considerable material costs upon their population.

A survey conducted in June 1992, for instance, suggested that 31 per cent of Poles would be happy to return to the conditions that had prevailed before the elections of June 1989, that is, before the victory of Solidarity and the collapse of communist rule. This form of historic nostalgia was less pronounced amongst the young, better educated, the more highly paid and those in those better jobs. As many as 45 per cent of the unemployed and 41 per cent of the low paid were however, not surprisingly, less enchanted by the prospect of capitalist democracy and the problems that had attended its development in post-communist Eastern Europe. It was such sentiments that under-laid the surprisingly good showing of the post-communist Democratic Left Alliance in the 1991 elections and the continuing attraction of the otherwise discredited communist period. Nor were Poles alone in holding such views. Around a third of Czechs, Hungarians, Poles and Slovaks thought that their conditions of life had not undergone an significant change since 1989. But while a further survey showed that 44 per cent of Poles thought that conditions had worsened, as many as 61 per cent of Hungarians expressed this distinctly negative view. Communist, as well as pre-communist, history is part of the East European present, and the conflicts and syntheses that emerge be-tween different affiliations and legacies of former orders contribute to the uncertainties and instabilities of contemporary political life there.

West of Centre? Post-Communist Europe between East and West

The awareness that 1989 had seen a transformation of major histori-cal proportions was closely linked with the evolution of attitudes towards Europe and changes in the views held by citizens of the former communist states concerning their identity as members of a broader international community. Developments in both West and East contributed to these changes. Part of the strengthening European identity derived from the dynamism of Western Europe and the success of the Community that many of its members had formed, which showed itself capable of maintaining and extending democratic practices whilst establishing relatively effective patterns of economic growth and technological development. A combination of this kind was strikingly different from the experience of the inter-war years. Eastern Europe had, indeed, not been wholly excluded from these processes. The special relation of the GDR with the *Bundesrepublik* gave it access to EC markets and effectively trans-formed it into a junior member of the West European organisation – although with the effect more of ameliorating some of its current problems than of providing any basis for a long-term solution to them.

Hungary and Poland had also sought closer relations with the West, but many of the ties formed had been designed to buttress the position of the crumbling communist elite and prop up existing structures of production and consumption. The net result of the opening to the West and exposure to the global processes of contemporary capitalism in both cases was the rapid accumulation of awesome levels of national debt whose effects have continued to bedevil processes of post-communist economic transformation. This, however, was primarily the fault of mismanagement and faulty judgement on the part of the East and did not reflect on the status or attractiveness of the western Community. Indeed, its relative success was all the more striking in view of the sluggish pace of development in the Eastern bloc and the nature of problems whose enormity even Mikhail Gorbachev did not realise at the outset of his *perestroika* crusade. While remaining communist in form the content of East European political life had gradually, as we have seen, become more national and traditional in content, a process that reflected further on the bankrupt nature of the Marxist-Leninist project and its failing capacity to offer any solution to the problems of late-twentieth-century Eastern Europe.

The importance of Europe, both past and present, and of specifically European traditions for the Eastern transformation was also reflected in other dimensions of the discussion that developed during the 1980s. As 'Eastern Europe' began to show signs of losing its primary post-war meaning, the idea of a 'Central Europe' re-emerged in some quarters and gained acceptance as an attractive and viable framework within which post-communist Czechoslovakia, Hungary and Poland could locate their future development. As a late-twentieth-century phenomenon the idea of Central Europe was particularly associated with the pervasive disenchantment that burdened communist rule within Europe during the 1980s and, understandably enough, took on a marked anti-Russian tinge. The key debate of the late communist period was launched by Czech writer Milan Kundera (1984) and cast in terms of a contrast identified between 'European' and 'Russian' culture. It was a view whose assumptions and implications were far from uncontested, and they provided a source of considerable intellectual controversy in the period immediately preceding the collapse of the communist regime (Schöpflin and Wood, 1989).

Much of this debate, then, hinged on perceptions of Russia itself and its relationship with Europe, a feature that could hardly fail to be prominent after several decades of conflict and repression throughout the region under the banner of Soviet Russian communism. But the roots of the Central European concept lay elsewhere and they, too, were surrounded by certain conflicts and uncertainties. In contrast to a German idea of *Mitteleuropa* promoted during the First World War, that of a modern Central Europe was particularly associated with the policies and activity of Tomas Masaryk, president of the newly formed Czechoslovakia. With the dissolution of the Austro-Hungarian empire his idea concerned the creation of a framework that could promote the association of the diverse, but individually less numerous, peoples and groups that lay between the Germans and Russians. It was a conception specifically referred to by a later president of Czechoslovakia, Vaclav Havel (1990), in his speech to the Polish parliament in January 1990. He noted there the 'real historic chance to fill with something meaningful the great political vacuum that appeared in Central Europe after the break-up of the Habsburg Empire. We have the chance to transform Central Europe from a phenomenon that has so far been historical and spiritual into a political phenomenon.'

The attempt at any such transformation is clearly an ambitious one, and it is not difficult to detect potential pitfalls. The resurrection of any sort of framework devised in the nineteenth century with a view to confronting the problems of the twenty-first must involve a robust optimism. Nor, of course, had the original empire been wholly successful in coping with the problems of its own time – not least in containing the ethnic tensions and patterns of multi-national relations that in retrospect lent Hapsburg culture much of its charm and vigour but which also contributed to the destruction of the political framework that contained it. It was not surprising in this context that the origins and main thrust of the modern Central European idea were cultural and that it was first launched by a Czech novelist. Masaryk's original conception was in fact also rather different from that of reviving the Hapsburg legacy, and signs of the influence of his particular views can also be detected in modern conceptions. Nor do all the countries of contemporary post-communist Central Europe fit into the traditional patterns evident earlier in the century. Relatively small areas of modern Poland, for example, formed part of the Austro-Hungarian empire, and it had not generally been a major participant in the traditions of early-twentieth-century Central

Europe. Changes in this area nonetheless occurred during the years of communist rule, as a cross-border awareness grew with the post-Helsinki civil rights movement and dissidents gained greater political prominence.

The cultural and political location of Central Europe and its relations with both East and West also raise a number of questions. If, as some of the vehement advocates argued, Russia lies outside Europe and was both culturally and politically antagonistic to major European traditions, what status does the idea of a European centre occupy? If Central Europeans represent an outpost of civilisation that first challenged and then, in 1989, reclaimed its inheritance from the Russian antagonist, is there any part of Europe to the east of the centre and is Central Europe to be regarded strictly as a non-geographical concept (it has clearly not been primarily a geographical one)? Such considerations, in combination with the strong post-communist impetus to 'return to Europe', strengthen suspicions that Central Europe in some conceptions is little different from Europe *per se* – and, perhaps, fundamentally Western in its identity (Kumar, 1992, p. 449). While the Soviet Union was, in military and political terms, emphatically able to stake its claim within Europe, it was easier in cultural terms to outline a distinctive identity for Central Europeans. With the lifting of the Cold War shutters such distinctions are more difficult to maintain.

In fact, as Havel made particularly clear in his Polish speech, the political and economic implications both of the Central European project and of the 'return to Europe' refer to closer ties with the West and greater integration within Europe as a whole:

> Paradise on earth has not been victorious and there are many difficult moments ahead. All we have is the hope that we will return to Europe as free, independent and democratic states and nations . . . Western Europe is substantially further forward in the process of integration. If we decide to return to Europe individually, it will be substantially more complicated than if we enter into a mutual agreement . . . We want a comity of European nations: independent and democratic states; a Europe which is stable, not divided into blocs and pacts; a Europe that does not need the protection of the superpowers.

The fundamentals of this programme, moreover, appeared to find wide acceptance among the inhabitants of the Central European states. In early 1991 78 per cent of Poles, 78 per cent of Czechs and

Slovaks and 74 per cent of Hungarians endorsed the plan to join the European Community in the near future.

Nevertheless, as CMEA collapsed and the dissolution of the Warsaw Treaty Organisation became imminent, the rest of 1990 saw little progress towards this objective, leaving a growing vacuum in terms of regional organisation and integration. Individual countries tended to play to their presumed international advantage – Hungarians approaching Austria, Czechs looking towards Germany. But few rapid results were obtained and a basis for closer Central European cooperation was only established at the Visegrad summit of leaders from the three Central European countries in February 1991. There initially turned out, in general, to be rather more obstacles involved in the attempt of post-communist Eastern Europe to return to Europe than many had previously thought. The formation of a broader and more integrated Europe was made that much more difficult by the openness and very democracy of the new post-communist systems (Linden, 1992, p. 22). One issue here was the sheer level of the costs involved, exemplified in the unforeseen consequences of German unification; the transfer of German public funds to the formerly communist east in 1991 was equivalent to 80 per cent of the entire Polish GDP. Other factors involved were the impact of the costs (economic and political) on the consumers and producers of Eastern Europe, the relative modesty of Western resources offered and the overall scale of the organisational problems faced in constructing institutional arrangements not just to fund but also to administer the diverse aspects of economic transformation.

Western conceptions were not always favourable to stronger processes of European integration and views that Central Europe should remain a buffer between the West and an unstable (and still Soviet) East remained influential during 1990 (Kuzniar, 1992, p. 50). The changing domestic situation of the post-communist states made its own contribution. The uncertainties of the late Gorbachev period within the Soviet Union in terms of hesitancy with regard both to economic reform and marketisation and to the ambiguities of political democratisation drew some of the Western attention away from Eastern Europe and heightened its concern about the possibility of a wholesale collapse of the Soviet political and economic system – a development that would have severe consequences throughout Europe and a major impact on Western security and economic concerns. The early experience of post-communist development also played a part. This was most striking and initially discernible in

Poland, where the first post-communist government had been established and early measures to liberalise the economy had been taken – with severe socio-economic consequences and, soon, significant political repercussions too.

By early 1991 a 'post-revolutionary hangover' could be detected in Poland, this now being explicitly linked with the return to Europe, which 'brought less satisfaction than we had expected' (*Polityka*, 27 April 1991). People began to feel that they had lost more than they had gained (in terms of living standards by mid-1992 it was estimated that 85 per cent of Poles were net losers and that only 15 per cent had improved their situation) and the view of the final form that the post-communist society might take remained an unclear one. But this, too, could hardly be surprising so long as the key question underlying the return to Europe was that of 'when we will become a normal, democratic, economically strong country, and a well-respected partner in international relations'. It remains an unfortunate fact that it is by no means normal within the international community for countries to be democratic or economically strong – and even less both at the same time. The general conception surrounding the return to Europe, as well as that of a 'return to normality', remained highly optimistic and this was a major cause of post-communist disillusion. The most that could be said was that the core Central European countries of Czechoslovakia, Hungary and Poland were in Europe – but only just.

Integration with the International Economy

Nevertheless, steady, if gradual, progress was made in the direction of European integration. At the end of 1991 the three Central European countries of Czechoslovakia, Hungary and Poland became associate members of the European Community. But major changes in trade flows, for example, were already evident before that date. Shifts in the direction of export and import flows could be seen by 1990, particularly in the case of Poland but also in Czechoslovakia. While the CMEA area had accounted for 69 per cent of Poland's exports in 1986, other countries of contemporary Eastern Europe (Czechoslovakia, Hungary and Romania) and those of the former Soviet Union accounted for only 19.2 per cent of them in 1992. The latter group of countries also accounted for 37.6 per cent of Czechoslovak exports in 1992. Much of Hungary's trade had been reoriented before 1989 and countries of the former communist bloc accounted for only 20 per cent of Hungarian exports in 1992. It should, nevertheless, be noted that trade flows per head of population were considerably higher in Hungary than either Czechoslovakia or (even more) Poland, so the proportions of Western trade flows were not a reflection of actual trade volumes. In terms of proportion, the level of Romanian exports to the countries of the former Soviet bloc was only slightly higher, at 40.3 per cent, in the same year. The situation with regard to Bulgaria, formerly the most CMEA-oriented of the East European countries, had understandably shown little change by early 1990.

Economic integration was not to be measured just in terms of trade flows, however. Joint ventures were another important aspect of this development; they numbered, in 1991, 7,000 in Hungary (more than in the whole of the still extant USSR), 2,893 in Czechoslovakia, 2,290 in Poland – but only 60 in Bulgaria and 10 in Romania. Early experiences raise some doubts, however, about the degree to which such ventures had passed the contract stage and were actually functioning. Post-communist development patterns were differentiated and considerably more advanced in some countries than others. But it was still possible to raise the question of whether any of the East European countries had reached a critical mass in terms of integration with the global economy – and one representative view was that the situation remained inconclusive and the answer broadly negative (*Polityka*, 4 January 1992). Conditions were most advanced in Hungary, although this was more due to policies followed over the past dozen years or so rather than to changes made since 1989. Enormous shifts had taken place in Poland, but their significance was qualified by the weak export orientation of the economy as a whole and the relative paucity of its international economic links. The condition of Bulgaria and Romania, like that of the countries of the former Soviet Union, was considerably less advanced.

Economic integration was undoubtedly given a boost by the EC accession agreements signed at the end of 1991. Although the response of the West to the new situation that emerged in 1989 was in the eyes of many Central Europeans slow and in practical terms meagre, agreement with the EC on the prospect of integration was reached surprisingly quickly and was, it appeared, by no means unfavourable even to the short-term interests of the East. In the Polish case diverse forms of agreement were reached over a range of sensitive areas. Polish expectations for steel products were largely met, but those for textiles (which accounted for 15 per cent of Polish exports in 1990) proved to be more contentious. In the latter case strict transitional arrangements were imposed for the first two years (and would remain longer than in other areas), although all restrictions on trade in industrial products would be lifted from the end of 1998. Such prospects were not on offer for agricultural produce, which has represented a major part of Polish exports to date and derives from a sector that continues to employ one-quarter of the national workforce. Trade in agricultural produce, it appeared, was unlikely to be freed from tariffs and administrative controls until well into the twenty-first century.

Such an agreement promised more in the area of integration and economic cooperation than in that of immediate assistance and material support, although some estimates projected an immediate gain of one billion dollars or more a year. The diverse forms of assistance and aid for the recovery and transformation of East European economies also, however, promised to play a significant part in enhancing international integration and cooperation – and they were in some ways as important, if not more so, in this respect as in terms of the direct assistance they offered. From July 1989 to the end of 1991, G-24 (the countries associated within the Organisation for Economic and Cultural Development: OECD), the World Bank and IMF had assembled a package for Czechoslovakia, Hungary and Poland worth 33.8 billion dollars, although, at least until September 1991, only 14 per cent of this took the form of direct financial allocations, the remainder loans or export credit guarantees. The sum total was equivalent to $795 for each member of the Hungarian population, $545 for each Pole and $310 for each Czech or Slovak. In Central Europe terms, such sums were not inconsiderable, particularly for Poland – the poorest of the three – where the national product was equivalent to $1,850 per capita in 1991.

The EC also played a major part in this process of assistance, as well as in the more complex relationship that led to the association agreements of 1991. In 1990, 700 million ecu were allocated to support post-communist economic reform in Central Europe and the Balkans (an ecu being equivalent to $1.2 in 1991). Further commitments of ecu 850 million and 1 billion were made for 1991 and 1992. In addition to these grants, Community institutions had by January 1991 provided ecu 2 billion in the form of loans, and member governments a further 1.6 billion as grants and 4.9 billion as loans (in addition to contributions made by the European Bank for

Reconstruction and Development). In sum this represented a further $13.3 billion and a not inconsiderable contribution to the economic development of Eastern Europe. The extent to which such funds went any way to meeting the needs of the region were nevertheless the subject of some doubt. According to one estimate, the provision of a physical structure capable of creating and sustaining the operation of competitive economies in Bulgaria, Czechoslovakia, Hungary, Poland and Romania – a clear prerequisite for the effective integration of their economies in the global economy – might range in cost from between $103 to $226 billion per year (Pinder, 1991, p. 47). The process of full economic integration thus promises both to be a complex and costly process.

States, Peoples and the Stability of Europe

The end of the Cold War and the changes set in motion in 1989 have not been restricted in their consequences to the transformation of the political and socioeconomic orders of individual states or to re-evaluation of their status within a broader Europe and relations with the West. They also affect, as we have seen to a limited extent in terms of the re-evaluation of relations between the Visegrad 'Triangle' of Czechoslovakia, Hungary and Poland, relations between states within that region as well as the lines of ethnic division that run within and across those sovereign territories. Most dramatically, for example, the tensions that resided in the complex structures of post-war Yugoslavia were initially exploited by the embattled Serbian communist Slobodan Milosevic and then increasingly blew apart with enormous violence under the force of their own contradictions. The early stages of economic transformation and transition to a market system also help to undermine social stability and fuel dissatisfaction. At the same time, newly formed party and parliamentary systems have struggled to establish conditions for their effective operation and construct new political channels through which these social currents might run. Relations both within and between the states of Eastern Europe, and the peoples that live within them, have thus become subject to considerable uncertainty and raise further questions about political order and the security both of that region and of Europe as a whole.

Perhaps more than during any other period of European history, developments in domestic East European politics stand in a close and highly complex relationship with changing international relations and create a situation of finely balanced interdependence. It is not difficult to identify situations where the pursuit of Western-promoted policies of economic transformation have swiftly produced antithetic domestic responses and strengthened forces of nationalism and traditional cultural revival. They have, surprisingly soon after the removal of extensively discredited communist rulers, also facilitated the resurgence of some elements of the former ruling parties who oppose the economic changes and their social effects on grounds not dissimilar to those of the more traditional conservative forces. The changing alignment of domestic East European political forces, now of course more visible and significant in terms of government and policy formation with the progress of democratisation, also feeds back directly into international relations and the prospects for further economic integration and European cooperation. Both aspects are also related to changing relations between different groups and peoples within and across state boundaries.

Political perceptions in Eastern Europe were hardly likely to be mellowed by the widespread conviction, clearly evident in opinion surveys throughout the region, that the economic situation was worsening during 1991. Particularly prevalent in Russia and the Baltic states, this view was also held by 65 per cent of Poles. Gallup polls taken throughout the region and published in January 1992 showed that only in Bulgaria did as many as 24 per cent think things had improved. The degree of stability that did prevail was likely to have been associated with the absence of any alternative vision or economic policies to those currently pursued, and significant (and in some cases overwhelming) majorities endorsed – with the sole exception of Romania – the continuing creation of market economies. The overall mood could, then, have been interpeted as one of belt-tightening in the anticipation of better economic times to come – if it were not for the fact that only in the Baltic states, the Balkans (Albania, Bulgaria, Romania) and, to a more limited extent in Czechoslovakia, did people think that things were going in the right direction. Leaders in the process of economic transformation like Poland and Hungary, but also respondents in Russia, were in fact more likely to think that things were going in the wrong direction. The greatest number holding this opinion (56 per cent) could be found in Poland – the trailblazer in terms of marketisation. In those with the longest experience of economic reform and transformation accordingly, the majority view was that economic conditions had worsened and were not likely to get better – fertile ground for the growth of further dissatisfaction and its political expression.

The somewhat negative view taken by East Europeans of their current situation, prospects for harmonious regional integration and, by implication, of the maintenance of stable European relations is one that finds some reflection in more theoretical projections. In an account which considers some themes similar to those introduced in this discussion, Jack Snyder (1990, pp. 24–8) outlines three broad approaches to the outcome of the end of the bipolar division of Europe: the optimistic 'end of history' vision in which the peaceful installation of liberal, market-oriented regimes occurs; a Hobbesian pessimistic account which foresees a reversion to patterns of multi-polar instability and nationalism; and a more considered optimistic scenario according to which Hobbesian anarchy is contained by the evolution of cooperative international institutions. The somewhat more optimistic vision of the latter option is, however, more likely to be realised if certain domestic conditions are also met – namely, if a civic polity or form of democratic corporatism is established rather than a praetorian pattern of largely unmediated political struggle.

Some specific international proposals and transnational proposals are, in turn, more likely to encourage domestic democratic variants than others. These include:

- a form of 'new Marshall Plan', not just to encourage interdependence *per se*, but rather to favour the development of appropriate institutional structures and changes in the pattern of domestic interests;
- the avoidance of threatening military situations whereby states with potentially irredentist ethnic claims are not militarily stronger than their neighbours;
- the creation of a cooperative security regime which would codify minority rights and responsibilities and thus help head off nationalist conflicts before they started.

These proposals were formulated soon after the changes of 1989 and the situation has already moved on quite far. It is worth considering at this point, in the search for a tentative conclusion, how far conditions for the success of the qualified optimistic variant have been met.

Firstly, on the positive side and as outlined at some length above, Czechoslovakia, Hungary and Poland have gained associate membership of the EC and are all, since Poland's free elections of October

1991, members of the Council of Europe. In the case of the latter organisation, although not the EC, the membership of the Baltic states and Bulgaria is likely to be imminent. Moreover, and this is a point of some importance, with the Visegrad summit the Central European 'Triangle' set up a new kind of security mechanism that reflects awareness not just of the need to follow Western initiatives and integrate with existing structures but also to build on autonomous East European capabilities and to combine more specialised regional cooperative activity with that of a broader pan-European nature. Such initiatives are likely to result in more complex forms of interdependence whose outcome will be more solidly based in individual East European countries. Following the Soviet coup the Triangle began to develop closer forms of cooperation and draw up a broader regional agenda (Spero, 1991, pp. 141–2). Detailed analysis of Central European developments, however, suggest that a substantial dose of scepticism is in order concerning the commitment to shared interests and the viability of effective policy coordination (Tokes, 1992). The uncertainties deriving from the division of Czechoslovakia can only add to such problems. In early 1993 Vaclav Klaus, prime minister of the newly separated Czech Republic, commented disparagingly on the position of the Visegrad group and looked forward to the swifter integration of the Czech lands with the EC. But this, too, was likely to require further negotiation following the division of the country itself. Moreover, the European Community link will remain restricted to the three Triangle countries and will not be extended to include the rest of Eastern Europe for some time. It, too, is limited in its reach and, of particular importance to Eastern Europe, contains only limited provisions for the removal of obstacles to the flow of agricultural produce. In Poland at least, where peasant parties remain an important parliamentary force, this restriction is likely to be of considerable political significance.

Secondly, the recommendation that states with potentially irredentist ethnic claims should not be stronger than their neighbours was soon nullified by the unification of Germany. The territorial issue was soon settled and may, with good fortune, not reappear on future political agendas.

More unsettling, thirdly, has been the total lack of progress on attempts to codify the rights and responsibilities of minorities. While the conflicts in former Yugoslavia obviously have profound domestic roots, the failure to pay any attention to the area identified in this recommendation in a situation where major international powers made haste to secure the recognition of Slovenia, Croatia and Bosnia, served to ignite the conflict and left international organisations with remarkably little leverage over the forces involved once the bloodshed began. The major importance of a European security regime has been clearly demonstrated by its near-total absence.

Developments since 1989–90 have thus largely substantiated the appropriateness of Snyder's expressed preference for a path that lies between the Hobbesian school of sceptical realists and the qualified optimism of the neo-liberal institutionalists. In a full-blown programme for European security the latter would have to provide for the speedy, multi-faceted integration of Russia as well as the rest of Eastern Europe, a condition that would clearly be grossly unrealistic. While, apart from the GDR, Czechoslovakia and Hungary were more cautiously proposed by Snyder for initial consideration for admission into the Western institutional framework it would now be sensible to include Poland in that group, both because of subsequent regional developments and the pioneering and thus symbolically important role of that country in processes of political and economic post-communist development. Although some of the premises of the institutionalist approach have been set in place in Eastern Europe, the conditions for stability prescribed by a full-blooded realism have also been relatively successfully preserved. Not all the features of the Cold War have been removed from Europe – and this is by no means regarded unfavourably by all analysts in terms of preserving the continent's security: the Warsaw Treaty Organisation has been disbanded, 'Soviet' troops are in the process of full withdrawal from Eastern Europe, but NATO still exists and a residual US presence remains (at least for the present) a long-term prospect (Mearsheimer, 1990).

Excessive emphasis on the role of cooperative institution would certainly be dangerous. Unsuccessful and regionally overambitious institution-building would, as Snyder makes clear, damage both West and East, by drawing the former into a complex of problems it is incapable of solving, and the latter by raising expectations that cannot be satisfied and undermining the islands of social stability that remained after the traumatic collapse of the communist regime. It might, indeed, be suggested that clear signs of both problems are already appearing. Political instabilities persist and processes of economic recovery in the East are considerably slower than anticipated. What can be viewed in some ways as the maladroit handling of German unification and the unfortunate basis on which monetary union was conducted have fed back negatively into the EC financial regime and the ERM just as political doubts were surfacing about the speed of West European integration and the practical implications of the Maastricht treaty. Following the virtuous spiral of European integration during the 1980s that centred on the West and exerted a significant pull on the Eastern countries just as the force of Soviet orthodoxy began to subside, so it appeared imperative in the 1990s to avoid a vicious spiral of disintegration which – if it also gained momentum in the West – could have dire consequences for sub-sequent developments in East European politics.

16

East European Voices

JUDY DEMPSEY

This final chapter is an unconventional approach towards trying to understand the transition from communism to democracy. Since the other chapters in this book deal with specific subjects and countries, it has opted for the rather different approach of relying on the voices of East Europeans themselves.

When I started writing, I realised there were many issues that needed consideration. But as I read through my notebooks, the themes which occurred over and over related to nationalism, relations with Germany, and the need for articulating one's identity. The clear impression is that nationalism, or a search for identity coupled with the deep need for certainty and security, forms one of the fragile bridges over which the countries of Eastern Europe must cross in the long road from communism to democracy.

Inevitably, by using voices, I have excluded many issues, and those which relate particularly to civil society: in other words, what institutions and political instruments may be needed to create a balance between state and society, to strengthen public accountability, and to create a politics which is built on a strong opposition and an accountable parliament.

The institutions necessary for this process require a firm commitment to a market economy. Without a market economy, the chances of creating a new entrepreneurial middle class, which has a vested interest in stability and democracy, are seriously undermined. A market economy also requires a commitment from the European Community to open up its markets to the countries of Eastern Europe. In this respect, the European Community has been painfully slow – and indeed short-sighted, since delays will slow up the integration of the two Europes, make Eastern Europe a less attractive region for foreign investors, and weaken rather than enhance stability and structural reforms.

A market also shapes the media. Here, the media in Eastern Europe remain highly politicised, in the sense that the reflex of the ruling elites is to control or influence the press. We have seen examples of this in Hungary, with the sacking of the heads of Hungarian radio and television in January 1992, and in Slovakia, when Vladimir Meciar, the prime minister, closed down some critical newspapers as soon as Slovakia gained its independence in January 1993.

Moreover, the press is heavily oriented towards editorialising – although this is also a trait of the German and Austrian press. Since Central Europe lost its journalists and small middle/intellectual class during the Second World War, and since 1945 the press was the ideological tool of the ruling communist parties, it is not surprising that the media is still trying to stabilise, and find a balance between editorialising and solid reporting. Nor is it surprising that the governments regard a critical media as often disloyal to the democratic process, instead of viewing it as a vital component of accountability.

Furthermore, the governments of Eastern Europe have inherited a precommunist and communist legacy of corruption. During the communist era, patronage and clientelism took precedence over merit and competence – the inevitable consequence of a 'shortage economy' – and acted as a route towards a very distorted form of social mobility.

The phenomenon of corruption, whether in the form of a black economy, or promotion through contacts, does of course exist in Western democracies. But an independent press, institutions of public accountability, and public perceptions, weaken its influence. The speed in which Pal Schluter, the former prime minister of Denmark, resigned in January 1993, is indicative of what the Danes expect from those holding public office. In communist Eastern Europe corruption was not only endemic; it was an institution.

Another hurdle in making the transition from communism to democracy involves the drafting of constitutions which spell out the role of government, the judiciary, and the powers of the executive and legislature. After 1989, the countries of Eastern Europe, generally, created constituent assemblies which had the task of drawing up constitutions, and of preparing for the first, free elections in the region since 1945. In retrospect, the constitutions are in some respects flawed, particularly with regard to the electoral law and citizenship rights.

In the desire to be democratic, the electoral laws are perhaps 'over democratic' in the sense that they have faciliated the proliferation of small parties which make stable government difficult. The outcome of many election results – Bulgaria and Romania, Poland and the Czech and Slovak republics – have lent themselves towards unwieldly coalitions wedded to poor compromises and trade-offs. This means that difficult decisions are either postponed, or else governments are constantly looking over their shoulders fearing the immiment defection of their coalition partners.

Citizenship is another problem. There remains a confusion between citizenship – an individual of a state, regardless of ethnic background, who has equal access to human and civil rights – and nationality anchored to a specific ethnic background. The electoral laws in Estonia and Croatia, in which ethnic background was a criteria for voting, and therefore citizenship, sets a worrying example for the other countries of Eastern Europe.

In the transition to democracy, the governments of Eastern Europe also require an independent civil service. They are not in a position to pick and choose because the repository of talent and experience is either nil, or suspect. Not only are there still lingering suspicions about those who worked – and many were competent – for the former communist regimes, and who still retain their jobs in the ministries; but governments – from Poland to Romania – tend to assume that a civil service owes its loyalty to the government of the day, rather than acting as independent servants for society. Creating an independent civil service will take at least a generation.

These then are some of the institutions and instruments the governments of Eastern Europe have to create in order to consolidate and strengthen the democratic process. The consultants in grey suits who rush from one East European capital to another are no substitute for open borders and free trade. Perhaps they are no substitute either for the voices of Eastern Europe.

The Voices

The dead pig had been hanging in the cellar for five days. It was time to take it down and divide it among the families. The six men –

Slovak peasants, foresters and a local government inspector – were in a good mood. After a round of vodkas, they set to work. One of them had brought a sausage-making machine into which he fed chunks of meat. He turned the wooden handle. Sausages slowly poured out and dropped into a plastic bucket. The European Community would never approve!

'It's warmer upstairs. You can talk to the womenfolk,' said one of the men in rubber boots.

Outside, a thick blanket of snow covered the small Slovak hamlet of Lednicke Rovne, a few miles from Europe's newest international frontier.

Earlier that day, the middle-aged porter at the small hotel tucked behind Prague's Wenceslas Square had been far from sentimental about the breakup of his country.

'Tell the Slovaks good riddance from us Czechs. We have had enough of their whingeing. We are better off with our own Czech Republic.' He paused. 'I still think it's the fault of the Germans. They wanted this split-up so that they can set up another Reich, here in the Czech Lands.' The cashier sighed, and rolled her eyes, as if to say, 'here he goes again'.

'And wait until what happens in 1993,' the porter continued. 'There will be more price rises. And then we will be importing food – from the Germans – which will be dumped on us. They will soon colonise us – just like the Second World War. Pah!'

In Lednicke Rovne, it was indeed much warmer upstairs, high above the cellar. The large, parquet-floored living room was filled with mothers, children and toys. Marta Rusanakova, who works in a forestry across the border in Moravia, one of the Czech Lands, dipped a large ladle into a barrel full of sauerkraut and filled my plate, already laden with pork.

'The truth is that those Czechs have been exploiting us since 1918. They stole everything from us,' she argued.

'I thought the Czechs had helped up build up Slovak industry after 1945,' I said.

'For themselves. Everthing was ruled by, and from, Prague.'

'Was the relationship that unequal? Slovaks could lobby for your interests in Prague. Your language and culture were not threatened. And you had a substantial presence in the federal foreign ministry.'

'The Czechs held the purse strings. They looked down on us as if we were second-class citizens. Now we are free. Life will be much better. We will become part of Europe. Slovakia will be for the Slovaks.'

'The six hundred thousand Hungarians living here will want to feel secure in an independent Slovakia.'

'The Hungarians have all the rights they deserve. They are always complaining. What more rights should they have when our Slovaks in Hungary do not have many rights?'

Ewa, the sister-in-law, interrupted. 'I worry about the break-up. I also work in the forestry in Moravia. Anton, my husband, who works for the federal army, has Czech relatives. He will have to choose his ethnic background once we take our separate citizenship papers. I don't know if I can keep my job once we become separate countries. It's all right now. But you never know about the future. We will be commuting to a foreign country.'

Marta said the Slovaks would cope very well without the Czechs. 'They are even now discrediting our new republic. Prague, and all those intellectuals who keep travelling abroad, are spreading lies about how we collaborated with the Germans during the war. You know, the Germans were not that bad. After all, they paid their bills on time.'

'The Czechs are also saying the Vladimir Meciar, our prime minister, is against a market economy, and that he is a communist. That's all lies. Meciar only wants to protect the national interests of the Slovaks,' she continued.

'Do you want more sauerkraut?' asked Ewa.

On a Sunday morning, the Catholic churches were packed. In the western Slovak town of Trencin, young and old stood outside, trying to catch the words of the priest's prayers.

'It's good we have the freedom to go to Mass now,' said Milan, an engineer in his thirties. 'But I don't want the church to start laying down the law about what our rights are – about abortion, for instance. They should keep out of politics and stop interfering in our private lives.'

'Is the church becoming stronger?'

'Of course it is. This is their chance now to make up for the past forty years. It is the same in Poland. The church should be free to speak its mind. But it should not tell us what to do. We have had enough of that for decades. We just want to be left alone,' he said.

The elderly lady wanted some bread. The small shop in Dzienkowice, in southern Poland, was still open, even though it was a Sunday evening. She asked for it in Polish, then broke into German. Her request was drowned by the man behind the counter who was shouting in German.

'Why are you stirring up trouble in Dzienkowice? You journalists are all the same. Why don't you go to Germany and write about how all those foreigners and refugees are ruining the country. Get out of here!' he said.

I thought about the brightly coloured shield, sited near the church in the centre of the village, on which were the words 'Frauenfeld [the German for Dzienkowice] O/S Grüsst Alle Gäste'.

'Why did the German National Offensive [a neo-Nazi group from Germany] come here and try to organise a cell?'

'None of your business,' said the man, storming out of the shop into the dimly lit street.

The lady with the bread began to speak. 'Ignore him. He's a bit tense. Dzienkowice is like a ghetto. There are only one thousand six hundred of us ethnic Germans in the village. We are confused. Everything has changed since the Berlin Wall came down. The Poles never allowed us to read, learn, or speak German since 1945. Now we are free again to be German, in Poland. The Poles are upset because they think we want to be part of Germany again. Everybody is afraid of history.'

She explained that she saw nothing wrong with the locals of Dzienkowice putting up war memorials for those German soldiers who had died during the First and Second World Wars.

'The Poles are getting upset about it. You know, our sons died too.' She walked into the dark evening.

Janusz didn't care about history, Poles, or the Germans.

'Thieves. That's the problem now,' he explained.

Janusz is the nightwatchman for the guests' cars at the central hotel in Opole, one of the main cities in Upper Silesia, which was part of Germany before 1945. Each evening, he sets up guard from a tiny caravan which is parked in front of the hotel.

He unlocked a heavy, U-shaped metal security device, parked my car between the pavement and the contraption, and locked it again. Ten thousand zlotys please.'

A Polish businessman, clearly acquainted with the East European attraction to expensive cars, had taken no chances. He had brought his own yellow steel clamp for his brand new BMW.

'All the politics is down the road and across the bridge in the Vojvod headquarters,' said Janusz, in a mixture of German and Polish.

The drab, former communist party building had some redeeming features. The paternoster was still functioning, even if it creaked. Stanislaw Skakuj, a former member of the Solidarity independent trade union, now head of the Vojvod's Department for Problems of Citizenship, said: 'Officially, there are no problems with the ethnic Germans. They just have to stick to the law. They did not ask if they could put up memorials to the Second World War. It's a very sensitive issue.'

'Why did you decide to expel Gunther Boschutz, the neo-Nazi, only recently, and not when he came to Dzienkowice in December 1991?'

'It was Warsaw which made the decision, not us. Despite the political and economic reforms, we are still uncertain about the powers of local government. It's a sort of reflex. It takes time to dilute the powers of the centralised state.'

'Are you afraid about the growing German influence in Poland?'

'Officially, no.'

'What will happen now? Do you think the ethnic Germans will seek, or should have more autonomy, especially if some of the hundred and eighty thousand ethnic Germans in Opole represent a majority in some of the villages?'

'Autonomy? Do you know what that word means? It means separatism. Then where would we be? Look at Yugoslavia. Look at Czechoslovakia. Look at Russia. Countries all around us are breaking up.'

Henryk Kroll, the 43-year-old head of the ethnic Germans in Opole, was standing outside Skakuj's office, engulfed in cigarette smoke.

'The problem, if one exists, is both simple and complex. It is about the Poles coming to terms with the ethnic Germans rediscovering their culture. After the war, all our rights were taken away,' he explained, chain-smoking his way through the history of identity.

'Our language and culture practically disappeared,' he explained in excellent German. 'We are Germans, but Polish citizens. We don't want to emigrate to Germany. Our home is here, in Upper Silesia. It would be good if those Germans who emigrated after 1945 came back. We need them to invest. We need new schools. More teachers. For our identity.'

Andrezj Olechowski, Poland's former finance minister, takes a more sanguine, pragmatic view about relations between Poland and Germany. 'We have to accept the fact that with a united Germany, Germany will play a much greater role both within the European Community and in Eastern Europe. That is a fact. We know that Germany is one of the largest investors here in Poland. Geography and traditions dictate this.' Which is why Mr Olechowski believes the EC must speed up the entry of Poland, and the other countries of Eastern Europe into the Community.

'Poland could act as a kind of counterweight to German influence in the EC. But it is up to the Community to decide if it really wants to integrate the economies of Eastern Europe with Western markets. If they are serious about a stable Europe – both in East and West – then it will have to lift trade barriers and let the Poles, and the other East European states, export their goods to the EC. If the EC is pro-market and pro-competition, then it should stop fearing competition from the East European market.'

Olechowski also believes that the longer the Community takes in reducing trade barriers and upgrading its relations with the countries of Eastern Europe, the greater the risk of a backlash.

'It is easy for populists and nationalists to create an anti-Western feeling, especially if living standards are falling, and unemployment is rising. The countries of Eastern Europe are looking for more than encouragement and signals from the Community. They want access to markets. Markets would help intergrate the two Europes,' he said.

Like other Polish technocrats, Olechowski worries about instability in Russia and in the Balkans, and how the international community, particularly the EC, has responded to the post-cold-war era.

'The EC has been slow in dealing with nationalism. It has been slow in understanding what role nationalism and identity have played in the transition from communism to democracy.'

'When I was much younger, my parents never questioned our identity. We never spoke about the past. We never observed the Sabbath.'

Tamas Lozsy stood outside the Sasz Chevra Orthodox Synogogue in Weselenyi street in Budapest. It was a damp, cold, Saturday morning. Aged 22, he is a teacher in a Jewish school. 'The sense of being different started when I was fourteen I wanted to know: What does it mean to be a Jew in Hungary today?'

'Do your parents feel assimilated?'

'If I say they are assimilated to the extent that they think and act like Hungarians, then they are assimilated. But they are not assimilated from this point of view – they are afraid.'

'Why are they afraid? Do they worry about the far right who are grouped around Istvan Csurka – who recently wrote that Hungary was being taken over by foreign Jewish financiers?'

'In the 1920s and 1930s, when the name of Hitler was mentioned in elegant homes, everyone laughed madly. They said he was a stupid guy. A house painter. And you know what happened. I hope that history will not repeat itself. I hope that it will not happen with Csurka.'

Sandor Haraszti interrupted his prayers. 'My parents never spoke about the past. They wanted to assimilate because of the war. In any case, the system did not allow us to be Jewish, and not be afraid,' he said.

'I am 17 years old. When I was much younger, I wanted to discover what I was. I began to read the Talmud. Today, I am insulted on the streets. I ignore it. I have not yet been attacked, yet. Excuse me, I must go back inside.'

Young and old Ashkenazi Jews in traditional orthodox dress prayed with the cantor. Outside, a solitary police car kept watch.

Further Reading

There are several good introductions to the modern history of Central and Eastern Europe, among them Joseph Held's *Columbia History* and Nigel and Geoffrey Swain's *Eastern Europe since 1945*. George Schöpflin, another contributor to this volume, has recently published *Politics in Eastern Europe*, covering the period from 1945 to 1992. Joseph Rothschild's *Return to Diversity* considers the whole post-war period, as does Misha Glenny's more popular *Rebirth of History*. On the transition from communist rule J.F. Brown's *Surge to Freedom* and David Mason's *Revolution in East-Central Europe* are particularly helpful. Judy Batt's *East Central Europe from Reform to Transformation* emphasises the politics and economics of the transition; Ralf Dahrendorf's *Reflections on the Revolution in Europe* is a thoughtful meditation on the changes and the meaning of 'Europe' in this connection.

A detailed reference guide to the changes of 1989 and 1990 is available in Stephen White's edited *Handbook of Reconstruction in Eastern Europe and the Soviet Union*; briefer summary volumes are Roger East's *Revolutions in Eastern Europe* and Keith Sword's *Times Guide to Eastern Europe*. Ray Taras's edited *Handbook of Political Science Research on the USSR and Eastern Europe* provides a comprehensive bibliographical survey with its emphasis on the communist period. Timothy Garton Ash's *We the People* is a more impressionistic journalist's account, emphasising developments in Poland, Czechoslovakia and Hungary; the same author's *Uses of Adversity* contains a series of reflective essays on the region as a whole.

Comprehensive general studies of individual countries towards the end of the communist period appeared in the 'Marxist regimes' series published under the general editorship of Bogdan Szajkowski. These included books by Hans-Georg Heinrich on *Hungary*, George Kolankiewicz and Paul Lewis on *Poland*, Robert McIntyre on *Bulgaria*, Bruce McFarlane on *Yugoslavia* and Michael Shafir on *Romania*. Sharon Wolchik's planned contribution appeared after the demise of 'Marxist regimes' and was entitled *Czechoslovakia in Transition*, with useful details of the early states of postcommunist politics in what later became two separate states.

Analogous studies of changes in Poland are George Sanford's edited work *Democratization in Poland, 1988–90* and George Blazyca and Ryszard Rapacki's *Poland into the 1990s*. Nigel Swain offers a general view of Hungarian developments in *Hungary: the Rise and Fall of Feasible Socialism*, while a more theoretical study is that by Agnes Horvath and Arpad Szakolczai on *The Dissolution of Communist Power*. More detailed political perspectives can be found in Bozoki, Korosenyi and Schöpflin's *Post-Communist Transition: Emerging Pluralism in Hungary*. Misha Glenny and Branka Magas have provided useful accounts of the 'former Yugoslavia', and Martin Rady a study of *Romania in Turmoil*.

Book-length studies of particular themes have, under the confusing and fast-moving conditions of postcommunist Eastern Europe, been slower to appear. On privatisation there is a recent study by Roman Frydman and others, *The Privatization Process in Central Europe*; Chris Corrin and others deal with *Superwomen and the Double Burden*; Bob Deacon and others consider changes in social policy in *The New Eastern Europe*; and other issues are examined in Paul Lewis's edited *Civil Society and Democracy in Eastern Europe*. Contemporary regional relations and international affairs are considered in Andrew Michta and Ilya Prizel's edited volume *Postcommunist Eastern Europe: Crisis and Reform*.

In a rapidly changing situation, developments and changing theoretical perspectives must be followed through the scholarly and more popular literature. There are several periodicals that deal specifically with Eastern and Central Europe, among them *East European Politics and Societies*, *East European Quarterly*, *Slavic Review*, *Europe-Asia Studies* (formerly *Soviet Studies*), the *Journal of Communist Studies*, and *Studies in Comparative Communism* (from 1993, *Communist and Post-Communist Studies*). More general politics periodicals often carry articles with an East European focus, among them the *British Journal of Political Science*, *Parliamentary*

Affairs, the *World Policy Journal* and *World Politics*.

East European Reporter, now appearing bimonthly, carries a range of articles on regional themes and reprints some interesting pieces from the East European press. Among several news and monitoring services, the Radio Free Europe/Radio Liberty *Research Report* is particularly valuable; it is published on a weekly basis and is also available on-line.

Bibliography

Adams, I. (1991) 'Can History Be Finished?', *Politics*, vol. 11, no. 2.
Almond, Gabriel and Powell, G. Bingham (eds) (1983) *Comparative Politics Today*, Boston: Little, Brown.
Andrejevich, Milan (1992) 'Slovenian Politics and the Economy in Year One', *RFE/RL Research Report*, vol. 1, 11 September.
Arendt, Hannah (1958) *The Origins of Totalitarianism*, London: Allen & Unwin.
Arriagarda, G. (1992) 'Reflections on Recent Elections in Latin America and Eastern and Central Europe', in L. Garber and E. Bjornlund (eds), *The New Democratic Frontier*, Washington, DC: National Democratic Institute for International Affairs.
Ash, Timothy G. (1983) *The Polish Revolution: Solidarity 1980–1982*, London: Cape.
Ash, Timothy G. (1989) *The Uses of Adversity*, New York: Random House.
Ash, Timothy G. (1990) *We the People: The Revolution of 1989*, Harmondsworth, Middlesex: Penguin.
Atkinson, A.B. (1992) 'Social Policy, Economic Organisation and the Search for a Third Way', in Z. Ferge and J.E. Kolberge (eds), *Social Policy in a Changing Europe*, Frankfurt: Campus Verlag.
Augarde, T. (1991) *The Oxford Dictionary of Modern Quotations*, New York: Oxford University Press.
Banac, Ivo (1984) *The National Question in Yugoslavia: Origins, History, Politics*, Ithaca: Cornell University Press.
Batt, Judy (1991) *East Central Europe from Reform to Transformation*, London: Pinter.
Bauman, Zygmunt (1987) 'Intellectuals in East-Central Europe: Continuity and Change', *East European Politics and Societies*, vol. 1, no. 2 (Spring).
Beck, Carl (1970) 'Career Characteristics of East European Leadership', in Farrell (1970).
Beck, Carl *et al.* (eds) (1973) *Comparative Communist Political Leadership*, New York: David McKay.

Bicanic, Ivo and Dominis, Iva (1992) 'Tujman Remains Dominant After Croatian Elections', *RFE/RL Research Report*, vol. 1, 18 September.

Bielasiak, Jack (1983) 'Inequalities and the Politicization of the Polish Working Class', in Nelson (1983).

Bielasiak, Jack (1992) 'Regime Transition, Founding Elections, and Political Fields in Post-Communist States', mimeo, June.

Blazyca, George and Rapacki, Ryszard (eds) (1991) *Poland into the 1990s: Economy and Society in Transition*, New York: St Martin's.

Boeri, T. and Sziracki, G. (1992) 'Labour Market Developments and Policies in Central and Eastern Europe', in OECD/ILO, *Labour Market and Social Policy Implications of Restructuring*, Paris: OECD.

Bozoki, A., Korosenyi, A. and Schopflin, G. (eds), (1992) *Post-Communist Transition: Emerging Pluralism in Hungary*, London: Pinter.

Brada, J. (1992) 'The Mechanics of the Voucher Plan in Czechoslovakia', in *RFE/RL Research Report*, vol. 1, no. 17, 24 April.

Brown, Archie and Wightman, Gordon (1977) 'Czechoslovakia: Revival and Retreat', in Archie Brown and Jack Gray (eds), *Political Culture and Political Change in Communist States*, London: Macmillan.

Brown, J.F. (1991) *Surge to Freedom*, Durham, NC: Duke University Press.

Bruszt, L. (1992) 'The Negotiated Revolution in Hungary', in A. Bozoki *et al.* (1992).

Brzezinski, Zbigniew (1966) *The Soviet Bloc*, rev. edn, Cambridge, MA: Harvard University Press.

Brzezinski, Zbigniew (1990) *The Grand Failure*, 2nd edn, New York: Collier.

Brzezinski, Zbigniew and Huntington, Samuel (1964) *Political Power: USA/USSR*, Cambridge, MA: Harvard University Press.

Bunce, Valerie (1981) *Do Leaders Make A Difference? Executive Succession and Public Policy under Capitalism and Socialist Systems*, Princeton, NJ: Princeton University Press.

Bunce, Valerie and Echols, John M. (1979) 'From Soviet Studies to Comparative Politics: The Unfinished Revolution', *Soviet Studies*, vol. 31 (January).

Butora, Martin *et al.* (1991) 'The Hard Birth of Democracy in Slovakia: One Year After the "Tender Revolution" ', *Journal of Communist Studies*, no. 4 (December).

Chirot, Daniel (ed.) (1989) *The Origins of Backwardness in Eastern Europe: Economics and Politics from the Middle Ages until the Early Twentieth Century*, Berkeley: University of California Press.

Cohen, Lenard J. (1991) 'Reform in Yugoslavia', in Ilpyong Kim and Jane Shapiro Zacek (eds), *Reform and Transformation in Communist Systems*, New York: Paragon House.

Connor, Walter (1979) *Socialism, Politics and Equality: Hierarchy and Change in Eastern Europe and the USSR*, New York: Columbia University Press.

Corrin, Chris (ed.) (1992) *Superwomen and the Double Burden: Women's Experience of Change in Central and Eastern Europe and the Former Soviet Union*, London: Scarlett Press.

Curry, Jane (1984) *The Black Book of the Polish Censorship*, New York: Praeger.

Dahrendorf, Ralph (1990) *Reflections on the Revolution in Europe*, London: Chatto & Windus.

Davies, Norman (1981) *God's Playground: A History of Poland*, 2 vols, New York: Columbia University Press.

Deacon, Bob (ed.) (1992) *Social Policy, Social Justice and Citizenship in Eastern Europe*, Aldershot, Hants: Avebury.

Deacon, Bob *et al.* (1992) *The New Eastern Europe: Social Policy, Past, Present and Future*, London: Sage.

Deacon, Bob and Szalai, Judith (1990) *Social Policy in the New Eastern Europe*, Aldershot, Hants: Avebury.

Dolling, Irene (1992) 'Between Hope and Hopelessness: Women in the GDR After the "Turningpoint" ', in Lewis (1992).

Duverger, Maurice (1963) *Political Parties*, New York: Wiley.

Duverger, Maurice (1986) 'Duverger's Law: Forty Years Later', in B. Grofman and A. Lijphart (eds), *Electoral Laws and their Political Consequences*, New York: Agathon Press.

East, Roger (1992) *Revolutions in Eastern Europe*, London: Pinter.

Echols, John M. (1981) 'Does Socialism Mean Greater Equality? A Comparison of East and West Along Several Major Dimensions', *American Journal of Political Science*, vol. 25, no. 1 (February).

Eckstein, Harry (1963) 'A Perspective on Comparative Politics, Past and Present', in Eckstein and Apter (1963).

Eckstein, Harry and Apter, David (eds) (1963) *Comparative Politics: A Reader*, New York: Free Press.

Farrell, R. Barry (ed.) (1970) *Political Leadership in Eastern Europe and the Soviet Union*, Chicago: Aldine.

Feher, A., Heller, A. and Markus, G. (1983) *Dictatorship Over Needs*, Oxford: Blackwell.

Fischer-Galati, Stephen (1992) 'Eastern Europe in the Twentieth Century: "Old Wine in New Bottles" ', in Joseph Held (1992).

Fleron, Frederic J. (ed.) (1969) *Communist Studies and the Social Sciences*, Chicago: Rand McNally.

Friedrich, Carl (1969) 'The Evolving Theory and Practice of Totalitarian Regimes', in Michael Curtis (ed.), *Totalitarianism in Perspective*, London: Pall Mall.

Friedrich, Carl and Brzezinski, Zbigniew (1956) *Totalitarian Dictatorship and Autocracy*, Cambridge, MA: Harvard University Press.

Frydman, Roman *et al.* (1993) *The Privatization Process in Central Europe*, London: Central European University Press.

Fukuyama, Francis (1989) 'The End of History?', *The National Interest*, vol. 16.

Gati, Charles (ed.) (1974) *The Politics of Modernization in Eastern Europe*, New York: Praeger.

Glenny, Misha (1992) *The Fall of Yugoslavia*, Harmondsworth, Middlesex: Penguin.

Glenny, Misha (1993) *The Rebirth of History*, 2nd edn, Harmondsworth, Middlesex: Penguin.

Goodwyn, Lawrence (1991) *Breaking the Barrier: The Rise of Solidarity in Poland*, New York: Oxford University Press.

Gotting, U. (1992) 'Coping with Unemployment in East Central Europe', mimeo, October.

Grosfeld, I. (1991) 'Privatization of State Enterprises in Eastern Europe: The Search for a Market Environment', *East European Politics and Societies*, vol. 5, no. 1 (Winter).

Hankiss, Elemer (1990) *East European Alternatives*, Oxford: Clarendon Press.

Hann, Chris (ed.) (1990) *Market Economy and Civil Society in Hungary*, London: Cass.

Hare, Paul (1991) 'The Assessment: Microeconomics of Transition in Eastern Europe', *Oxford Review of Economic Policy*, vol. 7, no. 4 (Winter).

Havel, Vaclav (1985) *The Power of the Powerless*, Armonk, NY: Sharpe.

Havel, Vaclav (1990) 'Return to Europe', *East European Reporter*, vol. 4, no. 2.

Havel, Vaclav (1991) *Letni premitani*, Prague: Odeon.

Heinrich, Hans-George (1986) *Hungary: Politics, Economics and Society*, London: Pinter.

Held, David (1992) 'Liberalism, Marxism and Democracy', in Stuart Hall *et al.* (eds), *Modernity and its Futures*, Cambridge: Polity.

Held, Joseph (ed.) (1992) *The Columbia History of Eastern Europe in the Twentieth Century*, New York: Columbia University Press.

Holmes, Leslie (1986) *Politics in the Communist World*, Oxford: Clarendon Press.

Horowitz, D.L. Lipset, S.M. and Linz, J. (1990) 'Debate: Presidents vs. Parliaments', *Journal of Democracy*, vol. 1, no. 4.

Horvath, Agnes and Szakolczai, Arpad (1992) *The Dissolution of Communist Power: The Case of Hungary*, London and New York: Routledge.

Huntington, Samuel (1991) *The Third Wave: Democratization in the Late Twentieth Century*, Norman: University of Oklahoma Press.

Jasiewicz, K. (1992) 'Polish Elections 1989–1991: Beyond the "Pospolite Ruszenie" ', in Peter Volten (ed.), *Bound to Change: Consolidating Democracy in Eastern Europe*, Boulder, CO: Westview.

Jorgensen, Knud Erik (1992) 'The End of Anti-Politics in Central Europe', in Lewis (1992).

Kolankiewicz, George and Lewis, Paul G. (1988) *Poland: Politics, Economics and Society*, Londosn: Printer.

Kaldor, Mary (1990) *The Imaginary War*, Oxford: Blackwell.

Kanet, Roger E. (ed.) (1971) *The Behavioral Revolution and Communist Studies*, New York: Free Press.

Kaminski, Bartolomiej (1991) *The Collapse of State Socialism: The Case of Poland*, Princeton, NJ: Princeton University Press.

Kaufman, Michael T. (1989) *Mad Dreams, Saving Graces: Poland, a Nation in Conspiracy*, New York: Random House.

Keane, John (ed.) (1988) *Civil Society and the State*, London: Verso.

Kiss, Elisabeth (1991) 'Democracy Without Parties?', *Dissent*, no. 1.

Kolarska-Bobinska, Lena (1992) 'Civil Society and Social Anomy in Poland', in Deacon, ed. (1992).

Konrad, George and Szelenyi, Ivan (1979) *The Intellectuals on the Road to Class Power*, New York: Harcourt Brace Jovanovich.

Kornai, Janos (1980) *Economics of Shortage*, Amsterdam: North-Holland.

Kornai, Janos (1990) *The Road to a Free Economy*, New York and London: Norton.

Krejci, Jaroslav (1990) *Czechoslovakia at the Crossroads of European History*, London: Tauris.

Kumar, K. (1992) 'The 1989 Revolutions and the Idea of Europe', *Political Studies*, vol. 50, no. 3.

Kundera, Milan (1984) 'The Tragedy of Central Europe', *New York Review of Books*, 26 April.

Kusin, Vladimir (1978) *From Dubcek to Charter 77: A Study of 'Normalization' in Czechoslovakia, 1968–1978*, Edinburgh: Q Press.

Kuzniar, R. (1992) 'Wszystkie drogi prowadza . . . na Zachod', in Kuzniar (ed.), *Krajobraz po transformacii*, Warsaw: Uniwersytet Warszawski.

Lasswell, Harold D. (1986) 'Democratic Leadership', in Barbara Kellerman (ed.), *Political Leadership*, Pittsburgh: University of Pittsburgh Press.

Lendvai, P. (1989) 'A majusi fordulat' (the May turnabout), *Hitel*, no. 5, pp. 16–17.

Lewis, Paul G. (1990) 'Democratization in Eastern Europe', *Coexistence*, vol. 27.

Lewis, Paul G. (ed.) (1992) *Democracy and Civil Society in Eastern Europe*, London: Macmillan.

Lijphart, Arend (1977) *Democracy in Plural Societies: A Comparative Perspective*, New Haven: Yale University Press.

Lijphart, Arend (1991) 'Consociational Choices for New Democracies', *Journal of Democracy*, vol. 2, no. 3.

Lijphart, Arend (1992) 'Democratization and Constitutional Choices in Czecho-Slovakia, Hungary and Poland', *Journal of Theoretical Politics*, no. 4.

Lindblom, Charles (1977) *Politics and Markets*, New York: Basic Books.

Linden, Ronald (1981) *Bear and Foxes*, Boulder, CO: East European Monographs.

Linden, Ronald (1992) 'The New International Political Economy of Eastern Europe', *Studies in Comparative Communism*, vol. 25, no. 1.

Linden, Ronald and Rockman, Bert (eds) (1984) *Elite Studies and Communist Politics*, Pittsburgh: University of Pittsburgh Press.

Linz, Juan (1990) 'The Perils of Presidentialism', *Journal of Democracy*, vol. 1, no. 1.

McFarlane, Bruce (1988) *Yugoslavia: Politics, Economics and Society*, London: Pinter.

McIntyre, Robert J. (1988) *Bulgaria: Politics, Economics and Society*, London: Pinter.

McMillan, J. and Naughton, B. (1992) 'How to Perform a Planned Economy: Lessons from China', *Oxford Review of Economic Policy*, vol. 8, no. 1 (Spring).

Macridis, Roy C. (1968) 'Comparative Politics and the Study of Government: The Search for Focus', *Comparative Politics*, vol. 1.

Magas, Branka (1993) *The Destruction of Yugoslavia*, London: Verso.

Maravall, Jose and Santamaria, Julian (1986) 'Political Change in Spain and the Prospects for Democracy', in O'Donnell *et al.* (1986).

Mason, David S. (1985) *Public Opinion and Political Change in Poland, 1980–1982*, Cambridge: Cambridge University Press.

Mason, David S. (1992a) 'Public Opinion in Poland's Transition to Market Democracy', in Deacon *et al.* (1992).

Mason, David S. (1992b) *Revolution in East-Central Europe*, Boulder, CO: Westview.

Mastnak, Tomaz (1991) in *The HCA's Founding Assembly*, Prague: Helsinki Citizens' Assembly.

Maxwell, Kenneth (1986) 'Regime Overthrow and the Prospects for Democratic Transition in Portugal', in O'Donnell *et al.* (1986).

Mearsheimer, J.J. (1990) 'Back to the Future: Instability in Europe After the Cold War', *International Security*, vol. 15, no. 1.

Michnik, Adam (1989) 'Does Socialism Have Any Future in Eastern Europe?', *Studium Papers*, vol. 13, no. 4 (October).

Michta, Andrew and Prizel, Ilya (eds) (1992) *Postcommunist Eastern Europe: Crisis and Reform*, New York: St Martin's.

Miliband, Ralph (1992) 'Fukuyama and the Socialist Alternative', *New Left Review*, no. 193 (May/June).

Millar, James R. (1987) *Politics, Work, and Daily Life in the USSR*, Cambridge: Cambridge University Press.

Moore, Patrick (1992) 'Issues in Croatian Politics', *RFE/RL Research Report*, vol. 1, 6 November.

Mora, M. (1990) *Az Allami Vallalatok (Al) privatizacioja (The (Pseudo) Privatization of State Enterprises)*, Budapest.

Murrell, Peter (1992a) 'Evolutionary and Radical Approaches to Economic Reform', *Economics of Planning*, vol. 25, no. 1.

Murrell, Peter (1992b) 'Conservative Political Philosophy and the Strategy of Economic Transition', *East European Politics and Societies*, vol. 6, no. 1 (Winter).

Nelson, Daniel N. (1977) 'Socioeconomic and Political Change in Communist Europe', *International Studies Quarterly*, June.

Nelson, Daniel N. (ed.) (1983) *Communism and the Politics of Inequalities*, Lexington, KY: Lexington Books.

Nelson, Daniel N. (1986a) *Alliance Behavior in the Warsaw Pact*, Boulder, CO: Westview.

Nelson, Daniel N. (1986b) 'The Diffusion of Non-Supportive Participatory Involvement in Eastern Europe', *Social Science Quarterly*, vol. 67 (Winter).

Nelson, Daniel N. (1992) 'The Rise of Public Legitimation in Communist States', in Ramet (1992).

Nelson, Daniel and White, Stephen (eds) (1982) *Communist Legislatures in Comparative Perspective*, Albany, NY: State University of New York Press.

Neubert, Erhart (1990) 'Die Opposition in der demokratischen Revolution der DDR', in Detlef Pollack (ed.), *Die Legitimität der Freiheit*, Frankfurt: Lang.

Nove, Alec (1964) *Was Stalin Really Necessary?*, London: Allen & Unwin.

O'Donnell, Guillermo *et al.* (eds) (1986) *Transitions from Authoritarian Rule: prospects of Democracy*, Baltimore, MD: Johns Hopkins University Press.

Olson, David M. and Simon, Maurice D. (1982) 'The Institutional Development of a Minimal Parliament: The Case of the Polish Sejm', in Nelson and White (1982).

Perry, Duncan (1992) 'Macedonian Politics', *RFE/RL Research Report*, vol. 1, 20 November.

Pinder, John (1991) *The European Community and Eastern Europe*, London: Pinter.

Pontusson, J. (1992) 'Sweden', in M. Kesselman and J. Krieger (eds), *European Politics in Transition*, Lexington and Toronto: D.C. Heath.

Pravda, Alex (1986) 'Elections in Communist Party States', in White and Nelson (1986).

Przeworski, Adam (1986) 'Some Problems in the Study of the Transition to Democracy', in O'Donnell *et al.* (1986).

Przeworski, Adam (1992) *Democracy and the Market*, Cambridge: Cambridge University Press.

Rady, Martin (1992) *Romania in Turmoil*, London: Tauris.

Rai, Shirin, Pilkington, Hilary and Phizacklea, Annie (1992) *Women in the Face of Change: The Soviet Union, Eastern Europe and China*, London: Routledge.

Ramet, Shirin (ed.) (1992) *Adaptation of Communist and Post-Communist Systems*, Boulder, CO: Westview.

Rigby, T.H. and Feher, F. (eds) (1982) *Political Legitimation in Communist States*, New York: St Martin's.

Riker, W.H. (1986) 'Duverger's Law Revisited', in B. Grofman and A. Lijphart (eds), *Electoral Laws and their Political Consequences*, New York: Agathon.

Ristic, Sinisa (ed.) (1989) *The Socialist Republic of Serbia in Reform*, Belgrad: KIZ.

Rose, Richard (1991) *Between State and Market: Key Indicators of Transition in Eastern Europe*, Glasgow: Centre for the Study of Public Policy.

Rose, Richard (1992a) 'Identifying Needs for Social Protection in Romania', mimeo, May.

Rose, Richard (1992b) *Making Progress and Catching Up: A Time–Space Analysis of Social Welfare Across Europe*, Glasgow: Centre for the Study of Public Policy.

Rose, Richard and Haerpfer, Christian (1992) *New Democracies between State and Market: A Baseline Report*, Glasgow: Centre for the Study of Public Policy.

Rothschild, Joseph (1989) *Return to Diversity*, New York: Oxford University Press.

Rupnik, Jacques (1982) 'The Roots of Czech Stalinism', in Ralph Samuel and Gareth Stedman Jones (eds), *Culture, Ideology and Politics*, London: Routledge.

Rychard, A. (1992) 'Politics and Society After the Breakthough', in George Sanford (ed.), *Democratization in Poland, 1988–90*, New York: St Martin's.

Ryczynski, T. (1991) 'The Sequencing of Reform', *Oxford Review of Economic Policy*, vol. 7, no. 4 (Winter).

Sachs, Jeffrey and Lipton, David (1990) 'Poland's Economic Reform', *Foreign Affairs*, vol. 69, no. 3 (Summer).

Sanford, George (ed.) (1992) *Democratization in Poland, 1988–90*, London: Macmillan.

Sartori, Giovanni (1976) *Parties and Party Systems: A Framework for Analysis*, Cambridge: Cambridge University Press.

Schöpflin, George (1990) 'The Political Traditions of Eastern Europe', *Daedalus*, no. 1.

Schöpflin, George (1991) 'Conservatism and Hungary's Political Transition', *Problems of Communism*, nos 1–2.

Schöpflin, George (1992) 'From Communism to Democracy in Hungary', in A. Bozoki *et al.* (1992).

Schöpflin, George (1993) *Politics in Eastern Europe 1945–1992*, Oxford: Blackwell.

Schöpflin, George and Wood, Nancy (eds) (1989) *In Search of Central Europe*, Cambridge: Polity.

Seroka, Jim (1988) 'The Interdependence of Institutional Revitalization and Intra-Party Reform in Yugoslavia', *Soviet Studies*, vol. 40, no. 1 (January).

Seroka, Jim (1989) 'Economic Stabilization and Communal Politics in Yugoslavia', *Journal of Communist Studies*, vol. 5, no. 2 (June).

Seroka, Jim (1990) 'Institutional Reform in Yugoslavia: Background to Crisis', in Anthony Jones (ed.), *Research on the Soviet Union and Eastern Europe*, London: JAI Press.

Seroka, Jim (1992) 'Nationalism and the New Political Compact in Yugoslavia', *History of European Ideas*, vol. 15 (April–June).

Shafir, Michael (1985) *Romania: Politics, Economics and Society*, London: Pinter.

Skilling, H. Gordon (1960) 'Soviet and Communist Politics: A Comparative Approach', *Journal of Politics*, vol. 22 (May).

Skilling, H. Gordon (1966) *The Governments of Communist East Europe*, New York: Crowell.

Skilling, H. Gordon (1976) *Czechoslovakia's Interrupted Revolution*, Princeton, NJ: Princeton University Press.

Skilling, H. Gordon (1981) *Charter 77 and Human Rights in Czechoslovakia*, London: Allen & Unwin.

Skilling, H. Gordon and Wilson, Paul (eds) (1991) *Civic Freedom in Central Europe: Voices from Czechoslovakia*, London: Macmillan.

Slay, B. and Tedstrom, J. (1992) 'Privatization in the Post-Communist Economies', *RFE/RL Research Report*, vol. 1, no. 17, 24 April.

Snyder, Jack (1990) 'Averting Anarchy in the New Europe', *International Security*, vol. 14, no. 4.

Spero, J.B. (1991) 'Central European Security', *Problems of Communism*, vol. 40, no. 6.

Standing, G. (ed.) (1992) *In Search of Flexibility: The New Soviet Labour Market*, Geneva: ILO.

Staniszkis, Jadwiga (1984) *Poland's Self-Limiting Revolution*, Princeton, NJ: Princeton University Press.

Staniszkis, Jadwiga (1985–6) 'Forms of Reasoning as Ideology', *Telos*, no. 66 (Winter).

Stepan, Alfred (1986) 'Paths Towards Redemocratization: Theoretical and Comparative', in O'Donnell *et al.* (1986).

Stone, Norman and Strouhal, Eduard (eds) (1989) *Czechoslovakia: Crossroads and Crises, 1918–1988*, London: Macmillan.

Swain, Nigel (1992) *Hungary: The Rise and Fall of Feasible Socialism*, London: Verso.

Swain, Nigel and Geoffrey (1993) *Eastern Europe Since 1945*, London: Macmillan.

Sword, Keith (ed.) (1991) *The Times Guide to Eastern Europe*, rev. edn, London: Times Books.

Szajkowski, Bogdan (ed.) (1991) *New Political Parties of Eastern Europe and the Soviet Union*, London: Longman.

Szalai, Judith (1992) 'Social Participation in Hungary in the Context of Restructuring and Liberalisation', in Deacon, ed. (1992).

Szelenyi, I. and Szelenyi, Sz. (1991) 'The Vacuum in Hungarian Politics: Classes and Parties', *New Left Review*, no. 187 (May/June) pp. 121–37.

Szelenyi, Ivan *et al.* (1992) 'The Making of Political Fields in Post-Communist Transition', in A. Bozoki *et al.* (1992).

Szoboszlai, Gyorgy (ed.) (1991) *Democracy and Political Transformation: Theories and East-Central European Realities*, Budapest: Hungarian Political Science Association.

Sztompka, Piotr (1991) 'The Intangibles and Imponderables of the Transition to Democracy', *Studies in Comparative Communism*, vol. 24, no. 3 (September).

Taras, Ray (ed.) (1992) *Handbook of Political Science Research on the USSR and Eastern Europe*, Westport, CT: Greenwood Press.

Tatur, Melanie (1992) 'Why Is There No Women's Movement in Eastern Europe?', in Lewis (1992).

Teune, Henry (1984) 'Eastern European Politics and Macro Political Theory', in Linden and Rockman (1984).

Tokes, Rudolf L. (1975) 'Comparative Communism: The Elusive Target', *Studies in Comparative Communism*, vol. 8 (Autumn).

Tokes, Rudolf L. (1992) 'From Visegrad to Krakow: Cooperation, Competition, and Coexistence in Central Europe', *Problems of Communism*, vol. 40, no. 6.

Touraine, Alain *et al.* (1983) *Solidarity: The Analysis of a Social Movement*, Cambridge: Cambridge University Press.

Tucker, Robert C. (1981) *Politics as Leadership*, Columbia: University of Missouri Press.

Ulc, O. (1974) 'Czechoslovakia: The Great Leap Backwards', in Gati (1974).

Vajda, Mihaly (1991) 'Hungary After the Local Elections', *East European Reporter*, vol. 4, no. 3 (Autumn/Winter).

Walesa, Lech (1987) *A Way of Hope*, New York: Holt.

Walesa, Lech (1992) *The Struggle and the Triumph: An Autobiography*, New York: Arcade.

Welsh, William A. (1973) 'The Comparative Study of Political Leadership in Communist Systems', in Beck *et al.* (1973).

White, Stephen (1986) 'Preface', in White and Nelson (1986).

White, Stephen (ed.) (1991) *Handbook of Reconstruction in Eastern Europe and the Soviet Union*, London: Longman.

White, Stephen and Nelson, Daniel N. (eds) (1986) *Communist Politics: A Reader*, New York: New York University Press.

White, Stephen and Simons, William B. (eds.) (1984) *The Party Statutes of the Communist World*, The Hague: Martinus Nijhoff.

Wightman, Gordon (1990a) 'The June 1990 Elections in Czechoslovakia: A Plebiscite for Democracy', *Representation*, vol. 29, no. 108 (Winter).

Wightman, Gordon (1990b) 'Czechoslovakia', *Electoral Studies*, vol. 9, no. 4 (December).

Wightman, Gordon (1991) 'The Collapse of Communist Rule in Czechoslovakia and the June 1990 Parliamentary Elections', *Parliamentary Affairs*, vol. 44, no. 1 (January).

Wightman, Gordon and Rutland, Peter (1991) 'Czechoslovakia', in White (1991).

Wolchik, Sharon (1991) *Czechoslovakia in Transition*, London: Pinter.

Wolfe, Bertram (1969) *An Ideology in Power*, London: Allen & Unwin.

Zubek, Voytek (1991) 'Walesa's Leadership and Poland's Transition', *Problems of Communism*, vol. 40, nos 1–2 (January–April).

Index

302

Index